STORIES OF PEOPLE & CIVILIZATION

KOREAN

ANCIENT ORIGINS

FLAME TREE PUBLISHING
6 Melbray Mews, Fulham,
London SW6 3NS, United Kingdom
www.flametreepublishing.com

24 26 28 27 25
1 3 5 7 9 10 8 6 4 2

ISBN: 978-1-80417-784-6

Cover and pattern art was created by Flame Tree Studio, with elements courtesy of Shutterstock.com/svekloid/PremiumStock. Additional interior decoration courtesy of Shutterstock.com/Bariskina.

Judith John (lists of Ancient Kings & Leaders) is a writer and editor specializing in literature and history. A former secondary school English Language and Literature teacher, she has subsequently worked as an editor on major educational projects, including *English A: Literature* for the Pearson International Baccalaureate series. Judith's major research interests include Romantic and Gothic literature, and Renaissance drama.

The text in this book is compiled and edited, with a new introduction and chapter introductions. The classic texts derive from: *The Story of Korea* by Joseph H. Longford (T. Fisher Unwin, 1911), *Corea: The Hermit Nation* by William Elliott Griffis (Charles Scribner's Sons, 1911), *The History of Korea* by Homer Hulbert (The Methodist Publishing House, 1905) and *The Korean Alphabet* by James Scarth Gale (Transactions of the Korea Branch of the Royal Asiatic Society, Volume 4, Part 1, 1912).

A copy of the CIP data for this book is available
from the British Library.

Designed and created in the UK | Printed and bound in China

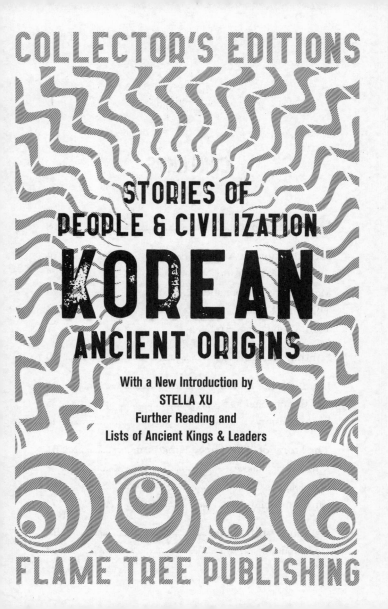

COLLECTOR'S EDITIONS

STORIES OF PEOPLE & CIVILIZATION
KOREAN
ANCIENT ORIGINS

With a New Introduction by

STELLA XU

Further Reading and

Lists of Ancient Kings & Leaders

FLAME TREE PUBLISHING

CONTENTS

Series Foreword **8**

Introduction to Ancient Korean Origins **14**

Ancient Korean History – Controversy 15

More Recent Interpretations 23

The Three Kingdoms Period 24

Writings on Premodern Korea 27

Further Reading **30**

Land, People & Early History **34**

The Country and Its People 35

Earliest History 46

The Story of The Three Kingdoms **61**

Kingdom of Hiaksai 62

Kingdom of Korai 68

Kingdom of Shinra 74

Relations with Japan **82**

Japan and Korea 83

CONTENTS

Early Medieval Korea **95**

From 890 to 1392 CE 96

The Koryŭ Dynasty 106

Wang-gön's Death and the Rule of His Successors 114

War and Peace with Kitan 130

Ever-changing Alliances 148

Turmoil and Strife 166

The Mongol Invasion **171**

The Mongols 172

Rebellion Against the Mongols 185

Kublai Khan and the Invasion of Japan 201

The Zenith of Mongol Influence 219

Beginning of the End of the Koryŭ Dynasty 235

Sin-don Becomes the Favourite 252

The Fall of Sin-don 267

Gen. Yi Defends Koryŭ 281

Rise of the Wang Dynasty 294

The Joseon Dynasty and King Se-jong the Great **311**

The Foundations of Modern Korea 312

A Phonetic Alphabet 328

The Korean Alphabet 328

Ancient Kings & Leaders **337**

STORIES OF PEOPLE & CIVILIZATION

KOREAN

ANCIENT ORIGINS

SERIES FOREWORD

Stretching back to the oral traditions of thousands of years ago, tales of heroes and disaster, creation and conquest have been told by many different civilizations, in ways unique to their landscape and language. Their impact sits deep within our own culture even though the detail in the stories themselves are a loose mix of historical record, the latest archaeological evidence, transformed narrative and the unwitting distortions of generations of storytellers.

Today the language of mythology lives around us: our mood is jovial, our countenance is saturnine, we are narcissistic and our modern life is hermetically sealed from others. The nuances of the ancient world form part of our daily routines and help us navigate the information overload of our interconnected lives.

The nature of a myth is that its stories are already known by most of those who hear or read them. Every era brings a new emphasiz, but the fundamentals remain the same: a desire to understand and describe the events and relationships of the world. Many of the great stories are archetypes that help us find our own place, equipping us with tools for self-understanding, both individually and as part of a broader culture.

For Western societies it is Greek mythology that speaks to us most clearly. It greatly influenced the mythological heritage of the ancient Roman civilization and is the lens through which we still see the Celts, the Norse and many of the other great peoples and religions. The Greeks themselves inherited much from their neighbours, the Egyptians, an older culture that became weary with the mantle of civilization.

Of course, what we perceive now as mythology had its own origins in perceptions of the divine and the rituals of the sacred. The earliest civilizations, in the crucible of the Middle East, in the Sumer of the third millennium BCE, are the source to which many of the mythic archetypes can be traced. Over five thousand years ago, as humankind collected together in cities for the first time, developed writing and industrial scale agriculture, started to irrigate the rivers and attempted to control rather than be at the mercy of its environment, humanity began to write down its tentative explanations of natural events, of floods and plagues, of disease.

Early stories tell of gods or god-like animals who are crafty and use their wits to survive, and it is not unreasonable to suggest that these were the first rulers of the gathering peoples of the earth, later elevated to god-like status with the distance of time. Such tales became more political as cities vied with each other for supremacy, creating new gods, new hierarchies for their pantheons. The older gods took on primordial roles and became the preserve of creation and destruction, leaving the new gods to deal with more current, everyday affairs. Empires rose and fell, with Babylon assuming the mantle from Sumeria in the 1800s BCE, in turn to be swept away by the Assyrians of the 1200s BCE; then the Assyrians and the Egyptians were subjugated by the Greeks, the Greeks by the Romans and so on, leading to the spread and assimilation of common themes, ideas and stories throughout the world.

The survival of history is dependent on the telling of good tales, but each one must have the 'feeling' of truth, otherwise it will be ignored. Around the firesides, or embedded in a book or a computer, the myths and legends of the past are still the living materials of retold myth, not restricted to an exploration of historical origins. Now we have devices and global communications that give us unparalleled access to a diversity of traditions. We can find out about Indigenous American, Indian, Chinese and tribal African mythology in a way that was denied to our ancestors, we can find connections, plot the archaeology, religion and the mythologies of the world to build a comprehensive image of the human experience that is both humbling and fascinating.

The books in this series introduce the many cultures of ancient humankind to the modern reader. From the earliest migrations across the globe to settlements along rivers, from the landscapes of mountains to the vast Steppes, from woodlands to deserts, humanity has adapted to its environments, nurturing languages and observations and expressing itself through records, mythmaking stories and living traditions. There is still so much to explore, but this is a great place to start.

Jake Jackson
General Editor

STORIES OF
PEOPLE & CIVILIZATION
KOREAN
ANCIENT ORIGINS

INTRODUCTION
& FURTHER READING

INTRODUCTION TO KOREAN ANCIENT ORIGINS

Often referred to as 'the Hermit Kingdom', Korea has been overshadowed in history by her two larger neighbours, China and Japan. In the 1950s the only time that Korea attracted global attention was during the Korean War; however, this conflict was soon reduced to 'the Forgotten War' after its conclusion. Until recently, typical news stories about the Korean peninsula have featured North Korean military manoeuvres and nuclear tests. Only in recent years have overall perceptions about Korea started to change. This came about partly because people started to notice South Korea's impressive economic success and because Korean popular culture reached neighbouring Asian countries for the first time. However, the country has now gone far beyond these early stages to become a global trendsetter to rival Europe and the US, long considered the cradles of popular culture.

Compared to China and Japan, Korea resembles 'a shrimp between two whales'. However, one fact makes Korea stand out against all odds: Korea represents one of the very few groups of people that has resisted all attempts at conquest, absorption and annexation into China. In particular, Korea has maintained its autonomy and unique identity until the present day, despite having always looked up to China as a source of cultural inspiration. In fact, over the past two thousand years, a number of ethnic groups have existed in China proper, some of which established formidable states or even conquered China, either in whole or in part. However, many of these groups dissolved or merged with other ethnic groups along the way, leaving minimal traces of their own history and culture.

ANCIENT KOREAN HISTORY – CONTROVERSY AND CHALLENGES

Premodern Korean history is conventionally divided into five phases by dynasties: the ancient period, the Three Kingdoms, Unified Silla, Koryŏ and the Chosŏn dynasty. Compared to Chinese history, Korea has experienced far fewer dynastic changes. Some Japanese colonial historians use this as evidence of Korea's historical stagnancy: most dynasties in Korea lasted 500 years or longer. On the other hand, Korean historians use this fact to prove the resilience of the Korean people. In their opinion, the leaders and ruling class were astute in adjusting to new circumstances, so that despite multiple crises their dynasties were not toppled and eventually thrived. Two Korean dynasties in particular came close to demise – the Koryŏ, during military rebellions and Mongol invasions, and the Chosŏn, confronted by the Toyotomi Hideyoshi invasion and two rounds of Manchu invasions. However, both the Koryŏ and Chosŏn managed to survive and to continue their respective dynastic journeys successfully.

Studying Korean history is a challenging task, due to the scarcity of primary sources compared to those about China and

Japan. The earliest sources about people living in Korea are Chinese documents, mostly derived from the series of Chinese Standard Dynastic Histories. Despite evidence of early historical writings in Korea having existed, the earliest sources extant today from the Korean side are *Samguk sagi* (the *History of the Three Kingdoms*), written in the twelfth century, and *Samguk yusa* (the *Memorabilia of the Three Kingdoms*), written in the thirteenth century. These were not only compiled more than one thousand years after the times they describe, but also heavily relied on Chinese sources. Because of the ambiguity and relative lack of historical records, the study of Korean history has involved piecing together fragmentary, sometimes contradictory documents. Such attempts have often led to contested and controversial interpretations.

East Asian countries have a long tradition of using historical writing primarily to justify political legitimacy and a didactic moral agenda. It has been common for the ruling class and court historians to look back to the past for inspiration and insights into both present and future. The rise of modern nationalism and the formation of the modern nation-state in East Asia in the late nineteenth century have made historical interpretation more complex and disputed. Some contested issues have far surpassed any other inquiries about the past. Foremost among these are questions about the origin of East Asian civilization, national ancestors, the first ancient state, the direction of cultural dissemination and the lineage of early Korea.

Tracing the origin of East Asian peoples and civilizations has been crucial to the construction of national history and identity. Since the 1950s most South Korean scholars have embraced a so-called migration hypothesis about the origin of the Korean people. That is to say, the earliest residents of the Korean peninsula were called Paleo-Asiatic people; they spread widely across Eurasia, northern China and the Korean peninsula. This account of northern origins became appealing because it offered the potential to counteract Japanese colonial scholarship that emphasized Korea's heteronomy – in other words, Korea's total and continual reliance on foreign influences, especially those of China. Korean scholars felt more comfortable connecting prehistoric Korean civilization to northern areas such as Altai and Siberia, while pushing the beginning of Chinese influence to as late a date as possible.

The Three Chosŏn

One of the most controversial issues in ancient Korean history is the lineage of the Three Chosŏn – namely Tan'gun, Kija and Wiman Chosŏn. Korean scholars made every effort to make Tan'gun a tangible national ancestor and putative founder of the first Korean state, Ko Chosŏn. He has thus long maintained unsurpassable significance in Korean history and consciousness. To go a step further, modern Korean historians shifted Tan'gun from the realm of myth to historical reality; in contrast, the long-venerated authenticity of Kija has been repeatedly challenged in the modern era. Kija had previously been highly respected as a most righteous sage who brought advanced Chinese civilization to Korea. Indeed, the Kija legend enabled the literati of the Chosŏn Dynasty (1392–1910) to claim their superiority and the authenticity of Chinese civilization over the Manchu people. However, the pride of being Kija's descendants diminished along with the weakening of China after the late nineteenth century.

Kija still remains a mysterious figure today. Did he really exist? Did he come to the Korean peninsula? Did he establish Kija Chosŏn? Where was Kija Chosŏn located? Having established Tan'gun as the starting point of Korean history, contemporary Korean scholars concur that Kija's emigration to the Korean peninsula is a fabrication, first introduced by Chinese historians during the Han dynasty (second century BCE); this story was later uncritically accepted and internalized by litarati of the Koryŏ and Chosŏn dynasties. Korean scholars presented various alternatives to this phase. For example, they posited that Kija Chosŏn should be renamed Hanssi Chosŏn or Yemaek Chosŏn and that it may have had a location outside of the Korean peninsula. Some argue further that Kija belonged to the *Tongi* or the Eastern Barbarians (that is, ancient Koreans). Kija Chosŏn has therefore been redeemed as an ancient Korean state instead of a Chinese refugee regime.

Wiman is another controversial figure in Korean history. From the Korean side, Wiman was first mentioned in *Samguk yusa,* the origin of the Three Chosŏn framework: Wiman Chosŏn was included in the lineage of Ko Chosŏn, along with Tan'gun and Kija Chosŏn. However, Wiman usurped the throne after deceiving and betraying King Kijun, the legitimate ruler of Kija Chosŏn. Wiman has therefore been regarded as a villain, and for centuries his role has been minimized or intentionally ignored. Interestingly, compared to Tan'gun and Kija Chosŏn, Wiman Chosŏn has been transformed the most dramatically in recent research. For almost two thousand years after the Wiman Chosŏn period, no historians ever questioned that Wiman was a member of the Yan people (and thus Chinese). However, the most prominent Korean historian of the twentieth century, Yi Pyŏngdo (1896–1989), contended that Wiman was actually a descendant of Ko Chosŏn; he highlighted Wiman's topknot hairdo and the barbarian dress that he wore when he fled to Korea, his insistence on the name Chosŏn for his new state and Wiman's determined resistance to the Han invasion. Consequently, Wiman Chosŏn has been transformed into a legitimate phase among Korean ancient states and Wiman himself resurrected as a Korean national hero who led his fellow compatriots in fighting against Chinese domination.

The Commanderies of Nangnang and Imna

If the Three Chosŏn framework is more about Korea's national history, Nangnang (C. *Lelang*) and Imna (*J. Mimana)* are more controversial, intertwined as they are with the history of China and Japan. Nangnang Commandery, established after Wiman Chosŏn collapsed following an invasion by troops of the Han Emperor Wudi, lasted from 108 BCE to 313 CE in the P'yŏngyang area. Japanese colonial scholars invested exceptional attention in Nangnang to prove the innate heteronomy of Koreans, positing that Korean history derived from a Chinese refugee regime. Post-1945 Korean scholars have intentionally avoided the issue of Nangnang. Nonetheless, they have had to address the large amount of Nangnang-related archaeological relics excavated near the P'yŏngyang area. Some recent scholars have therefore argued that Nangnang could have been located as far away as west of the Liao river in China. They have also attributed Nangnang relics in the P'yŏngyang area to an indigenous Korean state named *Nangnangguk*, or the State of Nangnang, believed to be irrelevant to the Han Lelang Commandery.

The issue of the Nangnang Commandery, along with the other three Han Commanderies, was crucial not only to the history of Korea, but also to the overall picture of premodern East Asia. There is little written and affirmed archaeological evidence about the other two Han Commanderies, i.e., Chinbŏn (C. *Zhenfan*) and Imdun (C. *Lintun*), mainly because these two commanderies only lasted for a brief 25 years. The fourth one, the Hyŏndo (C. *Xuantu*) Commandery, has also been neglected for a long time because it moved westward twice and remained outside the Korean peninsula thereafter. However, the Hyŏndo Commandery was pivotal because of its relationship with the later Koguryŏ Kingdom (C. *Gaogouli*, 37 BCE (?)–668 CE). According to *Hanshu*, or *The Historical Record of the Han Dynasty*,

After the Emperor Wu of the Han quashed Chaoxian, he made Gaogouli a county subject to Xuantu Commandery. Emperor Wu also invested musicians in Gaogouli.

This further contributed to the issues of Koguryŏ's historical sovereignty that have been the subject of enthusiastic debate between Chinese and Korean scholars since 2003. Some Chinese scholars insisted that because of the subjugation of Gaogouli to the Han Xuantu Commandery, Gaogouli was always a Chinese vassal state. In response, Korean scholars emphasized the independent formation of the Koguryŏ state and the stiff resistance raised by Koguryŏ against the expansion and invasion of the Chinese dynasties over the centuries. Despite its demise in 668, Koguryŏ continues to be remembered as one of the strongest and most prosperous phases of Korean history, especially in the sense of military strength and territorial scope.

Located on the southeastern coast of the Korean peninsula in the fourth century CE, Imna has been utilized for legitimizing Japan's colonization of Korea since the 1890s. Because of the limited and ambivalent written sources regarding Imna, the late nineteenth-century rediscovery of the King Kwanggaet'o (r. 391–413 CE) stele, erected in 414 CE, attracted tremendous political and academic attention. Japanese scholars demonstrated intense interest in this stele, which they believed to be the key for exploring not only the early history of Japan, but also the interstate relationships between Japan and Korea. The importance of this stele centred on a 14-character sentence that described the interstate relationships among the Three Kingdoms in the Korean peninsula and Japan. Based on the conventional reading by Japanese scholars, it observes that '*Wa* (Japan) came across the sea and defeated Paekche, and Paekche and Silla have been the subjects of Japan ever since'. Japanese scholars insisted that *Wa* actively intervened and even dominated interstate relationships in Northeast Asia. In other words, *Wa* came to the Korean peninsula under the request of Paekche, confronted Koguryŏ and invaded Silla. As a result, some Japanese scholars claimed this stele to be the most substantial evidence for the actual existence of Imna Colony and the dominance of Japan over the southeastern part of Korea.

The interpretation of this crucial sentence and some particular characters in it has been hotly debated among Japanese and Korean historians. Some Korean scholars have suspected a conspiracy in which lime was applied onto the stele so that the overall meaning would be beneficial to Japan, although a Chinese scholar later affirmed that the lime was applied by local Chinese workers in order to produce rubbings with readable quality. Due to its complexity and the crucial implications it inspires, Imna has unsurprisingly been one of the primary targets of Korean historians since the 1950s.

The debate over Imna continues. Although the colonial-era theories were consciously eroded, many postwar Japanese scholars still believe in the existence of a Japanese administration/outpost in the southern part of the Korean peninsula. Some Japanese scholars have suggested a much later date for the founding of Imna, 429 CE or even as late as around 530 CE, compared to the early hypothesis of 369 CE. There have also been new interpretations about the nature of Imna, with some arguing that Imna was more of a diplomatic or commercial station. Some Korean scholars further suggested that rather than *Wa* (Japan), it was Paekche that had suzerain power over Imna. According to this theory, the ruler of Imna was later mistakenly recorded as Japanese because the *Nihon shoki* or the *Historical Record of Japan* was written by Paekche refugees who escaped to Japan after the demise of the Paekche Kingdom in 660 CE; they consequently presented all Paekche-related records with Japanese protagonists. More recently scholars called for understanding Imna in the context of Kaya history and proposed that Imna was a branch office of Paekche for securing a trade route to Japan, as well as an intelligence outpost.

The issue of Imna has continually been spotlighted, especially when a discovery related to Korea and Japan occurs at archaeological sites. Interestingly, the fundamental question is always about the authenticity of Imna and the chronology of cultural relics – in other words, which side of the strait created and/or possessed certain items first. The dilemma of archaeology can be perceived in the opposite interpretations of the archaeological data: Japanese scholars used it to affirm the existence of a Japanese colony in Korea, while Korean scholars used it to prove the Korean origin of early Japanese culture and/or royal lineage.

MORE RECENT INTERPRETATIONS

With the prevalence of modern nationalism, colonialism and imperialism in the twentieth century, the interpretation of ancient history underwent tremendous changes. These can be observed, for example, in the way that history textbooks have been revised in South Korea. Tan'gun and Tan'gun Chosŏn have been transformed from myth to historical fact and, by using the vague term *seryŏk pŏmwi*, or the scope of power, the map of Ko Chosŏn was made to cover a wide range from northeast China to the Korean peninsula – a prime example of irredentism in historical inquiry. Despite the prominence of Kija in Korean history until the late nineteenth century, Kija and Kija Chosŏn were completely dismissed from the historical lineage of Korean history. Starting from Tan'gun, the textbooks implied a continuity of the Tan'gun lineage in the following period, conventionally named the Kija Chosŏn.

The nature and location of the Han Commanderies and Imna became two of the most contested issues since the late nineteenth century, thanks to their potential implications for the formation of a new East Asian order. Despite the complexity, importance and sensitivity of these issues, both the Han Commanderies and Imna have completely disappeared from current history textbooks in South Korea. Although these are ongoing debates, and there is room for different and/or opposite interpretations, revisionist views are still far from sufficient in counteracting the image of the Han Commanderies and Imna as foreign colonies located on the Korean peninsula. Therefore, without making any reference to the installation of the Four Han Commanderies, the textbook revisions have emphasized Korean resistance against foreign power and implied the eventual victory of the Korean nation.

Nationalist historiography is still prevalent among many Korean historians because of its contribution to counteracting Japanese colonialism and racism during the colonial period. With the disintegration of the Cold War framework and increasing cultural, economic and political interaction among countries, studies of ancient history have become yet more complex. This is because of the still valid burden of affirming a national essence/identity despite the ambivalent boundaries among 'national' cultures, especially regarding the early history of East Asia. As a result, the so-called 'history wars' have been frequently featured in mass media. They have consequently drawn tremendous and unprecedented attention not only from academics but also from the general public, with historians often condemning their colleagues in other countries for 'distorting history'.

THE THREE KINGDOMS PERIOD

The next stage in Korean history, the Three Kingdoms period, is one of the most dynamic phases of Korean and East Asian history. Initially far apart from one other, Koguryŏ, Paekche and Silla started to have intense conflicts with one another once their respective territorial expansion required them to share borders. The frequent warfare among the three kingdoms was not just for gaining the upper hand temporarily; it became a battle for survival. As they fought among themselves, they constantly switched sides and made alliances depending on their immediate and expedient needs. At the same time, all three kingdoms drew themselves closer to China and Chinese civilization and denigrated their peers as less civilized 'others'. Their various strategies for negotiation with China also employed the discourse of civility over barbarism. By claiming a relatively higher civility, each country tried to convince China to take sides with them and to support their attacks against their peers. Silla eventually secured an alliance with Tang China by showing their wholehearted willingness to adopt Chinese investitures, including official titles and clothing customs; this was a sign of accepting China's suzerainty.

The history of the Three Kingdoms of Korea is replete with warfare among themselves, diplomacy with China and Japan and interactive cultural exchange involving Confucianism, Buddhism and governance. The most unusual situation during this time is the first transnational warfare that had involved all neighbouring countries. It started with territorial disputes among the three kingdoms; the Sui dynasty waged multiple rounds of invasion against Koguryŏ, hoping to conquer Koguryŏ after China made peace with the Turks in the west. Such skirmishes soon developed into full-scale transnational warfare. Tang and Silla allied and attacked Paekche and Koguryŏ, while Yamato Japan also dispatched its massive navy, hoping to help their former ally Paekche resurrect herself from impending demise.

Against all odds, Silla ultimately won the unification war among the three kingdoms. However, scholars have constantly questioned the scale and value of the Silla unification and have developed dramatically opposing views on it. Some have praised Silla as orchestrating the first national unification of the Korean peninsula under one ruler, an event that laid a fundamental and indispensable foundation for later Korean history. Other scholars have been cynical and more sceptical, pointing out that Silla could not secure all the former territory of the Koguryŏ Kingdom, which had been mostly taken by the Tang dynasty and the Bohai (Parhae) Kingdom. Silla not only had merely two-thirds of the Korean peninsula, but also took the blame for inviting and collaborating with the Tang army in a Korean fraternal fight among the three kingdoms. Some scholars have further lamented that it would have been much better if Koguryŏ had unified Korea. Silla's unification achieved little and came at the cost of permanently losing a grip on Northeast China, a fertile and appealing land for Koreans that has been absent from the Korean historical scope ever since.

The first transnational war in East Asia left a tremendous legacy for the following period. China, Silla and Japan had all learned a hard lesson through their violent interactions, and the countries started to explore self-strengthening and peaceful engagement. East Asia enjoyed relative peace for the next 500 years until the rise of the Mongols. During those five centuries, consistent efforts at diplomatic and cultural exchanges were made. Many Japanese and Silla students came to study in China, with diplomatic missions often resulting in the exchange of books and ideas. Commercial activities flourished and transnational trade helped economic development across East Asia.

It was also this period that gave rise to the success of Chang Pogo (788(?)–841 or 846 CE). Despite his humble origin, Chang Pogo constructed a safe trans-East Asian maritime trading network and had a strong impact on all three countries in East Asia. During the following millennium Koryŏ and Chosŏn emerged as relatively stabilized dynasties, in the sense that people in the Korean peninsula had opportunities to develop far more distinctive Korean identities, separate from China. Despite multiple and repeated foreign invasions and internal strife, each dynasty endured the dynamic vicissitudes of a 500-year-long journey to develop that identity further.

WRITINGS ON PREMODERN KOREA AND THE TEXTS IN THIS BOOK

In spite of rising global interest in Korea, overall scholarship concerning the country is still far behind that of, for example, China and Japan. When did people outside of Korea or Asia begin to write about Korea? What kind of books and writings about Korea existed for English-speaking audiences in the early twentieth century? Who cared and wrote about Korea? How should we approach those writings about Korea from today's point of view?

This book is a collection of writings about premodern Korea by Joseph H. Longford, William Elliott Griffis, Homer Hulbert and James Scarth Gale. The four authors came from two types of backgrounds: early diplomats and officials stationed in Japan who extended their interests to Korea, and early missionaries stationed in Korea. Longford was a British consular official in Japan from 1869 to 1902; he later became the first professor of Japanese at King's College London. Longford wrote extensively about Japan and his interests also extended to Korea, with his work *The Story of Korea* published in 1911. William Elliot Griffis was an American educator who taught in Japan and conducted ministry work after returning to the US. A prolific author, Elliott Griffis wrote on diverse topics and subjects, including Japan and Korea. This collection features his discussion of Korea's Three Kingdoms period from his book, *Corea: The Hermit Nation*, published in 1911.

Homer Hulbert was one of the most influential US missionaries in Korea. He was an accomplished linguist who helped to compile an English–Korean dictionary. Koreans were also grateful to him for his wholehearted support of the Korean independence movement against Japanese colonial rule. Hulbert's chapters on Early Medieval Korea, the Chosun Dynasty and King Se-jong the Great comprise the largest portion of this book.

James Scarth Gale was a prominent Canadian-American missionary in Korea. Also a talented linguist, he made tremendous contributions to the translation of the Bible into Korean. His proficiency in the Korean language far surpassed that of other missionaries and, in addition to his mission work, he also became a serious scholar of Korean literature and history. Scarth Gale is often remembered as the first Koreanist, thanks to his outstanding translation of Korean classic fiction into English. In the late 1920s he donated his collection of rare books of Korean classics to the US Library of Congress; it was the first collection of Korean sources to be housed there.

Since the study of Korean history and historiography has evolved and transformed dramatically in recent years, it is interesting to take a closer look at the four authors included in this collection who wrote about Korea in the early twentieth century. In so doing we can learn more about how they perceived Korean history and understand what the most critical and important issues were from their point of view.

There are many controversial issues in the study of premodern history which the writers selected here have sought to address. The foremost of these in the early period concerns the lineage and legitimacy of Tan'gun, Kjia and Wiman Chosŏn. For the Unified Silla period, scholars have debated the place of Parhae history and its relation to Silla. Parhae had been considered the rival and enemy of Silla. Since the late seventeenth century, however, some Korean scholars have started to embrace Parhae history, and there is now a growing call to rename the Unified Silla the 'Southern and Northern States Period'. For the Koryŏ period, the most controversial debate concerns how to perceive the political and social impact of the Civil Service Examination and whether Koryŏ was an aristocratic or bureaucratic society. There have been relatively few dynastic changes in Korean history, with the result that the transition from Koryŏ to Chosŏn is a remarkable breaking point. Whether this change was more about continuity or a revolutionary departure remains the subject of debate.

Note: A portion of this introduction is revised from the author's book, *Reconstructing Ancient Korean History: The Formation of Korean-ness in the Shadow of History* (Lanham, MD: Lexington Books, 2016).

FURTHER READING

PRIMARY SOURCES

Siman Qian, *Records of the Grand Historian* (*Shiji*, 史記; Beijing: Zhonghua Shuju, 1959)

Ban Gu, *Book of Han* (*Hanshu*, 漢書; Beijing: Zhonghua Shuju, 1962)

Chen Shou, *Records of the Three Kingdoms* (*Sanguizhi*, 三國志; Beijing: Zhonghua Shuju, 1959)

Fan Ye, *Book of the Later Han* (*Houhanshu*; 後漢書; Beijing: Zhonghua Shuju, 1965)

Kim Pusik, *History of the Three Kingdoms* (*Samguk sagi*, 三國史記, annotated by Yi Pyŏngdo; Seoul: Ŭryu Munhwasa, 1977)

Iryŏn, *Memorabilia of the Three Kingdoms* (*Samguk yusa*, 三國遺事, annotated by Yi Pyŏngdo; Seoul: Myŏngmundang, 1992)

Chŏng Inji *et al.*, *History of Goryeo/Koryŏ* (*Koryŏsa*, 高麗史; Seoul: Kyŏngin Munhwasa, 1961)

Veritable Records of the Joseon/Chosŏn Dynasty (*Chosŏn wangjo sillok*, 朝鮮王朝實錄; Seoul: Kuksa P'yŏnch'an Wiwŏnhoe, 1955–63)

SECONDARY WORKS

Cummings, Bruce, *Korea's Place in the Sun: A Modern History* (New York: Norton, 1997)

Duncan, John, *The Origins of the Choson Dynasty* (Seattle: University of Washington Press, 2014)

Eckert, Carter et al., *Korea Old and New: A History* (Seoul: Ilchokak, 1990)

Hwang, Kyung Moon, *A History of Korea*, Bloomsbury Essential Histories, 3rd edition (New York: Bloomsbury Academic, 2022)

Lee, Ki-baek, *A New History of Korea*, translated by Edward W. Wagner, with Edward J. Shultz (Cambridge, Mass.: Harvard University Press, 1984)

Lee, Peter, *Sourcebook of Korean Civilization*, vols 1 & 2 (New York: Columbia University Press, 1996)

Pai, Hyung Il, *Constructing 'Korean' Origins: A Critical Review of Archaeology, Historiography, and Racial Myth in Korean State-formation Theories* (Cambridge, Mass.: Harvard U. Asia Center, 2000)

Palais, James B., *Confucian Statecraft and Korean Institutions: Yu Hyongwon and the Late Choson Dynasty*, Korean Studies of the Henry M. Jackson School of International Studies (Seattle: University of Washington Press, 2015)

Robinson, David M., *Empire's Twilight: Northeast Asia under the Mongols* (Cambridge, Mass.: Harvard East Asia Center, 2009)

Seth, Michael J., *A History of Korea: From Antiquity to the Present* (Lanham, MD: Rowman & Littlefield, 2010)

Shultz, J. Edward, *Generals and Scholars: Military Rule in Medieval Korea* (Honolulu: University of Hawaii Press, 2000)

Shultz, J. Edward, Hugh H. W. Kang, Daniel C. Kane and Kenneth J.J. Gardiner (translators), *The Koguryŏ Annuals of the Samguk Sagi* (Seoul: The Academy of Korean Studies Press, 2011)

Xu, Stella, *Reconstructing Ancient Korean History: The Formation of Korean-ness in the Shadow of History* (Lanham, MD: Lexington Books, 2016)

Stella Xu (Introduction) is John R. Turbyfill Endowed Chair and Professor of History at Roanoke College in Virginia, where she teaches East Asian history. She received her PhD at the University of California, Los Angeles. Her research topics include history and historiography of Korea; Korean-Chinese relations; nationalism in East Asia; history, memory and popular culture; contemporary historical disputes in East Asia; and early Korean-US relations from the late-nineteenth to the early-twentieth centuries. Her essays and book reviews have appeared in *Korean Studies*, *Journal of Korean Studies*, *Pacific Affairs*, *ASIANetwork Exchange: A Journal for Asian Studies in the Liberal Arts*, *Women and Social Movement in the United States, 1600–2000* and *Japanese Studies Association Journal*. Her book, *Reconstructing Ancient Korean History: The Formation of Korean-ness in the Shadow of History* (Lexington Books) was published in June, 2016.

LAND, PEOPLE & EARLY HISTORY

Joseph H. Longford (whose writings in *The Story of Korea*, published in 1911, make up this section) introduced the Korean land and people to others by providing information on geography, animals, climate, the origin of the people and their language. He placed special emphasis on the tiger, the most conspicuous animal in Korea due to its size and ferocity, as well as its complicated relations with humans – after all, tigers and humans can switch their roles of hunter and the hunted in winter and summer.

Longford also emphasized the close relationship between the Japanese and Korean people and languages. Korean people may consist of northern and southern streams, which have shown distinctions in language, customs, morals and physical characteristics. The northern immigrants came from Northeast China and beyond, while the southern immigrants arrived from the Malay Archipelago. Korean immigrants later landed on the west coast of Japan. They continued to be an important portion of the population during the formation of the Yamato people. There are close similarities in construction and vocabulary between Japanese and Korean. However, the Japanese language should be considered a branch of Korean, not vice versa as some patriotic Japanese philologists had claimed.

As for the earliest history of Korea, Longford introduced the Tan'gun myth – although he was mistaken about Tan'gun's origin: it was his father Hwan'ung who descended from heaven and conceived Tan'gun with a bear-woman (the female bear was transformed into a woman after observing taboos for 21 days). Longford attributed the origin of Korean civilization to the Chinese sage Ki Tse (Jizi) who, along with 5,000 faithful followers, came to Korea. Here he taught Koreans not only techniques of land cultivation and silk production and the rearing of silkworms, but also propriety and morals, proper relations and 'Eight Simple Laws' to keep peace and order.

Longford continued with a detailed account of the rise of Wiman, invasions of Korea from Han China and the consequences of this clash. He also claimed Fuyu (Puyŏ) for early Korean history, following that with information about Kaoli (Koguryŏ), Samhan and the formation of the Three Kingdoms. Longford's text here ends with his perception of Mimana; he disagreed with Japanese claims that Mimana was a Japanese protectorate or territory in Korea.

THE COUNTRY AND ITS PEOPLE

The kingdom of Korea, which possessed an authentic history extending over 3,000 years and traditional legends dating from a period more than 1,000 years prior to the dawn of its history, lay in the peninsula which extends southwards into the Sea of Japan from the north-eastern boundaries of the Chinese Empire and is fringed on its southern and western sides by numerous islands. Its existence first became known in

Europe through the Arab geographer Khordadbeh, who, in the ninth century of our era, described it in his book of roads and provinces, quoted in Baron Richtofen's great work on China, as 'an unknown land beyond the frontiers of Kantu' – the modern Shantung – 'rich in gold, and exporting ginseng, camphor, aloes, and deerhorn, and such manufactured products as nails, saddles, porcelain, and satin.' 'Mussulmans,' he said, 'who visited it were often so attracted by it that they were induced to settle there.' It was visited in the sixteenth century by one of the Jesuit priests from the mission in Japan, who was permitted to act as chaplain to the Christian soldiers who formed a large contingent of Hideyoshi's invading armies in the closing decade of the century; but the earliest European description of it which now survives was furnished by Hendrik Hamel, a Dutch seaman, who was shipwrecked in the year 1653 on the Island of Quelpart, when on a voyage from Texel to Japan, in the service of the Dutch East India Company....

The Peninsula

The peninsula extends from 43° 02' to 33° 12' north latitude and from 124° 18' to 130° 54' east longitude. Its extreme width in its widest part, from the mouth of the Yalu to that of the Tumen, is over 350 miles, but this narrows in the latitude of the capital to 120 miles. Its length is about 500 miles, and its total coastline is said to be over 1,700 miles. Its total area is estimated as 84,000 square miles, or, roughly, about that of Great Britain and half that of Japan. It is bounded on the north by the Russian Asiatic province of Primorsk, with which it is coterminous for 11 miles from the Pacific coast, and by Northeast China, its confines being delimitated by the River Tumen, flowing into the Pacific on the east, by the River Yalu, flowing into the Yellow Sea on the west, and between the two by the lofty Shan Yan Range or Ever White Mountains, in which are the sources of both rivers. On the east it has the Sea of Japan, and on the west the Yellow Sea. On the south it is separated from Kiusiu by the Straits of Korea, in which, midway between the Korean and Japanese coasts, lies the Japanese island of Tsushima, from which Korea is visible on clear days. The number of Korean islands exceeds 200.

One small, solitary island, Dagelet Island – so named by the French navigator La Perouse, who discovered it, in honour of the great French astronomer – lies in the Japan Sea, as lonely as St. Helena in the Great Ocean, 45 miles off the east coast, but with that exception all the islands are on the southern or western coasts of the peninsula. The majority of these are inhabited, cultivated or well wooded, but some are bare volcanic rocks, rising with picturesque precipitousness out of the sea, to a height of from 1,000 to 2,000 feet. The largest and most important among them is Quelpart … a well-cultivated island, 40 miles in length by 17 in breadth, with a resident population of 100,000 souls, lying about 60 miles from the southwest corner of the mainland. Thirty-six miles to the east of Quelpart is the Nan Hau Group of three islands[…].

The West and East Coasts

The picturesqueness of the seascapes throughout the whole length of the western coast is increased by numberless islets or rocks that rise boldly out of the deep waters of the sea, whose cliffs and fir-clad peaks are the joy of lovers of the grand in Nature, but whose presence is a source of anxiety to the navigator when, as is often the case, they are shrouded in the dense summer fogs of the Yellow Sea. So thickly do islands and islets duster together along the entire western shore of the peninsula that it is only at rare intervals the mainland can be seen at all from the deck of the passing seagoing steamer.

On the east, the long coast, from the Russian frontier to the south-east corner, where the harbour of Fusan fronts Tsushima and Kiusiu, is, with the one exception already mentioned, destitute of islands, and its line is broken only by what is called Broughton Bay, after the great British navigator, with its two harbours of Gensan and Port Lazareff. On the south coast are the capacious, deep, and well-sheltered harbours of Fusan and Masampo, each capable of affording safe anchorage for a fleet of the largest warships of the present day, the possession of which is therefore a most valuable asset to a power that aspires to the naval hegemony of the Pacific.

On the west coast there are many harbours, and also anchorages amid and under the shelter of the islands, but both their naval and commercial importance is discounted by the tides, which rise and fall, with great rapidity and violence, from 25 to 30 feet. On the east and south coasts the rise and fall are only a few feet. Quelpart has no harbour, but the Nan Hau Group enclose a deep and well-sheltered harbour, which could hold all the fleets on the Pacific, though they would have a poor time if seeking refuge from the guns of a blockading enemy. Both east and west coasts are bold and hilly, the east mountainous, only a narrow strip of cultivated plains separating the shore from the chain of lofty mountains which, after starting from the sacred Paik-Tu peak of the Ever White Range in the extreme north and passing through the centre of the north-eastern province of Ham Gyong, reaches the east coast about the fortieth parallel of latitude and then extends in a continuous line to the extreme south, here and there on its way throwing out spurs that wind towards the western coast.

Mountainous Areas

Among these spurs, nearly midway between the extreme north and south, are the Diamond Mountains, so called by the Koreans themselves, from the resemblance of their 'twelve thousand serrated peaks' to rough diamonds, the site of the great historic Buddhist monasteries of Korea, and famous, not only in Korea but in China and Japan, for the sublime grandeur of their scenery.

All Korea is mountainous, not so much so as is Japan, but still so broken that there is only one – perhaps two may be admitted – extensive plain, and the whole surface of the country was compared by the French missionaries to the sea in a heavy gale. The mountains in the north are thickly wooded and their deep valleys and gorges afford scenes of impressive beauty; but those along the coast are mostly bare, their surface covered with coarse bamboo grass, the monotony of which is only varied by scattered groves of stunted firs that rarely attain to a height of more than four to five feet. The 'land of treeless mountains' is a common epithet for Korea among Japanese. At a distance the coasts are not unlike the Sussex Downs, though they rise to a greater height from the sea level, but it is only distance that gives them this enchantment, the coarse grass which covers them being woefully different to the soft turf of the Downs.

Every mountain gorge and valley is watered by its own stream, that rushes over a shallow, pebbly bed; but, as could not be otherwise in so narrow a country, large rivers are few, and both their swiftness and shallowness render them unsuitable for purposes of transport. The Yalu (called by the Koreans, from the vividness of its colour after the melting of the snow and ice, the Am Nok or Green Duck) and the Tumen in the north have been already mentioned. Others, flowing into the Yellow Sea, are the Tatong, which flows through a great part of the north-western province of Phyong An, and, passing the old historical capital of the province, enters the sea at Chinampo about the thirty-ninth parallel, and the Han, which, rising in the eastern province of Kang Won and entering the sea at Chemulpo on the western coast, divides the entire peninsula into two almost equal portions. On it lies the capital Seoul. All these rivers receive many tributaries, and all are navigable for small craft for some distance from their mouths. The Naktong, which finds its way to the sea at Fusan in the south-eastern corner of the peninsula, after an almost direct southern course, is the only river of importance in the east, the proximity of the mountains to the coast preventing those which take their rise on the eastern slopes attaining any higher dignity than that of streams. There are no lakes in Korea sufficiently large to be marked on the map.

Domestic Animals

The domestic animals include horses, asses, mules, oxen, dogs, sheep, goats, and pigs. The horses are small, and long-continued cruelty has rendered them vicious in the extreme, but they possess great strength. The want of roads prevents their use in carriages or carts, and as the modern Koreans are not a nation of horsemen and prefer the more humble donkey for purposes of travelling, the principal service of the horse is that of pack carrying. For agricultural purposes only the ox is used. Cattle are abundant, especially in the south, and of excellent quality, bearing a marked resemblance to the English shorthorns, and are as remarkable for their tractability as the horses are the reverse. The Koreans are largely a meat-eating people, not disdaining even the flesh of dogs, and ox hides are an important article of export, furnishing the main supply for the requirements of the modern tanneries of Japan.

Wild Animals

Of the wild animals, the most noted is the tiger, which exists in great numbers in the mountains and forests of the north-eastern provinces, but is found all over the country, tigers having, it is said, been known to enter into the very streets of the capital. It is equally characterized by its size, boldness, and ferocity, qualities which have given it a prominent place in the folklore, proverbs, and customs of the people, and have also, it may be added, filled them with a very well-grounded dread. Its figure was a favourite device to be emblazoned on war banners.

The tiger hunters, who form a class by themselves, were always called upon to lead forlorn hopes when on military service, as those whose courage, strength, and activity had been developed in the best of schools. The skins, which are beautifully marked and, as is natural from the fact that its principal home is among mountains that are deeply clad in snow for nearly half the year, have a much thicker fur than the Indian variety, were highly prized for decorative purposes, not only as rugs but as military ornaments by the Japanese, among whom, ever since the days of Hideyoshi, the tiger-skin-covered scabbard was one of the most cherished outer marks of an officer of rank, while the claws were worn as jewels. The flesh was eaten and the bones were converted into a medicine which was highly prized in the Chinese pharmacopoeia as a courage-producing specific of infallible merit. Tigers were usually hunted in winter, when they floundered helplessly in the deep snow, the frozen surface of which was strong enough to bear the weight of nimble hunters on snowshoes and their dogs, but even under these circumstances, the courage of the hunters may be estimated from the fact that they seldom hesitated to attack the tiger single-handed and armed only with an old flintlock gun. In summer, on the other hand, when the dense undergrowth of the forests placed the hunter at its mercy, the advantage was on the side of the tiger, a fact which gave rise to the Chinese saying that the tiger is hunted by the Koreans during one half of the year and the Koreans by the tiger during the other half. Notwithstanding the terror caused by his known presence in their neighbourhood, villagers are so reckless as to sleep in midsummer with wide-open doors or even beneath sheds or in the open fields, where they fall an easy prey. The annual death roll is therefore very large.

The other wild animals include leopards, bears, deer, boars, and a variety of fur-bearing animals, including otters, martins, squirrels, and sables. Among the birds are eagles, hawks, pheasants, ducks, swans, geese, herons, cranes, snipe, rooks, storks, and many others in numbers large enough to render Korea, with its additional opportunities for the hunting of large game, a paradise for sportsmen, were it not for the physical discomforts of travelling and lodging in the mountain districts. The seas, especially on the east and south coasts, abound in fish, though the variety is much less than on the coast of Japan. They have long been a successful fishing ground for whales, which follow the shoals of herrings and sardines that are found in immense numbers. Only the most primitive methods of fishing are followed by the Koreans, and it is principally Japanese fishermen who reap the rich harvest of their seas on the east and Chinese on the west. Even in the days of national isolation, no prohibition was imposed on either Chinese or Japanese against fishing in Korean waters, the only limitation being that they should neither land on Korean soil nor communicate with the natives while on the sea. The last was easily evaded, either in the obscurity of the frequent fogs or under the shadows of the many islands whose lofty cliffs towered out of the sea, and extensive smuggling was successfully carried on by Chinese and Japanese, especially by the former, who, to this day, may be counted among the most astute smugglers in the world....

The Seasons

In a peninsula which extends over so wide an expanse of latitude the climate naturally varies. The winters in the two southern provinces are bright and mild. In the north and on the west coast they are also bright and clear, but the cold is intense. In both north and south there are clear, unclouded skies, and the dryness of the atmosphere renders even the most severe cold bearable. The river Han is usually frozen for two or even three months, the Yalu for a longer period, and the ice on both has been sufficiently strong to admit of the crossing of great armies with their baggage. In Ham Gyong the snow lies deep throughout the whole winter, and all the mountains, even in the south, have snow-clad summits from autumn to spring.

The autumn and spring are both delightful seasons, the spring genially warm and the autumn crisp and clear, and both are beautified by the flora and foliage, by the cherry trees of spring and the maples of autumn, which are hardly less varied and abundant than those which are the glory of Japan. Only the summer months are trying to Europeans. The rainy season, extending from the middle of June to the middle of July, is enervating and exhausting, and it is followed by two months of hot, glaring summer, when the deep valleys, encircled by the scorched, treeless hills, and cut off from all sea breezes, become almost natural furnaces. Generally, the climate may be described as colder in winter and hotter in summer than are the same latitudes in Europe. Europeans have not found it unhealthy.

Origin of the People

The origin of the people who inhabit the peninsula can only be a subject of conjecture, as is also the case in regard to that of the Japanese, with whom language and characteristics show that the Koreans are closely allied. Two great immigrations to Japan occurred in primeval ages: one from Korea, when the immigrants landed in the province of Izumo on the west coast of the main Island of Japan, directly facing Korea and separated from it by 100 miles of sea, and the second from the south, in which the landing took place at Hiuga, a province on the south-east coast of Kiusiu. Both finally united at Yamato, where they became fused into one people, the southerners, however, proving the dominant race and furnishing the national rulers. The ease with which they united, the fact that tradition recalls no complications between them caused by linguistic difficulties, have suggested the theory that both bodies had an ultimate common origin, that the southerners had, as was the case with those who landed at Izumo, their original home in the Steppes of Siberia, but reached Japan after more protracted wanderings through China and the

Malay Archipelago, during which they acquired a large admixture of Malay blood.

These theories are not supported by what history shows was the case in Korea. Before the dawn of the Christian era the tribal population of the peninsula south of the Han River were distinct in language, customs, moral and physical characteristics from those north of the river. Those in the south may, as did the Hiuga immigrants to Japan, originally have found their way from the Malay Archipelago, while the northerners undoubtedly came from Northeast China and beyond. Both, in the process of time, acquired a large admixture of Chinese and Japanese blood, hordes of Chinese immigrants pouring into the country in the centuries immediately prior to and succeeding the beginning of the Christian era, flying from the anarchy that then prevailed throughout their own empire, while Japanese founded permanent settlements over a considerable portion of the south. In later ages substantial numbers of Koreans of all ranks in life in their turn emigrated and became domiciled in Japan, infusing their own blood into the Japanese, both of the aristocratic and of the lower classes....

The Language

The languages of both Korea and Japan are of the same Turanian family, as closely allied as are the Dutch and German or the Italian and Spanish languages; in fact, patriotic Japanese philologists have gone so far as to claim that Korean is only a branch of Japanese, like the native language of the Loo Choo Islands. It might perhaps be more correctly said that Japanese is only a branch of Korean. Whichever may have been the original predominating tongue, not only Japanese but the most distinguished English authorities have clearly demonstrated from both construction and vocabulary a close similarity between both languages; and that the resemblance was anciently much closer than at the present day is shown by the fact that in the very earliest intercourse between the two countries no difficulty whatsoever seems to have been experienced in the interchange of ideas. It was not until a comparatively late period that interpreters and translators were first mentioned in the national records, and it was still later when they became recognized as necessary officials. [...] From the writings of both sailors and missionaries a fairly full description may be gleaned of the customs and institutions of the people when both were founded on the social and political systems of China, and when no attempt had yet been made to force on them the civilization of Europe, which Japan so eagerly, rapidly, and successfully assimilated.

EARLIEST HISTORY

Korea claims to date the beginning of her history from the year 2333 BCE, nearly 1,700 years prior to the accession of Jimmu Tenno to the Imperial throne of Japan, and, to take a Western parallel, nearly 1,600 years prior to the founding of the city of Rome. In that year the son of the Creator of Heaven descended with a retinue of heavenly spirits, alighting on a mountain in what is now the province of Phyong An, and there beneath the shade of a santal tree, in the presence of his attendant spirits, he proclaimed himself Lord of all the earthly world, assuming the name of 'Tan Gun' or the Lord of the Santal tree.

Though on earth he retained divine immortality, for his reign lasted for over 1,000 years, and then he did not die but resumed his original heavenly form and disappeared from the earth. Relics of him and his reign still remain. An altar built by him still exists on Mount Mari in the island of Kang Wha. Phyong An, a city famous throughout all the history of Korea, from his time to the present day, is said to have been his capital, and while he ascended to heaven without dying, his grave is still shown in the province at Kang Tong. He had a son who was driven from his father's kingdom by Ki Tse, and who, flying northwards, founded a new kingdom in the far north to which he gave the name of Puyu, which we shall find influencing the destinies of Korea after another 1,000 years have passed.

Founder of Korean Civilization

Ki Tse, before whom the son of Tan Gun fled, is regarded as the founder of Korean civilization. In the twelfth century preceding the Christian era the Yin dynasty of the Emperors of China, which had lasted from 1766 BCE, was tottering to its fall. The last of the race was the Emperor Chow, whose cruelty and vices made his subjects rise in rebellion and destroy him and all his family. He had been fortunate in having three sages as his ministers who had vainly endeavoured to divert him from his evil courses. Two of them were put to death at the instigation of a beautiful concubine with whom he was infatuated; and the third, Ki Tse, though closely allied by blood to the emperor, was in prison when the revolution took place. He was at once released, and the new Emperor offered to restore him to his old dignities. Notwithstanding all he had suffered, he was still loyal to the memory of his former master, and found it impossible to serve the usurper to whom that master owed his ruin, however well merited it was. He chose rather to expatriate himself and seek a home in a new land, and, accompanied in his exodus by 5,000 faithful followers, he migrated to Korea, and there founded a kingdom to which he gave the name of Chosen [also spelled Chosön, Cho-sen, Chosun, Joseon], the Land of the Morning Calm. This was in the year 1122 BCE.

Whether his migration took place by sea or land is not known, nor is the precise locality of the new kingdom definitely acknowledged. Some historians say that it was entirely outside the boundaries of modern Korea, and that it lay where the Chinese province Sheng King now is. But the version dear to the hearts of Koreans is that he came by sea and landed somewhere south of the Han River; that his capital was, as was that of Tan Gun, at the city of Phyong An, and that his kingdom was originally in the Korean provinces of Phyong An and Hoanghai, though it subsequently spread in the north until its boundary became the River Liao. Whatever be the truth, Ki Tse and his followers brought with them the elements of civilization, of industry, and of good government. Before his coming the land which he occupied was peopled by nine wild tribes who dressed in grass, lived under the trees in summer and in holes in the earth in winter, and fed on berries. He introduced among them the arts and industries of China, taught them tillage and sericulture; above all, he taught them propriety, the proper relations that exist among civilized mankind, those of king and subject, parent and child, husband and wife, old and young, master and servant, and gave them the 'eight simple laws', under which peace and order were so well maintained that robbery was unknown, doors and shutters were never closed, not even during the night, and women were rigidly chaste.

Death of Ki Tse

Ki Tse reigned for thirty-one years, and, dying in 1083 BCE, left a kingdom which was ruled by his direct descendants for nearly 900 years. The last of the dynasty was Ki Jun, who reigned at his ancestral capital of Phyong An from 221 to 193 BCE. His fall was an indirect consequence of wars in the North of China. Yen, a tributary state of that Empire, coterminous with Chosen, from which it was separated by the River Liao, rose in rebellion against its suzerain, and in the wars which followed and culminated in the total defeat of the rebel state, many of its inhabitants sought refuge from the invading Chinese armies in the neighbouring kingdom of Chosen. Among them was one of their generals, named Wiman.

Coming to Korea a beaten refugee, he was kindly received by the king, and given land in the north of the kingdom, whereon he established himself and his followers, where he promised to act as a frontier guard. He was, however, ambitious and treacherous. He had already his own followers; there were many of his own compatriots who had preceded him in his flight and were already settled in the north, and from the first he laid himself out to win the goodwill of the local tribes. When he felt secure in his strength, in the union of all three – his own followers, his countrymen who had preceded him, and the local tribes – he suddenly marched on Phyong An, treacherously announcing that he was coming to guard the capital and the King against an apocryphal Chinese invasion. Too late his treachery was discovered. No defence could be made against him, and all that was left for the last of the Ki Tse dynasty to do was to find personal safety in flight to the south of the peninsula, while Wiman entered Phyong An and proclaimed himself king in his stead.

Wiman's Administration

Wiman's administration was vigorous and successful. He soon procured his investiture as King from the Emperor of China, who seemed not only to have overlooked the fact that he had shortly before been a rebel, but to have now sought his services as a check against barbarian inroads to his own Empire from the north. Secure in his position, with the moral support of China and the material support of his own army of adventurers, he considerably enlarged the original Chosen territory and was able to secure the succession to his own descendants. But once their position was assured, both he and they, in the pride of their triumph, neglected their duty as vassals of sending tribute-bearing missions to the emperor, and no one went from their dominions 'to see the emperor's face'. During the reign of Wiman's grandson, Yu Ku, a Chinese envoy, came to his capital and reproved him for this neglect but without result. Yu Ku still refused to fulfil his duty, and the envoy, forced to return without accomplishing his mission, and vexed at his failure, when near the frontier on his way back to his own country, caused his charioteer to murder the prince to whom Yu Ku had deputed the task of courteously escorting him. Having accomplished this treachery, the envoy hastily crossed the frontier and reported to the emperor that he had killed a Korean general, and for his feat, his report of which was received without question, he was rewarded with the appointment of 'Protector of the Eastern Tribes of Liao Tung'.

At this time the kingdom of Korea was coterminous with Liao Tung and comprised all that portion of modern Northeast China that extends as far as the sources of the Sugari as well as the three northern provinces of modern Korea, its boundaries being the sea on the east and west and the River Han on the south, and all the tribes throughout this great extent of territory had submitted to the authority of Wiman and his successors. Yu Ku could therefore call to arms a fighting force, powerful in numbers and rendered by their mode of life as nomads and hunters formidable as fighting units. With such means at his disposal, it was not likely that he should permit the treacherous murder of his officer and relative to go unavenged. He promptly gathered his army and, marching into Liao Tung, attacked and killed the 'Protector of the Eastern Tribes'. By this action he had thrown the gauntlet of defiance in the face of the emperor – one of the powerful and vigorous Han dynasty – and knew he would have to pay the penalty. Withdrawing, therefore, at once to his own territories, he made preparations to meet the invasion that would soon be on him.

China Invades

The emperor sent two forces against him. One, of 50,000 men, commanded by an admiral, was sent by sea from Shantung and consisted of men of that province, all of powerful physique and capable of great endurance. The other, composed of Liao Tung men, many of them released criminals, marched by land under the command of a lieutenant general, the objective of both being Yi Ku's capital. The plans of the invaders were badly laid, and instead of concentrating simultaneously before the capital, as did three Japanese armies in our own day on the outbreak of the China war with Japan in 1894, the marine force appeared first by itself, and the garrison at once attacked and scattered it, the admiral himself being obliged to fly to the mountains and ten days passing before he was able to reassemble his fugitive men. The general was not more fortunate. 'His men nearly all exposed themselves to the penalty of decapitation by breaking into disorder and running back at the first onslaught,' and he could make no impression on the division of the Korean army that faced him.

Both sides were now at a deadlock. The two Chinese armies were in Korea, and though kept at bay by the victorious Koreans could not be dislodged, while the Chinese on their side could not break the Korean resistance. So recourse was once more had to diplomacy, and a second envoy was sent by the Emperor 'to deliver a lecture to Yu Ku'. The latter professed his regret for what had passed and his readiness to tender his submission as vassal to the emperor, but he feared that the officers who represented him might again be treacherously murdered as was the first. Neither side could trust the other. Yu Ku would not send his son, who was proposed as messenger, within the Chinese lines without a strong escort, which the Chinese would not admit. So the negotiation fell through. The Chinese envoy, having reported his failure to the emperor, was promptly executed, and the war was resumed.

Both Chinese commanders were now more successful. The general, reinforced by troops from Chihli and Shansi, who showed more courage than the released criminals from Liao Tung, defeated the Koreans, and, advancing on the capital, invested it on the north, while the admiral, having reorganised his beaten men, co-operated with him by investing it on the south. The relations between the two were, however, not cordial, and the spirit of their two armies was not the same. One, flushed with recent victory, was anxious for more glory, and its commander wished to press the siege to the utmost. The other had not yet recovered from its first defeat, and its admiral, depressed and humiliated, sought rather to come to terms with the besieged. Between the two nothing was done, and the Koreans then, as now and ever in their history, fighting stoutly behind their walls, held out for many months. Wearied with the long delay, the emperor sent a high military commissioner with full powers to settle the differences between the two commanders. He accepted the general's explanation that the weakness and pusillanimity of the admiral were the cause of the long delay, and that they must eventuate, if they continued, in the destruction of both armies. So the admiral was placed under arrest, and the siege continued under the general.

The Capital Falls

Still the city held out, and it was only taken at last, in the summer of 108 BCE, when Yu Ku, who to the end refused to talk of surrender, had been murdered by his own officers and the gates opened by the murderers. This was the end of the ancient kingdom of Chosen. Its dominions were incorporated into the Chinese Empire and divided into four military provinces under Chinese governors, and for over 100 years remained under Chinese domination. The fate of the two military commanders who had contributed to its downfall is a curious illustration of the Chinese methods of dealing with their officers. The weak and timorous admiral, who had done nothing but thwart the designs of his colleague, was sentenced to death, but was permitted to condone the death penalty by a fine and reduction to the rank of commoners. The general, who had won victories, who had vigorously endeavoured to hasten the siege, and had, throughout all the campaign, the confidence of his men, was on his return to his own capital 'convicted of desire for glorification, jealousy, and wrongheaded strategy, and was cut to pieces in the marketplace'.

The northern boundaries of old Chosen are not clearly known, and were probably never delineated while the kingdom existed. Beyond them, the vast plains of Northeast China were inhabited by numbers of tribes who, in the last century preceding the Christian era, began to organise themselves into petty states. While professing a nominal allegiance to the Emperor of China, these states were perfectly independent in both their internal and external administration, governing themselves and making war on or alliances with each other as they pleased, without reference to their suzerain. One of them, lying immediately to the south of the River Sungari, was called Puyu, and was said … to have been founded in the Dark Ages by the son of the mythical Tan Gun. North, and separated from it by the Sungari, was another tribe or state, which found its home in the delta formed by the rivers Sungari and Amur to the west of their junction, and was called Korea or Kaoli [also spelled Korai], but the time at which it existed was so ancient 'that even the Chinese historians mention it with a degree of scepticism'.

Tung Ming

While the chief of this barbarian tribe was once absent, on a hunting excursion, one of his damsels was found to be with child. She said that she had seen in the sky a vapour as large as an egg which descended on her, in consequence of which she conceived. The chief, who had at first meditated killing her, on hearing this explanation of her condition, put her in prison, where a son was born to her in due course of time. The chief was equally afraid to kill or preserve a child so miraculously born, and it was by his orders thrown to the pigs, but the pigs breathed upon it and kept it alive. Then it was thrown among the horses, but they did as the pigs had done, and so the babe still lived, and the chief, now convinced that it was of supernatural birth, restored it to its mother.

It was named Tung Ming (Eastern Brightness), and when the babe grew up a brave youth and a skilful archer, the old chief became jealous of him and sought to slay him. Then the youth fled southwards until he found himself stopped by the river. In despair, he shot his arrows into the water, when all the fish and tortoises of the river came to the surface, and, crowding together to avoid his arrows, formed with their backs a bridge upon which he crossed in safety. He was now in Puyu and became its king. The people of Puyu had already emerged from barbarism; their home was in the largest of the Eastern plains, which were rich and fertile and produced the five cereals in abundance, and they had many of the elements of primitive civilization.

'They had circular stockades in place of city walls, palace buildings, granaries, stores, and prisons. They were of an uncouth, robust, and hardy habit, and yet scrupulously honest and not given to plundering raids. In eating and drinking they used dishes and platters, and when they met together they observed the etiquette of the table. They were wont to be severe in their punishments and the household of the condemned were always relegated to slavery. Robberies were visited with twelvefold amercement. Lewdness was punished with the death of both man and woman, and they were particularly severe on jealous wives. If the elder brother died, the younger married his sister-in-law. Homicides were kept for burying alive at funerals, sometimes a whole hundred of them being used.'

Foundation of Kaoli

From this tribe, after many generations from Tung Ming's reign had passed, about the beginning of the Christian era, some families moved southwards under the leadership of a chief named Kao and settled themselves among the valleys and mountains in the land which now forms the south-western part of the modern Chinese province of Kirin. There they founded, in the year 37 BCE, a new nation, to which they gave the name of Kaoli, a combination formed of the name of their leader and that of the country in the faraway north from which the King of Puyu, the ancestor of their own leader, had fled. The new state was at first as insignificant in influence as it was in the number of its people, and when Chosen was governed by China, it was included in one of the four military provinces into which Chosen was divided for administrative purposes. But it quickly grew in strength and aggressiveness, and before a century had passed it had become a formidable power which threatened even the safety and peace of Liao Tung, while it had also absorbed all the country which lay to its east and extended to the sea. Its population was rapidly increased by refugees from the miseries of anarchy in China, and it became a powerful political and military factor in the wars which were continually taking place on the northern frontier of China.

During these wars Kao-Kaoli steadily pursued its conquering career westwards, and, though more slowly, southwards across the River Yalu and into the peninsula, and before the beginning of the fifth century it was recognized as a powerful kingdom and a highly valued tributary of the empire, extending from the River Tatong on the south to the River Liao on its west, and comprising all the territory that constituted the old Chosen. The prefix was dropped from its original name, and it became known simply as Kaoli, or to use the pronunciation employed by the people themselves, Korea. Before telling its story, we must turn aside for a while to describe the southern part of the peninsula and its people.

The Three Districts

It has been already told how Kijun, the last of the Ki Tse, when driven from his capital by the treacherous Wiman, fled to the south. At this time the peninsula south of the River Tatong was divided into three districts called Han, and distinguished as Ma-han, Ben-han, and Shin-han, the inhabitants of the first of which differed in language and customs from the other two. Although the latter lived together promiscuously, they presented some minor differences among themselves, and all three differed so fundamentally from the northerns of Korea, that it has been assumed that their origin, of which nothing definite is known, is to be looked for in Southern Asia, whence they migrated to Korea by sea, while that of the northerns is, as has been seen, looked for among the nomadic tribes of the plains of Northeast China.

Each district was formed of a congery of tribes, those of Ma-han numbering fifty-four and the other two twelve each, and not even those in the same district were united under any one central and predominant authority. Any indication as to the geographical limits of each district can only be based on pure conjecture, and all that can be safely said in this respect is that Ma-han was on the west-central coast of the peninsula, probably occupying the whole of the province of Chhung-Chyong and part of Cholla, Ben-han on the south, and Shin-han on the east. It was among the Ma-han that Kijun, landing at what is now Iksan, took refuge, and he was accompanied by a band of followers sufficiently strong to enable him to assume authority over all the tribes who had no union among themselves and were less vigorous and far less civilized than the northern refugees. His own reign over them was, however, of short duration, he and his son being destroyed by the people, but his descendants continued to rule till 16 BCE.

The civilization of all three districts was of a lower order than that of the people of the north. The Ma-han were acquainted, however, with tillage, sericulture, and weaving.

'They lived in mixed settlements and had no cities. They built their houses of mud, in shape like a gravemound, with an opening or door at the top. They were not acquainted with the kneeling form of obeisance, and drew no distinction of age or sex. They did not value gold, jewels, embroidery, or rugs, were ignorant of the way to ride oxen or horses, and only esteemed pebbles and pearls as ornaments for setting off their garments, and as necklaces and eardrops. The majority had no head covering beyond their coiled chignons, cloth robes, and straw sandals. The people were robust and brave, and the young men, when exerting themselves to build a house, would take a rope and run it through the skin of the back, and trail a huge log by it, amid cheers for their sturdiness. After the cultivation was finished in the fifth moon, they always worshipped the spiritual powers, and had a drinking bout, day and night, assembling in groups to dance and sing, when several dozen men would follow each other in keeping time by stamping on the ground.'

Settled among the Ma-han tribes, and so assimilated as to form with them one of the fifty-four tribes, was a colony descended from Chinese refugees, who had crossed from China at some remote period, and who, from the number of their party, which their traditions put at ten barons and their followers, were called Pekche, or 'the hundred crossers', the larger number being taken instead of ten to mark the fidelity of the followers. It was among this particular tribe that Kijun found his home. The tribes, both on the east and on the west, in the progress of time combined and formed two nations. That on the west, formed of the Ma-han, assumed the name of Pekche, originally only that of one alien settlement among them. The other two Han united into one nation, to which they gave the name of Shinra.

Formation of the Three Kingdoms

We have now arrived at the formation of the three independent kingdoms among which Korea was divided during the first six centuries of the Christian era: Korea, or Kaoli, on the north, known as Koma to the Japanese, founded in 35 BCE, and comprising all the north-west of the peninsula and a great part of what is now Northeast China; Pekche, called by the Koreans Baiji and by the Japanese Kudara, occupying all the west as far north as the River Tatong, tracing its foundation back to the year 16 BCE; and Shinra, subsequently euphonized into Silla, called by the Japanese Shiragi, occupying the whole of the east coast as far north as the Korea boundary, the precise location of which is impossible to fix, and dating its foundation as a united state from the year 57 BCE. In the south of the peninsula, a few tribes managed to preserve their independence against both Pekche and Silla for a few centuries, and to form a confederacy which they called the kingdom of Karak. It was originally not inferior in the extent of its dominions to Silla, but as time went on it was gradually absorbed by the latter, the last part of it to survive being the state known to the Japanese as Imna or Mimana, which eventually became what might not be improperly termed a Japanese protectorate or residency, and was mentioned by the Japanese historians as a 'Miyake' or 'state granary'. It lay as a blunt wedge on the south coast between the southern parts of Silla and Pekche.

THE STORY OF THE THREE KINGDOMS

William E. Griffis started his account of the Three Kingdoms (the text which makes up this section, from his *Hermit Nation*, 1911) with Hiaksai (Paekche) because he believed that Paekche was once the lowliest civilization but became the leading state on the Korean peninsula. Japan also owed a great deal to Paekche for initiating their impulse toward civilization. He described Paekche's struggle with Silla in detail, explaining how it collapsed after facing a joint attack by Tang and Silla. Despite their efforts at restoration, and even after receiving massive military aid from Japan, Paekche was doomed. One silver lining was that many people of Paekche emigrated as refugees to Japan, where they flourished thanks to outstanding skills in art and manufacture. Korai (Koguryŏ) managed to repel multiple attacks by China, though their efforts eventually failed due to internal strife among the ruling class.

Griffis was sceptical of Japan's legend concerning Empress Jingu's conquest and domination of Sinra (Silla); he believed that Silla was far superior to the Japan of the early Christian centuries. Silla's *Nido*, or Korea syllabary, is probably the inspiration for Japanese *katakana*, invented a century later. Unified Silla stood for a golden era of learning, and Kion-chiu (Kyŏngju) was highly regarded as a sacred city, even long after Silla's decline. This period was also beneficial to Japan because the country finally started to receive developments in arts and sciences directly from China, rather than second-hand through the Korean peninsula. Griffis was critical of modern Korea, exclaiming that 'Nihon increased in wealth and civilization while Chō-sen remained stationary or retrograded'. He justified Japanese colonization of Korea, whether intentionally or not, by observing that Japan 'has stretched forth willing hands to do for her neighbour now, what Korea did for Japan in centuries long gone by'.

KINGDOM OF HIAKSAI

The history of the peninsular states from the time in which it is first known until the tenth century, is that of almost continuous civil war or border fighting. The boundaries of the rival kingdoms changed from time to time as raid and reprisal, victory or defeat, turned the scale of war. A series of maps of the peninsula expressing the political situation during each century or half-century would show many variations of boundaries, and resemble those of Great Britain when the various native and continental tribes were struggling for its mastery. Something like an attempt to depict these changes in the political geography of the peninsula has been made by the Japanese historian, Otsuki Tōyō, in his work entitled *Historical Periods and Changes of the Japanese Empire.*

Yet though our narrative, through excessive brevity, seems to be only a picture of war, we must not forget that Hiaksai, once lowest in civilization, rapidly became, and for a while continued, the leading state in the peninsula. It held the lead in literary culture until crushed by China. The classics of Confucius and Mencius, with letters, writing, and their whole train of literary blessings, were introduced first to the peninsula in Hiaksai. In 374 CE Ko-ken was appointed a teacher or master of Chinese literature, and enthusiastic scholars gathered at the court. Buddhism followed with its educational influences, becoming a focus of light and culture. As early as 372 CE an apostle of northern Buddhism had penetrated into Liao Tung, and perhaps across the Yalu. In 384 CE the missionary Marananda, a Thibetan, formally established temples and monasteries in Hiaksai, in which women as well as men became scholastics. Long before this new element of civilization was rooted in Shinra or Korai, the faith of India was established and flourishing in the little kingdom of Hiaksai, so that its influences were felt as far as Japan. The first teacher of Chinese letters and ethics in Nippon was a Korean named Wani, as was also the first missionary who carried the images and sutras of northern Buddhism across the Sea of Japan. To Hiaksai more than to any other Korean state Japan owes her first impulse toward the civilization of the west.

Hiaksai came into collision with Kokorai as early as 345 CE, at which time also Shinra suffered the loss of several cities. In the fifth century a Chinese army, sent by one of the emperors of the Wei dynasty to enforce the payment of tribute, was defeated by Hiaksai. Such unexpected military results raised the reputation of 'the eastern savages' so high in the imperial mind, that the emperor offered the King of Hiaksai the title of 'Great Protector of the Eastern Frontier'. By this act the independence of the little kingdom was virtually recognized. In the sixth century, having given and received Chinese aid and comfort in alliance with Shinra against Korai, Hiaksai was ravaged in her borders by the troops of her irate neighbour on the north. Later on, we find these two states in peace with each other and allied against Shinra, which had become a vassal of the Tang emperors of China.

From this line of China's rulers the kingdoms of Korai and Hiaksai were to receive crushing blows. In answer to Shinra's prayer for aid, the Chinese emperor, in 660, despatched from Shantung a fleet of several hundred sail with 100,000 men on board. Against this host from the west the Hiaksai army could make little resistance, though they bravely attacked the invaders, but only to be beaten. After a victory near the mouth of the Rin-yin River, the Chinese marched at once to the capital of Hiaksai and again defeated, with terrible slaughter, the provincial army. The king fled to the north, and the city being nearly empty of defenders, the feeble garrison opened the gates. The Tang banners fluttered on all the walls, and another state was absorbed in the Chinese empire. For a time Hiaksai, like a fly snapped up by an angry dog, is lost in China.

Fuku-Shin

Not long, however, did the little kingdom disappear from sight. In 670 a Buddhist priest, fired with patriotism, raised an army of monks and priests, and joining Fuku-shin (Fu-sin), a brave general, they laid siege to a city held by a large Chinese garrison. At the same time they sent word to the emperor of Japan praying for succor against the 'robber kingdom'. They also begged that Hōsho (Fung), the youthful son of the late king, then a hostage and pupil at the mikado's court, might be invested with the royal title and sent home. The mikado despatched a fleet of 400 junks and a large body of soldiers to escort the royal heir homeward. On his arrival Hōsho was proclaimed king.

Meanwhile the priest-army and the forces under Fuku-shin had reconquered nearly all their territory, when they suffered a severe defeat near the seacoast from the large Chinese force hastily despatched to put down the rebellion. The invaders marched eastward and effected a junction with the forces of Shinra. The prospects of Hiaksai were now deplorable.

For even among the men of Hiaksai there was no unity of purpose. Fuku-shin had put the priest-leader to death, which arbitrary act so excited the suspicions of the king that he in turn ordered his general to be beheaded. He then sent to Japan, appealing for reinforcements. The mikado, willing to help an old ally, and fearing that the Chinese, if victorious, might invade his own dominions, quickly responded. The Japanese contingent arrived and encamped near the mouth of the Han River, preparatory to a descent by sea upon Shinra. Unsuspecting the near presence of an enemy, the allies neglected their usual vigilance. A fleet of war junks, flying the Tang streamers, suddenly appeared off the camp, and while the Japanese were engaging these, the Chinese land forces struck them in flank. Taken by surprise, the mikado's warriors were driven like flocks of sheep into the water and drowned or shot by the Chinese archers. The Japanese vessels were burned as they lay at anchor in the bloody stream, and the remnants of the beaten army got back to their islands in pitiable fragments. Hōsho, after witnessing the destruction of his host, fled to Korai, and the country was given over to the waste and pillage of the infuriated Chinese. The royal line, after thirty generations and nearly seven centuries of rule, became extinct. The sites of cities became the habitations of tigers, and once fertile fields were soon overgrown. Large portions of Hiaksai became a wilderness.

Though the Chinese Government ordered the bodies of those killed in war and the white bones of the victims of famine to be buried, yet many thousands of Hiaksai families fled elsewhere to find an asylum and to found new industries. The people who remained on their fertile lands, as well as all Southern Korea, fell under the sway of Shinra.

The fragments of the beaten Japanese army gradually returned to their native country or settled in Southern Korea. Thousands of the people of Hiaksai, detesting the idea of living as slaves of China, accompanied or followed their allies to Japan. On their arrival, by order of the mikado, 400 emigrants of both sexes were located in the province of Omi, and over 2,000 were distributed in the Kuantō, or Eastern Japan. These colonies of Koreans founded potteries, and their descendants, mingled by blood with the Japanese, follow the trade of their ancestors.

Musashi Colony Formed

In 710 another body of Hiaksai people, dissatisfied with the poverty of the country and tempted by the offers of the Japanese, formed a colony numbering 1,800 persons and emigrated to Japan. They were settled in Musashi, the province in which Tōkiō, the modern capital, is situated. Various other emigrations of Koreans to Japan of later date are referred to in the annals of the latter country, and it is fair to presume that tens of thousands of emigrants from the peninsula fled from the Tang invasion and mingled with the islanders, producing the composite race that inhabit the islands ruled by the mikado. Among the refugees were many priests and nuns, who brought their books and learning to the court at Nara, and thus diffused about them a literary atmosphere. The establishment of schools, the awakening of the Japanese intellect, and the first beginnings of the literature of Japan, the composition of their oldest historical books, the *Kojiki* and the *Nihongi* – all the fruits of the latter half of the seventh and early part of the eighth century – are directly traceable to this influx of the scholars of Hiaksai, which being destroyed by China, lived again in Japan. Even the pronunciation of the Chinese characters as taught by the Hiaksai teachers remains to this day. One of them, the nun Hōmiō, a learned lady, made her system so popular among the scholars that even an imperial proclamation against it could not banish it. She established her school in Tsushima, CE 655, and there taught that system of [Chinese] pronunciation [*Go-on*] which still holds sway in Japan, among the ecclesiastical literati, in opposition to the Kan-on of the secular scholars. The Go-on, the older of the two pronunciations, is that of ancient North China, the *Kan-on* is that of medieval Southern China (Nanking). Korea and Japan having phonetic alphabets have preserved and stereotyped the ancient Chinese pronunciation better than the Chinese language itself, since the Chinese have no phonetic writing, but only ideographic characters, the pronunciation of which varies during the progress of centuries.

Buddhism Grows

Hiaksai had given Buddhism to Japan as early as 552 CE, but opposition had prevented its spread, the temple was set on fire, and the images of Buddha thrown in the river. In 684 one Sayéki brought another image of Buddha from Korea, and Umako, son of Inamé, a minister at the mikado's court, enshrined it in a chapel on his own grounds. He made Yeben and Simata, two Koreans, his priests, and his daughter a nun. They celebrated a festival, and henceforth Buddhism grew apace.

The country toward the sunrise was then a new land to the peninsulars, just as 'the West' is to us, or Australia is to England; and Japan made these fugitives welcome. In their train came industry, learning, and skill, enriching the island kingdom with the best infusion of blood and culture.

Hiaksai was the first of the three kingdoms that was weakened by civil war and then fell a victim to Chinese lust of conquest.

The progress and fall of the other two kingdoms will now be narrated. Beginning with Korai, we shall follow its story from the year 613 CE, when the invading hordes of the Tang dynasty had been driven out of the peninsula with such awful slaughter by the Koraians.

KINGDOM OF KORAI

After the struggle in which the Korean tiger had worsted the Western Dragon, early in the seventh century, China and Korai were for a generation at peace. The bones of the slain were buried, and sacrificial fires for the dead soothed the spirits of the victims. The same imperial messenger, who in 622 was sent to supervise these offices of religion, also visited each of the courts of the three kingdoms. So successful was he in his mission of peaceful diplomacy, that each of the Korean states sent envoys with tribute and congratulation to the imperial throne. In proof of his good wishes, the emperor returned to his vassals all his prisoners, and declared that their young men would be received as students in the Imperial University at his capital. Henceforth, as in many instances during later centuries, the sons of nobles and promising youth from Korai, Shinra, and Hiaksai went to study at Nanking, where their envoys met the Arab traders.

Korai having been divided into five provinces, or circuits, named respectively the Home, North, South, East, and West divisions, extended from the Sea of Japan to the Liao River, and enjoyed a brief spell of peace, except always on the southern border; for the chronic state of Korai and Shinra was that of mutual hostility. On the north, beyond the Tumen River, was the kingdom of Pu-hai, with which Korai was at peace, and Japan was in intimate relations, and China at jealous hostility.

The Chinese court soon began to look with longing eyes on the territory of that part of Korai lying west of the Yalu River, believing it to be a geographical necessity that it should become their scientific frontier, while the emperor cherished the hope of soon rectifying it. Though unable to forget the fact that one of his predecessors had wasted millions of lives and tons of treasure in vainly attempting to humble Kokorai, his ambition and pride spurred him on to wade through slaughter to conquest and revenge. He waited only for a pretext.

This time the destinies of the Eastern Kingdom were profoundly influenced by the character of the feudalism brought into it from ancient times, and which was one of the characteristic institutions of the Fuyu race.

The government of Korai was simply that of a royal house, holding, by more or less binding ties of loyalty, powerful nobles, who in turn held their lands on feudal tenure. In certain contingencies these noble landholders were scarcely less powerful than the king himself.

Death of the King

In 641 one of these liegemen, whose ambition the king had in vain attempted to curb and even to put to death, revenged himself by killing the king with his own hands. He then proclaimed as sovereign the nephew of the dead king, and made himself prime minister. Having thus the control of all power in the state, and being a man of tremendous physical strength and mental ability, all the people submitted quietly to the new order of things, and were at the same time diverted, being sent to ravage Shinra, annexing all the country down to the 37th parallel. The Chinese emperor gave investiture to the new king, but ordered this Korean Warwick to recall his troops from invading Shinra, the ally of China. The minister paid his tribute loyally, but refused to acknowledge the right of China to interfere in Korean politics. The tribute was then sent back with insult, and war being certain to follow, Korai prepared for the worst. War with China has been so constant a phenomenon in Korean history that a special term, Ho-ran, exists and is common in the national annals, since the 'Chinese wars' have been numbered by the score.

Chinese Invasion

Again the sails of an invading fleet whitened the waters of the Yellow Sea, carrying the Chinese army of chastisement that was to land at the head of the peninsula, while two bodies of troops were despatched by different routes landward. The Tang emperor was a stanch believer in Whang Ti, the Asiatic equivalent of the European doctrine of the divine right of kings to reign – a tenet as easily found by one looking for it in the Confucian classics, as in the Hebrew scriptures. He professed to be marching simply to vindicate the honour of majesty and to punish the regicide rebel, but not to harm nobles or people. The invaders soon overran Liao Tung, and city after city fell. The emperor himself accompanied the army and burned his bridges after the crossing of every river. In spite of the mud and the summer rains he steadily pushed his way on, helping with his own hands in the works at the sieges of the walled cities – the ruins of which still litter the plains of Liao Tung. In one of these, captured only after a protracted investment, 10,000 Koraians are said to have been slain. In case of submission on summons, or after a slight defence, the besieged were leniently and even kindly treated. By July all the country west of the Yalu was in possession of the Chinese, who had crossed the river and arrived at Anchiu, only forty miles north of Ping-an city.

By tremendous personal energy and a general levy in mass, an army of 150,000 Korai men was sent against the Chinese, which took up a position on a hill about three miles from the city. The plan of the battle that ensued, made by the Chinese emperor himself, was skilfully carried out by his lieutenants, and a total defeat of the entrapped Koraian army followed, the slain numbering 20,000. The next day, with the remnant of his army, amounting to 40,000 men, the Koraian general surrendered. Fifty thousand horses and 10,000 coats of mail were among the spoils. The foot soldiers were dismissed and ordered home, but the Koraian leaders were made prisoners and marched into China.

Koraians Refuse to Surrender

After so crushing a loss in men and material, one might expect instant surrender of the besieged city. So far from this, the garrison redoubled the energy of their defence.... The Koreans themselves knew both their forte and their foible, and so understood how to foil the invader from either sea. Shut out from the rival nations on the right hand and on the left by the treacherous sea, buttressed on the north by lofty mountains, and separated from China by a stretch of barren or broken land, the peninsula is easily secure against an invader far from his base of supplies. The ancient policy of the Koreans, by which they over and over again foiled their mighty foe and finally secured their independence, was to shut themselves up in their well-provisioned cities and castles, and not only beat off but starve away their foes. In their state of feudalism, when every city and strategic town of importance was well fortified, this was easily accomplished. The ramparts gave them shelter, and their personal valour secured the rest. Reversing the usual process of starving out a beleaguered garrison, the besiegers, unable to fight on empty stomachs, were at last obliged to raise the siege and go home. Long persistence in this resolute policy finally saved Korea from the Chinese colossus, and preserved her individuality among nations.

Faithful to their character, as above set forth, the Koraians held their own in the city of Anchiu, and the Chinese could make no impression upon it. In spite of catapults, scaling ladders, movable towers, and artificial mounds raised higher than the walls, the Koraians held out, and by sorties bravely captured or destroyed the enemy's works. Not daring to leave such a fortified city in their rear, the Chinese could not advance further, while their failing provisions and the advent of frost showed them that they must retreat.

Hungrily they turned their faces toward China.

In spite of the intense chagrin of the foiled Chinese leader, so great was his admiration for the valour of the besieged that he sent the Koraian commander a valuable present of rolls of silk. The Koraians were unable to pursue the flying invaders, and few fell by their weapons. But hunger, the fatigue of crossing impassable oceans of worse than Virginia mud, cold winds, and snowstorms destroyed thousands of the Chinese on their weary homeward march over the mountain passes and quagmires of Liao Tung. The net results of the campaign were great glory to Korai; and besides the loss of ten cities, 70,000 of her sons were captives in China, and 40,000 lay in battle graves.

According to a custom which Californians have learned in our day, the bones of the Chinese soldiers who died or were killed in the campaign were collected, brought into China, and, with due sacrificial rites and lamentations by the emperor, solemnly buried in their native soil. Irregular warfare still continued between the two countries, the offered tribute of Korai being refused, and the emperor waiting until his resources would justify him in sending another vast fleet and army against defiant Korai. While thus waiting he died.

Peace for a Time

After a few years of peace, his successor found occasion for war, and, in 660 CE, despatched the expedition which crushed Hiaksai, the ally of Korai, and worried, without humbling, the latter state. In 664 Korai lost its able leader, the regicide prime minister – that rock against which the waves of Chinese invasion had dashed again and again in vain.

His son, who would have succeeded to the office of his father, was opposed by his brother. The latter, fleeing to China, became guide to the hosts again sent against Korai 'to save the people and to chastise their rebellious chiefs'. This time Korai, without a leader, was doomed. The Chinese armies having their rear well secured by a good base of supplies, and being led by skilful commanders, marched on from victory to victory, until, at the Yalu River, the various detachments united, and breaking the front of the Korai army, scattered them and marched on to Ping-an. The city surrendered without the discharge of an arrow. The line of kings of Korai came to an end after twenty-eight generations, ruling over 700 years.

All Korai, with its five provinces, its 176 cities, and its four or five millions of people, was annexed to the Chinese empire. Tens of thousands of Koraian refugees fled into Shinra, thousands into Pu-hai, north of the Tumen, then a rising state; and many to the new country of Japan. Desolated by slaughter and ravaged by fire and blood, war and famine, large portions of the land lay waste for generations. Thus fell the second of the Korean kingdoms, and the sole dominant state now supreme in the peninsula was Shinra, an outline of whose history we shall proceed to give.

KINGDOM OF SHINRA

When Shinra becomes first known to us from Japanese tradition, her place in the peninsula is in the southeast, comprising portions of the modern provinces of Kang-wen and Kiung-sang. The people in this warm and fertile part of the peninsula had very probably sent many colonies of settlers over to the Japanese Islands, which lay only 100 miles off, with Tsushima for a stepping stone. It is probable that the 'rebels' in Kiushiu, so often spoken of in old Japanese histories, were simply

Koreans or their descendants, as, indeed, the majority of the inhabitants of Kiushiu originally had been.

The Yamato tribe, which gradually became paramount in Japan, were probably immigrants of old Kokorai stock, that is, men of the Fuyu race, who had crossed from the north of Korea over the Sea of Japan, to the land of Sunrise, just as the Saxons and Engles pushed across the North Sea to England. They found the Kumaso, or Kiushiu 'rebels', troublesome, mainly because these settlers from the west, or southern mainland of Korea, considered themselves to be the righteous owners of the island rather than the Yamato people. At all events, the pretext that led the mikado Chiu-ai, who is said to have reigned from 192 to 200 CE, to march against them was that these people in Kiushiu would not acknowledge his authority. His wife, the Amazonian queen Jingu, was of the opinion that the root of the trouble was to be found in the peninsula, and that the army should be sent across the sea.

The Narrative of Jingu

Her husband, having been killed in battle, the queen was left to carry out her purposes, which she did at the date said to be 202 CE. She set sail from Hizen, and reached the Asian mainland probably at the harbor of Fusan. Unable to resist so well-appointed a force, the king of Shinra submitted and became the declared vassal of Japan. Envoys from Hiaksai and another of the petty kingdoms also came to the Japanese camp and made friends with the invaders. After a two months' stay, the victorious fleet, richly laden with precious gifts and spoil, returned.

How much of truth there is in this narrative of Jingu it is difficult to tell. The date given cannot be trustworthy. The truth seems at least this, that Shinra was far superior to the Japan of the early Christian centuries. Buddhism was formally established in Shinra in the year 528; and as early as the sixth century a steady stream of immigrants – traders, artists, scholars, and teachers, and later Buddhist missionaries – passed from Shinra into Japan, interrupted only by the wars which from time to time broke out. [...]

Meanwhile, in the peninsula the leading state expanded her borders by gradual encroachments upon the little 'kingdom' of Mimana to the southwest and upon Hiaksai on the north. The latter, having always considered Shinra to be inferior, and even a dependent, war broke out between the two states as soon as Shinra assumed perfect independence. Korai and Hiaksai leagued themselves against Shinra, and the game of war continued, with various shifting of the pieces on the board, until the tenth century. The three rival states mutually hostile, the Japanese usually friends to Hiaksai, the Chinese generally helpers of Shinra, the northern nations beyond the Tumen and Sungari assisting Korai, varying their operations in the field with frequent alliances and counterplots, make but a series of dissolving views of battle and strife, into the details of which it is not profitable to enter.

Though Korai and Hiaksai felt the heaviest blows from China, Shinra was harried oftenest by the armies of her neighbours and by the Japanese. Indeed, from a tributary point of view, it seems questionable whether her alliances with China were of any benefit to her. In times of peace, however, the blessings of education and civilization flowed freely from her great patron. Though farthest east from China, it seems certain that Shinra was, in many respects, the most highly civilized of the three states. Especially was this the case during the Tang era (618–905 CE), when the mutual relations between China and Shinra were closest, and arts, letters, and customs were borrowed most liberally by the pupil state. Even at the present time, in the Korean idiom, 'Tang-yang' (times of the Tang and Yang dynasties) is a synonym of prosperity. The term for 'Chinese', applied to works of art, poetry, coins, fans, and even to a certain disease, is 'Tang', instead of the ordinary word for China, since this famous dynastic title represents to the Korean mind, as to the student of Kathayan history, one of the most brilliant epochs known to this longest-lived of empires. What the names of Plantagenet and Tudor represent to an Anglo-Saxon mind, the terms Tang and Sung are to a Korean.

Buddhism Steadily Propagated

During this period, Buddhism was being steadily propagated, until it became the prevailing cult of the nation.... In the civilization of a nation, the possession of a vernacular alphabet must be acknowledged to be one of the most potent factors for the spread of intelligence and culture. It is believed by many linguists that the Choctaws and Koreans have the only two perfect alphabets in the world. It is agreed by natives of Chō-sen that their most profound scholar and ablest man of intellect was Chul-chong, a statesman at the court of Kion-chiu, the capital of Shinra. This famous penman, a scholar in the classics and ancient languages of India as well as China, is credited with the invention of the Nido, or Korean syllabary, one of the simplest and most perfect 'alphabets' in the world. It expresses the sounds of the Korean language far better than the *katakana* of Japan expresses Japanese.

Chul-chong seems to have invented the *Nido* syllabary by giving a phonetic value to a certain number of selected Chinese characters, which are ideographs expressing ideas but not sounds. Perhaps the Sanskrit alphabet suggested the model both for manner of use and for forms of letters. The Nido is composed almost entirely of straight lines and circles, and the letters belonging to the same class of labials, dentals, etc., have a similarity of form easily recognized. The Koreans state that the Nido was invented in the early part of the eighth century, and that it was based on the Sanskrit alphabet. It is worthy of note that, if the date given be true, the Japanese katakana, invented a century later, was perhaps suggested by the Korean.

One remarkable effect of the use of phonetic writing in Korea and Japan has been to stereotype, and thus to preserve, the ancient sounds and pronunciation of words of the Chinese, which the latter have lost. These systems of writing outside of China have served … in registering and reproducing the manner in which the Chinese spoke, a whole millennium ago. This fact has already opened a fertile field of research, and may yet yield rich treasures of discovery to the sciences of history and linguistics.

An Era of Learning

Certainly, however, we may gather that the Tang era was one of learning and literary progress in Korea, as in Japan – all countries in pupilage to China feeling the glow of literary splendour in which the Middle Kingdom was then basking. The young nobles were sent to obtain their education at the court and schools of Nanking, and the fair damsels of Shinra bloomed in the harem of the emperor. Imperial ambassadors frequently visited the court of this kingdom in the far east. Chinese costume and etiquette were, for a time, at least, made the rigorous rule at court. On one occasion, in 653 CE, the envoy from Shinra to the mikado came arrayed in Chinese dress, and, neglecting the ceremonial forms of the Japanese court, attempted to observe those of China. The mikado was highly irritated at the supposed insult. The premier even advised that the Korean be put to death; but better counsels prevailed. During the eighth and ninth centuries this flourishing kingdom was well known to the Arab geographers, and it is evident that Mussulman travellers visited Shinra or resided in the cities of the peninsula for purposes of trade and commerce, as has been shown before.

Kion-chiu, the capital of Shinra, was a brilliant centre of art and science, of architecture and of literary and religious light. Imposing temples, grand monasteries, lofty pagodas, halls of scholars, magnificent gateways and towers adorned the city. In campaniles, equipped with water-clocks and with ponderous bells and gongs, which, when struck, flooded the valleys and hilltops with a rich resonance, the sciences of astronomy and horoscopy were cultivated. As from a fountain, rich streams of knowledge flowed from the capital of Shinra, both over the peninsula and to the court of Japan. Even after the decay of Shinra's power in the political unity of the whole peninsula, the nation looked upon Kion-chiu as a sacred city. Her noble temples, halls, and towers stood in honour and repair, enshrining the treasures of India, Persia, and China, until the ruthless Japanese torch laid them in ashes in 1596.

Shinra the Supreme State

The generation of Korean people during the seventh century, when the Chinese hordes desolated large portions of the peninsula and crushed out Hiaksai and Korai, saw the borders of Shinra extending from the Everlasting White Mountains to the Island of Tsushima, and occupying the entire eastern half of the peninsula. From the beginning of the eighth until the tenth century, Shinra is the supreme state, and the political power of the Eastern Kingdom is represented by her alone. Her ambition tempted, or her Chinese master commanded, her into an invasion of the kingdom of Pu-hai beyond her northern border, 733 CE. Her armies crossed the Tumen, but met with such spirited resistance that only half of them returned. Shinra's desire of conquest in that direction was appeased, and for two centuries the land had rest from blood.

Until Shinra fell, in 934 CE, and united Korea rose on the ruins of the three kingdoms, the history of this state, as found in the Chinese annals, is simply a list of her kings, who, of course, received investiture from China. On the east, the Japanese, having ceased to be her pupils in civilization during times of peace, as in time of war they were her conquerors, turned their attention to Nanking, receiving directly therefrom the arts and sciences, instead of at second-hand through the Korean peninsula. They found enough to do at home in conquering all the tribes in the north and east and centralizing their system of government after the model of the Tangs in China. For these reasons the sources of information concerning the eighth and ninth centuries fail, or rather it is more exact to say that the history of Shinra is that of peace instead of war. In 869 we read of pirates from her shores descending upon the Japanese coast to plunder the tribute ships from Buzen province, and again, in 893, that a fleet of fifty junks, manned by these Korean rovers, was driven off from Tsushima by the Japanese troops, with the loss of 300 slain. Another descent of 'foreign pirates', most probably Koreans, upon Iki Island, in 1019, is recorded, the strangers being beaten off by reinforcements from the mainland.

The very existence of these marauders is, perhaps, a good indication that the power of the Shinra government was falling into decay, and that lawlessness within the kingdom was preparing the way for some mighty hand to not only seize the existing state, but to unite all Korea into political, as well as geographical, unity. In the far north another of those great intermittent movements of population was in process, which, though destroying the kingdom of Puhai beyond the Tumen, was to repeople the desolate land of Korai, and again call a dead state to aggressive life. From the origin to the fall of Shinra there were three royal families of fifty-five kings, ruling 993 years, or seven years less than a millennium.

RELATIONS WITH JAPAN

Griffis (whose text continues in this section) believed that both Korean and Japanese people originated from common ancestors, the Fuyu people, and that they were related by blood more closely to one another than with the Chinese. The relationship between Korea and Japan has been extremely controversial and contested throughout history. On the one hand, there is predominant evidence of a close relationship between Koreans and Japanese; their similarities in language, culture and religions, for example, have long been noted. On the other hand, the countries have always been in dispute over which is superior to the other. In early Japanese historical records such as *Kojiki* and *Nihonshogi*, Japan tended to be depicted in a far superior position. In addition, a series of military campaigns in which Japanese emperors had defeated the states of Silla and Paekche, and made both send tributes to Japan to affirm their inferior status, were highlighted in these records. Silla had sent mirrors, jade stone and swords to Japan; these were new to the country and later become emblems of the Japanese imperial family.

The alleged Japanese colony in southern Korea, Mimana, has often been used as justification of Japanese expeditions in Korea, particularly for Japan's colonization of Korea in 1910.

Many Koreans emigrated to Japan over the years for various reasons, and there they founded industries and intermarried with Japanese. Their identities have thus evolved, been transformed and often lost by living for generations among the Japanese. The relationship between early Japan and Korea remains an ongoing debate among scholars today.

JAPAN AND KOREA

It is as nearly impossible to write the history of Korea and exclude Japan, as to tell the story of medieval England and leave out France....

From about the beginning of the Christian era until the fifteenth century the relations between the two nations were very close and active. Alternate peace and war, mutual assistance given, and embassies sent to and fro are recorded with lively frequency in the early Japanese annals, especially the *Nihongi* and *Kojiki*. A more or less continual stream of commerce and emigration seems to have set in from the peninsula. Some writers of high authority, who are also comparative students of the languages of the two countries, see in these events the origin of the modern Japanese. They interpret them to mean nothing less than the peopling of the archipelago by continental tribes passing through the peninsula, and landing in Japan at various points along the coast from Kiushiu to Kaga. Some of them think that Japan was settled wholly and only by Tungusic races of Northeastern Asia coming from or through Korea. They base their belief not only on the general stream and tendency of Japanese tradition, but also and more on the proofs of language.

The first mention of Korea in the Japanese annals occurs in the fifth volume of the *Nihongi*, and is the perhaps half-fabulous narrative of ancient tradition. In the 65th year of the reign of the tenth mikado, Sujin (97–30 BCE), a boat filled with people from the west appeared off the southern point of Chō-shiu, near the modern town of Shimonoséki. They would not land there, but steered their course from cape to cape along the coast until they reached the Bay of Keji no Wara in Echizen, near the modern city of Tsuruga. Here they disembarked and announced themselves from Amana Sankan (Amana of the Three Han or Kingdoms) in Southern Korea. They unpacked their treasures of finely wrought goods, and their leader made offerings to the mikado Sujin. These immigrants remained five years in Echizen, not far from the city of Fukui, till 28 BCE. Before leaving Japan, they presented themselves in the capital for a farewell audience. The mikado Mimaki, having died three years before, the visitors were requested on their return to call their country Mimana, after their patron, as a memorial of their stay in Japan. To this they assented, and on their return named their district Mimana.

Some traditions state that the first Korean envoy had a horn growing out of his forehead, and that since his time, and on account of it, the bay near which he dwelt was named Tsunaga (Horn Bay) now corrupted into Tsuruga….

Six years later an envoy from Shinra arrived, also bringing presents to the mikado. These consisted of mirrors, jade stone, swords, and other precious articles, then common in Korea but doubtless new in Japan.

According to the tradition of the *Kojiki* (Book of Ancient Legends) the fourteenth mikado, Chiu-ai (CE 192–200) was holding his court at Tsuruga in Echizen, in CE 194, when a rebellion broke out in Kiushiu. He marched at once into Kiushiu, against the rebels, and there fell by disease or arrow. His consort, Jingu Kōgō, had a presentiment that he ought not to go into Kiushiu, as he would surely fail if he did, but that he should strike at the root of the trouble and sail at once to the west.

After his death she headed the Japanese army and, leading the troops in person, quelled the revolt. She then ordered all the available forces of her realm to assemble for an invasion of Shinra. Japanese modern writers have laid great stress upon the fact that Shinra began the aggressions which brought on war, and in this fact justify Jingu's action and Japan's right to hold Korea as an honestly acquired possession.

All being ready, the doughty queen regent set sail from the coast of Hizen, in Japan, in the tenth month CE 202, and beached the fleet safely on the coast of Shinra. The King of Shinra, accustomed to meet only with men from the rude tribes of Kiushiu, was surprised to see so well-appointed an army and so large a fleet from a land to the eastward. Struck with terror he resolved at once to submit. Tying his hands in token of submission and in presence of the queen Jingu, he declared himself the slave of Japan. Jingu caused her bow to be suspended over the gate of the palace of the king in sign of his submission. It is even said that she wrote on the gate 'The King of Shinra is the dog of Japan'. Perhaps these are historic words, which find their meaning today in the two golden dogs forming part of the mikado's throne....

The followers of Jingu evidently expected a rich booty, but after so peaceful a conquest the empress ordered that no looting should be allowed, and no spoil taken except the treasures constituting tribute. She restored the king to the throne as her vassal, and the tribute was then collected and laden on eighty boats with hostages for future annual tribute. The offerings comprised pictures, works of elegance and art, mirrors, jade, gold, silver, and silk fabrics.

Preparations were now made to conquer Hiaksai also, when Jingu was surprised to receive the voluntary submission and offers of tribute of this country.

Results of Japanese Invasion

The Japanese army remained in Korea only two months, but this brief expedition led to great and lasting results. It gave the Japanese a keener thirst for martial glory, it opened their eyes to a higher state of arts and civilization. From this time forth there flowed into the islands a constant stream of Korean emigrants, who gave a great impulse to the spirit of improvement in Japan. The Japanese accept the story of Jingu and her conquest as sound history, and adorn their greenback paper money with pictures of her foreign exploits. Critics reject many elements in the tradition, such as her controlling the waves and drowning the Shinra army by the jewels of the ebbing and the flowing tide, and the delay of her accouchement by a magic stone carried in her girdle. The Japanese ascribe the glory of victory to her then unborn babe, afterward deified as Ojin, god of war, and worshipped by Buddhists as Hachiman or the Eight-bannered Buddha. Yet many temples are dedicated to Jingu, one especially famous is near Hiōgo, and Koraiji (Korean village) near Oiso, a few miles from Yokohama, has another which was at first built in her honour. Evidently the core of the narrative of conquest is fact.

At the time when the faint, dim light of trustworthy tradition dawns, we find the people inhabiting the Japanese archipelago to be roughly divided, as to their political status, into four classes.

In the central province around Kiōto ruled a kingly house – the mikado and his family – with tributary nobles or feudal chiefs holding their lands on military tenure. This is the ancient classic land and realm of Yamato. Four other provinces adjoining it have always formed the core of the empire, and are called the Go-Kinai, or five home provinces, suggesting the five clans of Kokorai.

To the north and east stretched the little known and less civilized region, peopled by tribes of kindred blood and speech, who spoke nearly the same language as the Yamato tribes, and who had probably come at some past time from the same ancestral seats in Northeast China, and called the Kuan-tō, or region east (*tō*) of the barrier (*kuan*) at Ozaka; or poetically Adzuma.

Still further north, on the main island and in Yezo, lived the Ainos or Ebisŭ, probably the aborigines of the soil—the straight-eyed men whose descendants still live in Yezo and the Kuriles. The northern and eastern tribes were first conquered and thoroughly subdued by the Yamato tribes, after which all the far north was overrun and the Ainos subjugated.

In the extreme south of the main island of Japan and in Kiushiu, then called Kumaso by the Yamato people, lived a number of tribes of perhaps the same ethnic stock as the Yamato Japanese, but further removed. Their progenitors had probably descended from Northeast China through Korea to Japan. Their blood and speech, however, were more mixed by infusions from Malay and southern elements. Into Kiushiu – it being nearest to the continent – the peninsulars were constantly coming and mingling with the islanders.

The allegiance of the Kiushiu tribes to the royal house of Yamato was of a very loose kind. The history of these early centuries, as shown in the annals of Nihon, is but a series of revolts against the distant warrior mikado, whose life was chiefly one of war. He had often to leave his seat in the central island to march at the head of his followers to put down rebellions or to conquer new tribes. Over these, when subdued, a prince chosen by the conqueror was set to rule, who became a feudatory of the mikado.

The attempts of the Yamato sovereign to wholly reduce the Kiushiu tribes to submission, were greatly frustrated by their stout resistance, fomented by emissaries from Shinra, who instigated them to 'revolt', while adventurers from the Korean mainland came over in large numbers and joined the 'rebels', who were, in one sense, their own compatriots.

Idea of Korea as Japanese Dependency

From the time of Jingu, if the early dates in Japanese history are to be trusted, may be said to date that belief, so firmly fixed in the Japanese mind, that Korea is, and always was since Jingu's time, a tributary and dependency of Japan. This idea … led to frequent expeditions from the third to the sixteenth century, and which … lay at the root of three civil wars.

All these expeditions, sometimes national, sometimes filibustering, served to drain the resources of Japan, though many impulses to development and higher civilization were thus gained, especially in the earlier centuries. It seemed, until 1877, almost impossible to eradicate from the military mind of Japan the conviction that to surrender Korea was cowardice and a stain on the national honour....

The Koreans taught the Japanese the arts of peace, while the Koreans profited from their neighbours to improve in the business of war. We read that, in 316 CE, a Korean ambassador, bringing the usual tribute, presented to the mikado a shield of iron which he believed to be invulnerable to Japanese arrows. The mikado called on one of his favourite marksmen to practice in the presence of the envoy. The shield was suspended, and the archer, drawing bow, sent a shaft through the iron skin of the buckler to the astonishment of the visitor. In all their battles the Koreans were rarely able to stand in open field before the archers from over the sea, who sent true cloth-yard shafts from their oak and bamboo bows.

The paying of tribute to a foreign country is never a pleasant duty to perform, though in times of prosperity and good harvests it is not difficult. In periods of scarcity from bad crops it is well-nigh impossible. To insist upon its payment is to provoke rebellion. Instances are indeed given in Japanese history where the conquerors not only remitted the tribute but even sent ship loads of rice and barley to the starving Koreans. When, however, for reasons not deemed sufficient, or out of sheer defiance, their vassals refused to discharge their dues, they again felt the iron hand of Japan in war.

Japan Invades Korea

During the reign of Yuriaki, the twenty-second mikado (CE 457–477), the three states failed to pay tribute. A Japanese army landed in Korea, and conquering Hiaksai, compelled her to return to her duty. The campaign was less successful in Shinra and Korai, for after the Japanese had left the Korean shores the 'tribute' was sent only at intervals, and the temper of the half-conquered people was such that other expeditions had to be despatched to inflict chastisement and compel payment.

The gallant but vain succor given by the Japanese to Hiaksai during the war with the Chinese, in the sixth century, which resulted in the destruction of the little kingdom, has already been detailed. Among the names, forever famous in Japanese art and tradition, of those who took part in this expedition are Saté-hiko and Kasi-wadé. The former sailed away from Hizen in the year 536, as one of the mikado's bodyguard to assist their allies the men of Hiaksai. A poetical legend recounts that his wife, Sayohimé, climbed the hills of Matsura to catch the last glimpse of his receding sails. Thus intently gazing, with straining eyes, she turned to stone. The peasants of the neighbourhood still discern in the weather-worn rocks, high up on the cliffs, the figure of a lady in long trailing court dress with face and figure eagerly bent over the western waves. Not only is the name Matsura Sayohimé the symbol of devoted love, but from this incident the famous author Bakin constructed his romance of 'The Great Stone Spirit of Matsura'.

Kasiwadé, who crossed over to do 'frontier service' in the peninsula a few years later, was driven ashore by a snow squall at an unknown part of the coast. While in this defenceless condition his camp was invaded by a tiger, which carried off and devoured his son, a lad of tender age. Kasiwadé at once gave chase and followed the beast to the mountains and into a cave. The tiger leaping out upon him, the wary warrior bearded him with his left hand, and buried his dirk in his throat. Then finishing him with his sabre, he skinned the brute and sent home the trophy. From olden times Chō-sen is known to Japanese children only as a land of tigers, while to the soldier the 'marshal's baton carried in his knapsack' is a tiger-skin scabbard, the emblem and possession of rank.

As the imperial court of Japan looked upon Shinra and Hiaksai as outlying vassal states, the frequent military movements across the sea were reckoned under 'frontier service', like that beyond the latitude of Sado in the north of the main island, or in Kiushiu in the south. 'The three countries' of Korea were far nearer and more familiar to the Japanese soldiers than were Yezo or the Riu Kiu Islands, which were not part of the empire till several centuries afterward. Kara Kuni, the country of Kara (a corruption of Korai?), as they now call China, was then applied to Korea. Not a little of classic poetry and legend in the Yamato language refers to this western frontier beyond the sea. The elegy on Ihémaro, the soldier-prince, who died at Iki Island on the voyage over, and that on the death of the Korean nun Riguwan, have been put into English verse by Mr. Chamberlain (named after the English explorer and writer on Korea, Basil Hall), in his *Classical Poetry of the Japanese*. This Korean lady left her home in 714, and for twenty-one years found a home with the mikado's prime minister, Otomo, and his wife, at Nara. She died in 735, while her hosts were away at the mineral springs of Arima, near Kobé; and the elegy was written by their daughter. One stanza describes her life in the new country:

'And here with aliens thou didst choose to dwell,
Year in, year out, in deepest sympathy;
And here thou builtest thee a holy cell,
And so the peaceful years went gliding by.'

An interesting field of research is still open to the scholar who will point out all the monuments of Korean origin or influence in the mikado's empire, in the arts and sciences, household customs, diet and dress, or architecture; in short, what by nature or the hand of man has been brought to the land of Sunrise from that of Morning Calm. One of the Korean princes, who settled in Japan early in the seventh century, founded a family which afterward ruled the famous province of Nagatō or Chōshiu. One of his descendants welcomed Francis Xavier, and aided his work by gifts of ground and the privilege of preaching. Many of the temples in Kiōto still contain images, paintings, and altar furniture brought from Korea. The 'Pheasant Bridge' still keeps its name from bygone centuries; in a garden nearby pheasants were kept for the supply of the tables of the Korean embassies….

Koreans in Japan

The many thousands of Koreans, who, during the first ten centuries of the Christian era, but especially in the seventh, eighth, and ninth, settled in Japan, lived peaceably with the people of their adopted country, and loyally obeyed the mikado's rule. An exception to this course occurred in 820, when 700 men who some time before had come from Shinra to Tōtōmi and Suruga revolted, killed many of the Japanese, seized the rice in the storehouses, and put to sea to escape. The people of Musashi and Sagami pursued and attacked them, putting many of them to death.

The general history of the Koreans in Japan divides itself into two parts. Those who came as voluntary immigrants in time of peace were in most cases skilled workmen or farmers, who settled in lands or in villages granted them, and were put on political and social equality with the mikado's subjects. They founded industries, intermarried with the natives, and their identity has been lost in the general body of the Japanese people.

With the prisoners taken in war, and with the labourers impressed into their service and carried off by force, the case was far different. These latter were set apart in villages by themselves – an outcast race on no social equality with the people. At first they were employed to feed the imperial falcons, or do such menial work, but under the ban of Buddhism, which forbids the destruction of life and the handling of flesh, they became an accursed race, the 'Etas' or pariahs of the nation. They were the butchers, skinners, leather makers, and those whose business it was to handle corpses of criminals and all other defiling things....

Relations of the Two Countries

From the ninth century onward to the sixteenth, the relations of the two countries seem to be unimportant. Japan was engaged in conquering northward the barbarians of her main island and Yezo. Her intercourse, both political and religious, grew to be so direct with the court of China, that Korea, in the Japanese annals, sinks out of sight except at rare intervals. Nihon increased in wealth and civilization while Chō-sen remained stationary or retrograded. In the nineteenth century the awakened Sunrise Kingdom has seen her former self in the hermit nation, and has stretched forth willing hands to do for her neighbour now, what Korea did for Japan in centuries long gone by.

Still, it must never be forgotten that Korea was not only the bridge on which civilization crossed from China to the archipelago, but was most probably the pathway of migration by which the rulers of the race now inhabiting Nihon reached it from their ancestral seats around the Sungari and the Ever-White Mountains. True, it is not absolutely certain whether the homeland of the mikado's ancestors lay southward in the sea, or westward among the mountains, but that the mass of the Korean and Japanese people are more closely allied in blood than either are with the Chinese, Manchius, or Malays, seems to be proved, not only by language and physical traits, but by the whole course of the history of both nations, and by the testimony of the Chinese records. Both Koreans and Japanese have inherited the peculiar institutions of their Fuyu ancestors – that race which alone of all the peoples sprung from Northeast China migrated toward the rising, instead of toward the setting, sun.

EARLY MEDIEVAL KOREA

Homer Hulbert attempted to provide as much information as possible in his account about early medieval Korea (*The History of Korea*, 1905, an extract from which makes up this section). Compared to dynasties in China, Koryŏ lasted an impressively long time: 474 years. However, Koryŏ suffered heavily due to many military attacks and both political and economic pressure from Khitan and Jurchen. The founder Wang Kŏn represented a different power group that had started to emerge during the last phase of Silla. It consisted of local strongmen who had accrued tremendous financial resources through maritime trade; these they used to fund their private army. Taking advantage of the declining power of Silla and rebellions from multiple regions, Wang eventually established a new dynasty.

Wang Kŏn was successful not only for his military prowess, but also, even more so, for his strategic skill in securing moral superiority over his opponents. Even the Silla king voluntarily walked to his camp and surrendered his title to his opponent. Wang Kŏn also managed to eliminate his last obstacle of Later Paekche successfully, when its king Kyŏnhwŏn came to take refuge under Wang after a military coup in which he had been imprisoned by his son. Wang Kŏn left behind a strong power infrastructure for his descendants as well as his famous Ten Injections for the Koryŏ kings to follow.

Koryŏ's major challenges had been the threats from northern nomads, Khitan and Jurchen, as well as the persistent clash between Confucianism and Buddhism. Despite implementing the Civil Service Examination early on, Buddhism won the upper hand. Most Koryŏ kings and royal family members were devout Buddhists and dedicated vast resources to temples. More importantly, priests became senior advisors for kings. They assumed full control not only of the spiritual sphere, but also of every aspect of secular matters in politics and daily life throughout the Koryŏ period.

FROM 890 TO 1392 CE

Kung-ye was the son of King Hön-gang by a concubine. He was born on the least auspicious day of the year, the fifth of the fifth moon. He had several teeth when he was born which made his arrival the less welcome. The king ordered the child to be destroyed; so it was thrown out of the window. But the nurse rescued it and carried it to a place of safety where she nursed it and provided for its bringing up. As she was carrying the child to this place of safety she accidentally put out one of its eyes. When he reached man's estate he became a monk under the name of Sŭn-jong. He was by nature ill fitted for the monastic life and soon found himself in the camp of the bandit Ki-whŭn at Chuk-ju. Soon he began to consider himself ill-treated by his new master and deserted him, finding his way later to the camp of the bandit Yang-gil at Puk-wŭn now Wŭn-ju. A considerable number of men accompanied him. Here his talents were better appreciated and he was put in command of a goodly force with which he soon overcame the districts of Ch'un-Ch'ŭn, Nă-sŭng, Ul-o and O-jin. From this time Kung-ye steadily gained in power until he quite eclipsed his master. Marching into the western part of Silla he took ten districts and went into permanent camp.

The following year another robber, Kyŭn-whŭn, made head against Silla in the southern part of what is now Kyŭng-sang Province. He was a Sang-ju man. Having seized the district of Mu-ju he proclaimed himself king of Southern Silla. His name was originally Yi but when fifteen years of age he had changed it to Kyŭn. He had been connected with the Silla army and had risen step by step and made himself extremely useful by his great activity in the field. When, however, the state of Silla became so corrupt as to be a by-word among all good men, he threw off his allegiance to her, gathered about him a band of desperate criminals, outlaws and other disaffected persons and began the conquest of the south and west. In a month he had a following of 5,000 men. He found he had gone too far in proclaiming himself king and so modified his title to that of 'Master of Men and Horses'. It is said of him that once, while still a small child, his father being busy in the fields and his mother at work behind the house, a tiger came along and the child sucked milk from its udder. This accounted for his wild and fierce nature.

At this time the great scholar Ch'oé Ch'i-wŭn, whom we have mentioned, was living at Pu-sŭng. Recognizing the abyss of depravity into which the state was falling he formulated ten rules for the regulation of the government and sent them to Queen Man. She read and praised them but took no means to put them in force. Ch'oé could no longer serve a queen who made light of the counsels of her most worthy subjects and, throwing up his position, retired to Kwang-ju in Nam-san and became a hermit.

After that he removed to Ping-san in Kang-ju, then to Ch'ŭng-yang Monastery in Hyŭp-ju, then to Sang-gye Monastery at Ch'i-ri San but finally made his permanent home at Ka-ya San where he lived with a few other choice spirits. It was here that he wrote his autobiography in thirteen volumes.

Wang-gön Origin

In 896 Kung-ye began operating in the north on a larger scale. He took ten districts near Ch'ŭl-wŭn and put them in charge of his young lieutenant Wang-gön [today typically spelled as Wang Gon] who was destined to become the founder of a dynasty. We must now retrace our steps in order to tell of the origin of this celebrated man.

Wang-yŭng, a large-minded and ambitious man, lived in the town of Song-ak. To him a son was born in the third year of King Hön-gang of Silla, CE 878. The night the boy was born a luminous cloud stood above the house and made it as bright as day, so the story runs. The child had a very high forehead and a square chin, and he developed rapidly. His birth had long since been prophesied by a monk named To-sŭn who told Wang-yŭng, as he was building his house, that within its walls a great man would be born. As the monk turned to go Wang-yŭng called him back and received from him a letter which he was ordered to give to the yet unborn child when he should be old enough to read. The contents are unknown but when the boy reached his seventeenth year the same monk reappeared and became his tutor, instructing him especially in the art of war. He showed him also how to obtain aid from the heavenly powers, how to sacrifice to the spirits of mountain and stream so as to propitiate them. Such is the tradition that surrounds the origin of the youth who now in the troubled days of Silla found a wide field for the display of his martial skill.

Kung-ye first ravaged the country from Puk-wŭn to A-Silla, with 600 followers. He there assumed the title of 'Great General'. Then he reduced all the country about Nang-ch'ŭn, Han-san, Kwan-nă and Ch'ŭl-wŭn. By this time his force had enormously increased and his fame had spread far and wide. All the wild tribes beyond the Ta-dong River did obeisance to him. But these successes soon began to turn his head. He styled himself 'Prince' and began to appoint prefects to various places. He advanced Wang-gön to a high position and made him governor of Song-do. This he did at the instigation of Wang-yŭng who sent him the following enigmatical advice: 'If you want to become King of Cho-sŭn, Suk-sin and Pyön-han you must build a wall about Song-do and make my son governor.' It was immediately done, and in this way Wang-gön was provided with a place for his capital.

Kung-ye Proclaims Himself a King

In 897 the profligate Queen Man of Silla handed the government over to her adopted son Yo and retired. This change gave opportunities on every side for the rebels to ply their trade. Kung-ye forthwith seized thirty more districts north of the Han River and Kyŭn-whŭn established his headquarters at Wan-san, now Chŭn-ju and called his kingdom New Păk-je. Wang-gön, in the name of Kung-ye, seized almost the whole of the territory included in the present provinces of Kyŭng-geui and Ch'ung-ch'ŭng. Finally in 901 Kung-ye proclaimed himself king and emphasized it by slashing with a sword the picture of the king of Silla which hung in a monastery. Two years later Wang-gön moved southward into what is now Chŭl-la Province and soon came in contact with the forces of Kyŭn-whŭn. In these contests the young Wang-gön was uniformly successful.

In 905 Kung-ye established his capital at Ch'ŭl-wŭn in the present Kang-wŭn province and named his kingdom Ma-jin and the year was called *Mut*. Then he distributed the offices among his followers. By this time all the north and east had joined the standards of Kung-ye and Wang-gön even to within 120 miles of the Silla capital. The king and court of Silla were in despair. There was no army with which to take the field and all they could do was to defend the position they had as best they could and hope that Kyung-ye and Kyŭn-whŭn might destroy each other. In 909 Kung-ye called Silla 'The Kingdom to be Destroyed' and set Wang-gön as military governor of all the south-west. Here he pursued an active policy, now fitting out ships with which to subjugate the neighbouring islands and now leading the attack on Kyŭn-whŭn who always suffered in the event. His army was a model of military precision and order. Volunteers flocked to his standard. He was recognized as the great leader of the day. When, at last, Na-ju fell into the hands of the young Wang-gön, Kyŭn-whŭn decided on a desperate venture and suddenly appearing before that town laid siege to it. After ten days of unsuccessful assault he retired but Wang-gön followed and forced an engagement at Mok-p'o, now Yŭng-san-p'o, and gave him such a whipping that he was fain to escape alone and unattended.

Meanwhile Kung-ye's character was developing. Cruelty and capriciousness became more and more his dominant qualities. Wang-gön never acted more wisely than in keeping as far as possible from the court of his master. His rising fame would have instantly roused the jealousy of Kung-ye.

Silla had apparently adopted the principle 'Let us eat and be merry for tomorrow we die'. Debauchery ran rife at the court and sapped what little strength was left. Among the courtiers was one of the better stamp and when he found that the king preferred the counsel of his favourite concubine to his own, he took occasion to use a sharper argument in the form of a dagger, which at a blow brought her down from her dizzy eminence.

Kung-ye Proclaims Himself a Buddha

In 911 Kung-ye changed the name of his kingdom to Tă-bong. It is probable that this was because of a strong Buddhistic tendency that had at this time quite absorbed him. He proclaimed himself a Buddha, called himself Mi-ryŭk-pul, made both his sons Buddhists, dressed as a high priest and went nowhere without censers. He pretended to teach the tenets of Buddhism. He printed a book, and put a monk to death because he did not accept it as canonical. The more Kung-ye dabbled in Buddhism the more did all military matters devolve upon Wang-gön, who from a distance beheld with amazement and concern the dotage of his master. At his own request he was always sent to a post far removed from the court. At last Kung-ye became so infatuated that he seemed little better than a madman. He heated an iron to a white heat and thrust it into his wife's womb because she continually tried to dissuade him from his Buddhistic notions. He charged her with being an adulteress. He followed this up by killing both his sons and many other of the people near his person. He was hated as thoroughly as he was feared.

The year 918 was one of the epochal years of Korean history. The state of the peninsula was as follows. In the south-east, the reduced kingdom of Silla, prostrated by her own excesses, without an army, and yet in her very supineness running to excess of riot, putting off the evil day and trying to drown regrets in further debauchery. In the central eastern portion, the little kingdom of Kung-ye who had now become a tyrant and a madman. He had put his whole army under the hand of a young, skillful, energetic, and popular man who had gained the esteem of all classes. In the south-west was another sporadic state under Kyŭn-whŭn who was a fierce, unscrupulous bandit, at swords points with the rising Wang-gön.

Wang-gön Accused

Suddenly Kung-ye awoke to the reality of his position. He knew he was hated by all and that Wang-gön was loved by all, and he knew too that the army was wholly estranged from himself and that everything depended upon what course the young general should pursue. Fear, suspicion, and jealousy mastered him and he suddenly ordered the young general up to the capital. Wang-gön boldly complied, knowing doubtless by how slender a thread hung his fortunes. When he entered his master's presence the latter exclaimed 'You conspired against me yesterday.' The young man calmly asked how. Kung-ye pretended to know it through the power of his sacred office as Buddha. He said 'Wait, I will again consult the inner consciousness.' Bowing his head he pretended to be communing with his inner self. At this moment one of the clerks purposely dropped his pen, letting it roll near to the prostrate form of Wang-gön. As the clerk stooped to pick it up, he whispered in Wang-gön's ear 'Confess that you have conspired.' The young man grasped the situation at once. When the mock Buddha raised his head and repeated the accusation Wang-gön confessed that it was true. The king was delighted at this, for he deceived himself into believing that he actually had acquired the faculty of reading men's minds. This pleased him so greatly that he readily forgave the offence and merely warned the young man not to repeat it. After this he gave Wang-gön rich gifts and had more confidence in him than ever.

Forced to Take the Throne

But the officials all besieged the young general with entreaties to crush the cruel and capricious monarch and assume the reins of government himself. This he refused to do, for through it all, he was faithful to his master. But they said 'He has killed his wife and his sons and we will all fall a prey to his fickle temper unless you come to our aid. He is worse than the emperor Chu.' Wang-gön, however, urged that it was the worst of crimes to usurp a throne. 'But' said they 'is it not much worse for us all to perish? If one does not improve the opportunity that heaven provides it is a sin.' He was unmoved by this casuistry and stood his ground firmly. At last even his wife joined in urging him to lay aside his foolish scruples and she told the officials to take him by force and carry him to the palace, whether he would or not. They did so, and bearing him in their arms they burst through the palace gate and called upon the wretch Kung-ye to make room for their chosen king. The terrified creature fled naked but was caught at Pu-yang, now P'yŏngyang, and beheaded.

Tradition says that this was all in fulfillment of a prophecy which was given in the form of an enigma. A Chinese merchant bought a mirror of a Silla man and in the mirror could be seen these words: 'Between three waters – God sends his son to Chin and Ma – First seize a hen and then a duck – In the year Ki-ja two dragons will arise, one in a green forest and one east of black metal.' The merchant presented it to Kung-ye who prized it highly and sought everywhere for the solution of the riddle. At last the scholar Song Han-hong solved it for him as follows. 'The Chin and Ma mean Chin-han and Ma-han. The hen is Kye-rim (Silla). The duck is the Am-nok (duck-blue) River. The green forest is pine tree or Song-do (Pine Tree Capital) and black metal is Ch'ŭl-wŭn (Ch'ŭl is metal). So a king in Song-do must arise (Wang-gön) and a king in Ch'ŭl-wŭn must fall (Kung-ye).'

Wang-gön Does Justice

Wang-gön began by bringing to summary justice the creatures of Kung-ye who seconded him in his cruelty; some of them were killed and some were imprisoned. Everywhere the people gave themselves up to festivities and rejoicings.

But the ambitious general, Whan Son-gil, took advantage of the unsettled state of affairs to raise an insurrection. Entering the palace with a band of desperadoes he suddenly entered the presence of Wang-gön who was without a guard. The king rose from his seat, and looking the traitor in the face said 'I am not king by my own desire or request. You all made me king. It was heaven's ordinance and you cannot kill me. Approach and try.' The traitor thought that the king had a strong guard secreted nearby and turning fled from the palace. He was caught and beheaded.

Wang-gön sent messages to all the bandit chiefs and invited them to join the new movement, and soon from all sides they came in and swore allegiance to the young king. Kyŭn-whŭn, however, held aloof and sought for means to put down the new power. Wang-gön set to work to establish his kingdom on a firm basis. He changed the official system and established a new set of official grades. He rewarded those who had been true to him and remitted three years' revenues. He altered the revenue laws, requiring the people to pay much less than heretofore, manumitted over 1,000 slaves and gave them goods out of the royal storehouses with which to make a start in life. As P'yŏngyang was the ancient capital of the country he sent one of the highest officials there as governor. And he finished the year with a Buddhist festival, being himself a Buddhist of a mild type. This great annual festival is described as follows: There was an enormous lantern, hung about with hundreds of others, under a tent made of a network of silk cords. Music was an important element. There were also representations of dragons, birds, elephants, horses, carts, and boats. Dancing was prominent and there were in all 100 forms of entertainment. Each official wore the long flowing sleeves and each carried the ivory memo tablet. The king sat upon a high platform and watched the entertainment.

The next year he transferred his court to Song-do which became the permanent capital. There he built his palace and also the large merchants' houses and shops in the centre of the city. This latter act was in accordance with the ancient custom of granting a monopoly of certain kinds of trade and using the merchants as a source of revenue when a sudden need for money arose. He divided the city into five wards and established seven military stations. He also established a secondary capital at Ch'ŭl-wŭn, the present Ch'un-Ch'ŭn, and called it Tong-ju. The pagodas and Buddhas in both the capitals were regilded and put in good order. The people looked with some suspicion upon these Buddhistic tendencies but he told them that the old customs must not be changed too rapidly, for the kingdom had need of the help of the spirits in order to become thoroughly established, and that when that was accomplished they could abandon the religion as soon as they pleased. Here was his grand mistake. He riveted upon the state a baneful influence which was destined to drag it into the mire and eventually bring it to ruin.

THE KORYŬ DYNASTY

In 920 Silla first recognized Koryŭ [today also spelled as Koryo or Goryeo] as a kingdom and sent an envoy with presents to the court at Song-do.

Wang-gön looked out for the interests of the people in the distant parts of the country as well as for those near the capital. In order to break the force of the attacks of the wild people beyond the Tu-man River he built a wall across the northern border of Ham-gyŭng Province. It is said to have been 900 *li* long. But there was a still stronger enemy on the south. Kyŭn-whŭn had by this time come to see that he had no hope of overcoming the young kingdom of Koryŭ and so he bent his energies to the securing of his position against the danger of interference, especially in his plans against Silla. For this reason he sent a messenger to Song-do with presents and tried to make friends with his old time enemy. His next move was to attack Silla. Wang-gön took up the cudgels in support of the king of Silla and by so doing secured the lasting enmity of the bandit who from this time determined upon war without quarter against his northern enemy. Wang-gön said to the Silla envoys, 'Silla has three treasures; the nine-story pagoda, the Buddha six times the height of a man, and the jade belt. As long as these three remain intact Silla will stand.

The first two are in Silla. Where is the jade belt?' The envoy answered that he did not know, whereupon Wang-gön blamed him sharply and sent him home. When Silla finally fell, the jade belt passed into the hands of Wang-gön.

In 921 the Mal-gal tribe, Heuk-su, made a treaty with Wang-gön. This bears evidence to the rapidly growing power of the young king. The Heuk-su Mal-gal were the most feared of all the semi-savage tribes of the north. The following year the Kŭ-ran, usually called Kitan in Chinese histories, followed the example of the Heuk-su people by sending an envoy with presents. It was not till 923 that Wang-gön thought fit to send an envoy to China to offer his compliments.

Kyŭn-whŭn Becomes Wang-gön's Enemy

When the last king of Silla, but one, ascended the throne in 924 important events were following thick and fast upon each other. Silla was now so weak that the records say the king had nothing left but his genealogy. Kyŭn-whŭn sent a force to begin operations against Koryŭ, but without success, and in the following year Wang-gön retaliated with such good success that Kyŭn-whŭn was fain to send his son to Song-do as a hostage. He thus bound himself to keep the peace. Having done this he sent to China desiring to secure backing against Koryŭ. The emperor so far complied as to confer upon him the title of King of Păk-je, thus following the time-honoured policy of pitting one power against another.

The year 926 saw the first envoy come from the kingdom of T'am-na on the island of Quelpart. He arrived at the capital of Koryŭ, where he was well received. The fame of Wang-gön was spreading far and wide among the northern tribes. The Kŭ-ran, or Kitan tribe, having overcome the Păl-ha tribe, made overtures to Wang-gön relative to annexation. These advances were cordially responded to but we are not informed that the union was actually effected.

Kyŭn-whŭn, who was at this time on the island Chŭl-yong-do, sent a present of horses to Wang-gön but a few days later he found a book of prophecy which said that in the year when he should send a gift of horses to Song-do his power would come to an end. He therefore sent a swift messenger begging Wang-gön to return the gift. The King laughed long and loud when he saw this message and good-naturedly sent back the horses.

Loots the Capital of Silla

The last King of Silla, Kyŭng-sun, ascended the throne in 927. It happened on this wise; Kyŭn-whŭn was keeping up a double fight, one against Wang-gön and the other, an offensive one, against Silla. He was badly defeated in an engagement with Koryŭ forces but had good success in his other venture. He burned and pillaged right up to the gates of Silla's capital, and, while a Silla envoy was posting to Song-do to ask for aid, entered the city with a picked band of men. Succor in the shape of 10,000 Koryŭ troops was on its way but came too late. At the hour when Kyŭn-whŭn entered the city the king, his son, the queen and many of the courtiers were feasting at Po-sŭk summer house. When the unwelcome news arrived, there was no time for preparation. The king and queen fled south without attendants. The palace women were seized and the palace occupied. The king was soon run to earth and was compelled to commit suicide. Kyŭn-whŭn ravished the queen and delivered over the palace women to the soldiery. The palace was looted and the entire band, sated with excess and debauchery, and loaded down with the treasures of the palace, started back on the homeward road. But not until Kyŭn-whŭn had appointed a relative of the murdered king to succeed him.

War

When Wang-gön heard of these atrocities, he hastened forward his troops and overtook the army of Kyŭn-whŭn in O-dong forest where a sharp engagement ensued. For some reason, whether it be because the soldiers of Kyŭn-whŭn were more familiar with the locality or because the Koryŭ soldiers were exhausted by their long forced march, the assault was unsuccessful and the Koryŭ forces withdrew. This was doubly unfortunate for it not only did not punish the ruffians for their atrocities at the Silla capital but it inspired them with confidence in their own power. Shortly after this Kyŭn-whŭn sent a letter to Wang-gön saying 'I became Silla's enemy because she sought aid from you. You have no cause for warring against me. It is like a dog chasing a rabbit; both are tired out to no purpose. It is like a kingfisher trying to catch a clam; when he thrusts his bill into the shell the clam closes it and he finds himself caught'. To this epistle Wang-gön replied 'Your actions at the Silla capital are so outrageous that I cannot endure the thought of any compromise. Your present course will lead you to speedy ruin'.

Elated over his successful repulse of Wang-gön's army, Kyŭn-whŭn took the field the following year, with a strong force, and was prepared to assume the offensive. He assaulted and took two Koryŭ fortresses and even, at one time, surrounded Wang-gön in Ch'ŭng-ju and caused him no little anxiety.

In the battle which followed Kyŭn-whŭn lost 300 men and was pushed back, thus freeing the king from an embarrassing position; but before the campaign was over Kyŭn-whŭn scored another victory by capturing the district of Ok-ch'ŭn. In his next campaign he was still successful, and Eui Fortress fell into his hands and he killed the general in charge. Here his successes ended, for Wang-gön awoke to the necessity of using strong measures against him. The following year Koryŭ forces inflicted a crushing defeat upon the southern leader, at An-dong. The fight had lasted all day and neither side had gained any advantage, but that night a picked band of Koryŭ men ascended Hog's Head Mountain and made a rush down upon the unsuspecting camp of the enemy, causing a panic and a stampede in which 8,000 men were killed. Kyŭn-whŭn himself sought safety in flight. This seemed conclusive and all the countryside sent in their allegiance to the victors. A hundred and ten districts in eastern Korea came over to Wang-gön in a body. Dagelet Island, or Ul-leung as the Koreans call it, sent presents to Koryŭ.

The next year after these stirring events, namely 931, Wang-gön made a visit to Silla taking with him an escort of only fifty soldiers. The king of Silla came out to meet him and they feasted there at the meeting-place together. The king of Silla lamented the smallness and weakness of his kingdom and deplored the ravages of Kyŭn-whŭn. The evils, he said, were beyond estimation; and he broke down and wept. The courtiers did the same and even Wang-gön could scarce restrain his tears. After this they had a friendly talk and the king of Koryŭ remained as a guest for some twenty days. As he left the capital of Silla the people vied with each other in doing him honour. Poor old

Silla had gone out of fashion and the minds of all men were turned Koryŭ-ward.

Wang-gŏn had a strong predilection for P'yŏngyang, the ancient capital of the country. He had already established a school there with professorships of literature, medicine, and incantation. He now in 932 conceived the project of moving his capital northward to that place. To this end he erected barracks there for his troops and was making other preparations for the change, when he was dissuaded from it by some evil omens. A great wind blew down some of the houses in P'yŏngyang and, so the story goes, a hen became a cock. These portents made it impossible to carry out the plan. It was about this time that he built a guest house outside the walls of Song-do to be used as a reception hall for envoys and messengers from the wild tribes of the north. Suspicion as to the object of their coming may have made it seem undesirable to allow them to enter the city proper, or it may have been simply to impress them with the importance of the place.

Kyŭn-whŭn's Last Stand

Kyŭn-whŭn's right hand man came and swore allegiance even though, at the time, his two sons and his daughter were hostages in the hands of his former master. When Kyŭn-whŭn heard of it he burned the first son alive and would have treated the second son and the daughter in like manner had they not effected their escape to a retreat where they lay in hiding till his death. This desertion seems to have roused the old man's ire, and he longed for the din of battle once more. He could still command a considerable force; so he entered upon another campaign and as usual was at first successful. He seized three districts in the east country and set fire to a large number of towns. It was not until the next year that Wang-gön sent an expedition against him. This was under the command of Gen. Yu Gön-p'il, whom the king had banished but had pardoned and recalled because of his lively efforts while in exile to raise a company of soldiers. He never seemed to know when he was beaten. He routed the forces of Kyŭn-whŭn and returned in triumph to Song-do, where he was hailed as the savior of the people. We may judge from this that Kyŭn-whŭn was still considered formidable. In another fight Gen. Yu captured seven of Kyŭn-whŭn's captains and one of his sons as well.

As things seemed quiet now, the king made a royal progress through the north and west, helping the poor, inspecting fortresses, supplanting unpopular prefects; but when he got back he found his old enemy still active, and at Un-ju he had his last great fight with him. In this struggle 3,000 of the enemy were killed and thirty-two fortresses were taken. The year 935 CE is another milestone in Korean history. It marks the end of a dynasty which lacked but eight years of completing a millennium. But we must relate the events of the year in order. Kyŭn-whŭn had many concubines and more than ten sons. Of the latter the fourth named Keum-gang, was the one he loved the best, a boy of robust body and great intelligence. The old man passed by his other sons and named this one as his successor. This of course made trouble at once. The first son, Sin-geum, led a conspiracy and the old gentleman was seized and imprisoned in Keum-san monastery, the young Keum-gang was put to death and Sin-geum ascended the insecure throne of his father, now doubly insecure, since it had lost the masterly genius which of late years had been its only support. But old Kyŭn-whŭn had not played his last card. After three months imprisonment he succeeded in getting his guards drunk (jolly monks those) and escaped to Ka-ju from which point he had the colossal impudence to send a letter to Wang-gön surrendering and asking for asylum in Koryŭ against his own son. It was granted and soon a ship of war arrived with a high official on board to escort the grey old wolf of the south to the Koryŭ capital, where he was received as a guest, given a comfortable house and plenty of servants and the revenues of Yang-ju prefecture. From that point we may believe that he waited patiently to see the overthrow of his sons.

Silla Expires

But these are small events compared with what followed. The king of Silla determined to abdicate and hand over the remnant of his kingdom to Wang-gön. When he broached the matter to his officials no man raised his voice. They could not assent and they knew there was no use in demurring. The crown prince urged his father to submit the question to the people and to abide by their decision, but the king was determined and so sent a letter to Song-do offering to lay his sceptre at the feet of Wang-gön. The crown prince was in despair, refused to see his father, retired to a mountain retreat and ate coarse food as a token of his grief. He died there of chagrin and sorrow.

Wang-gön answered by sending one of the highest officials to escort the ex-king to Song-do. The royal procession was ten miles long, as it slowly wound its way out of the deserted city amidst the clamorous grief of the people. Wang-gön met him in person at the gate of Song-do. He did not want the ex-king to bow to him but the courtiers had decided that as the country could have but one king this must be done. So the new arrival did obeisance. Wang-gön gave him his daughter to wife and made him prime minister, set aside the revenues of an entire district to his use and conferred high rank upon the Silla courtiers.

And so ended the ancient kingdom of Silla which had existed for 992 years, from 57 BCE to 935 CE. Her line of kings included fifty-six names, which gives an average of about eighteen years to each reign. From that day the capital of Silla was called simply by the name Kyŏng-ju. We believe that history shows few instances of greater generosity, forbearance, delicacy, and tact than are shadowed forth in the life of this same Wang-gŏn. Does history show a nobler act than that of providing a comfortable home where his old enemy Kyŭn-whŭn might spend his last days in comfort and ease? Does it show more delicacy than was shown by Wang-gŏn when he took every means to cover the chagrin of the retiring king of Silla by treating him as a royal guest?

WANG-GŎN'S DEATH AND THE RULE OF HIS SUCCESSORS

Before leaving the kingdom of Silla to be swallowed up in antiquity we must notice a few corollaries. We will notice that Silla was the first power to gain the control of the whole peninsula. It was the language of Silla that became at least the official language of the entire country. The *yi-t'u*, or system of diacritical marks, tended to stereotype the agglutinative endings, so that we find today the general characteristics running through the grammar of Korean are those which characterized the language of ancient Silla. This fact, clearly grasped, goes a long way toward opening a way for the solution of the question of the origin of the language.

As the year 936 opens we see king Wang-gön with his two former rivals, the peaceful one and the warlike one, gathered under his wing, and the only cloud upon his horizon the attitude of Kyŭn-whŭn's sons in the south. This was soon settled. The king in company with Kyŭn-whŭn, at the head of an army of 87,000 men, marched southward and engaged the pitiable force that was all the malcontents could now muster. When they saw this tremendous army approaching and knew that Kyŭn-whŭn was there in person, surrender was immediate. Wang-gön's first demand was, 'Where is Sin-geum?' He was told that he was in a fortress in the mountains with a small force and was prepared to fight to a finish. He was there attacked and 3,200 men were taken and 5,700 killed, which shows how desperate the battle was. Sin-geum and his two brothers were captured. The two other sons of Kyŭn-whŭn were executed, because they had driven their father away, but Sin-geum in some way showed that he had not been a principal actor in that disgraceful scene and so escaped what we may well believe was merited punishment. There on the field the old man Kyŭn-whŭn died. It is said that his death was caused by chagrin that Sin-geum was not killed with his brothers.

It was in 938 that Wang-gön went outside the walls of the capital to meet a celebrated monk named Hong-bŭm, who had come originally from Ch'un-ch'uk monastery in the land of Sŭ-yŭk.

All this time interesting reforms were in progress. The names of all the prefectures throughout the country were changed. This has always been customary in Korea with a change of dynasty. The next year, 939, the new king of Koryŭ was formally recognized by the emperor who sent and invested him with the insignia of royalty. The crown prince of T'am-na, on Quelpart, came and did obeisance at the court of Koryŭ. A redistribution of the farming lands throughout the country was affected, by which, the records say, the worthy received more while others received less. It would be interesting to know in what way the test of worthiness was applied.

In 942 the Kitan power in the north tried to make friendly advances and sent a present of thirty camels. But Wang-gön remembered the way in which Kitan had feigned friendship for Pal-hă and then treacherously seized her; and for this reason he showed his opinion of Kitan now by banishing the thirty men and tying the thirty camels to Man-bu bridge and starving them to death.

Wang-gön's Ten Rules

King Wang-gön was now sixty-five years old. His life had been an active one; first as a warrior and then as the administrator of the kingdom which he had founded. Feeling that his end was approaching, he set himself to the task of formulating rules for his successor. As a result he placed in the hands of his son and heir ten rules which read as follows:

(1) Buddhism is the state religion.

(2) Build no more monasteries.

(3) If the first son is bad let the second or some other become king.

(4) Do not make friends with Kitan.

(5) Do honour to P'yŏngyang, the ancient capital.

(6) Establish an annual Buddhist festival.

(7) Listen to good men and banish bad ones.

(8) As the south is disaffected towards us do not marry from among the people of that section.

(9) Look after the interests of the army.
(10) Be always ready for emergencies.

After urging his son to lock all these precepts in his heart the aged king turned to the wall and died. These ten laws are typical of the man. They inculcated reverence for the best religion that had come under his notice, but in the same breath forbade the disproportionate growth of priestcraft, for he had seen what a seductive influence lay hidden within the arcana of this most mystical of all heathen cults. He advised temperance in religion. He forbade the throning of a man simply because he was the king's firstborn. By so doing he really proclaimed that the king was for the people and not the people for the king. He hated treachery and forbade making alliances with the forsworn. He believed in doing honour to the best of the old traditions and ordered that the ancient city of P'yŏngyang be remembered. He believed in loving his friends and hating his enemies and forbade descendants taking a wife from among the people of the south who had so desperately supported the claims of Kyŭn-whŭn, the one-time bandit. He was a military man and believed in having a strong army and in treating it in such a way as to insure its perfect loyalty.

It was in the last injunction, however, that he struck the keynote of his character. Be always ready for emergencies. Reading his character in the light of his actions we can well imagine one more precept that would have been characteristic of him; namely, that it is better to make a friend of an honest enemy than to kill him. And so in the year 942 the great general, reformer, king, and administrator was laid to his fathers and his son Mu reigned in his stead. The latter's posthumous title is Hye-jong.

The King Marries His Sister

The reign of this second king of Koryŭ starts with the statement that the king gave his own sister to his brother for a wife. It was one of the peculiar institutions of the dynasty that whenever possible the king married his own sister. In this instance he gave his sister to his brother, but the king had probably already married another of his sisters. This custom, which has prevailed in other countries besides Korea, notably in ancient Egypt, rests upon the assumption that by marrying one's own sister more of royalty is preserved in the family and the line is kept purer, the royal blood not being mixed with any of baser quality. We are told that, in order to make it seem less offensive, the sister, upon marrying her brother, took her mother's family name. This shows that the custom was looked down upon, else this device would not have been resorted to. We find also that the kings of Koryŭ were accustomed to have more than one real wife, contrary to the custom of the present dynasty. We read that this king, who had none of the elements of his father's greatness, took as his sixteenth wife the daughter of one Wang-gyu and by her had a son. Through her influence Wang-gyu had risen to the position of prime minister and it was his ambition to see his daughter's son ascend the throne.

It had been the king's plan to give the throne to his brother Yo and the prime minister began by plotting against the life of this possible successor. The king learned of this and frustrated it by immediately abdicating in favour of his brother. Wang-gyu seems to have possessed considerable power independently of the king for we learn that he not only was not punished but that he continued to plot against Yo even after he had assumed the reins of power. An assassin whom he had hired to kill the king was himself killed by the king while attempting to carry out the deed. When the king fell ill he was advised to move secretly to another palace for safety. He did so and that very night the myrmidons of Wang-gyu broke into the palace that he had left, but found that their bird had flown. In spite of all this the king did not proceed against his minister but went about with an armed escort. This signal failure to punish a traitor is said to have been the reason why, during the whole dynasty, the officials overruled the king and made a puppet of him. In fact many times during the dynasty we find the condition of affairs somewhat like those in Japan where the emperor himself had little practical power but the government was carried on by a shogun. But at last this Wang-gyu met his deserts for he was banished to Kap-whan and there executed, and with him 300 men who had been in his pay.

It is interesting to notice how soon after the death of Wang Gon his ill-considered advice about Buddhism was to bear its legitimate fruit. The third king of Koryŭ was thoroughly in the hands of the sacerdotal power. He was a devout worshipper of Buddha and spent large sums of money upon the priesthood. He favoured the monks in every way and thus added one more blow to the wedge which ultimately split the land and brought the dynasty to a close.

P'yŏngyang

Following the directions of Wang-gön in regard to the city of P'yŏngyang, he decided to make this town a secondary capital. In the prosecution of this work many people were compelled to give their time and labour, and great suffering was the natural result. Many of the people of Song-do were compelled to move to the northern capital. This was very distasteful to them, and, joined with the king's blind adherence to Buddhism, made it easy for the people to rejoice when in 970 he died and his younger brother So became king. His posthumous title is Kwang-jong. He in turn married his own sister, and the records intimate that another reason for marrying in the family was that it kept out undesirable connections who would naturally expect to receive positions under the government.

When in 953 the emperor sent an envoy to the court of Koryŭ approving of the coronation of the new king, he was accompanied by a great scholar, Sang Geui, who found such favour in the eyes of the king that he remained and took office under the government. It is said that this caused a serious setback to the fortunes of Buddhism. Well would it have been could he have seen that insidious power crushed and driven from the country. But it had gained too strong a foothold to be overcome by the teaching or example of a single man or coterie of men. It is not unlikely that it was at the suggestion of this man that the king changed the law concerning slavery. Heretofore slavery had been the punishment for comparatively venial offences and the country was overrun with slaves. The king manumitted many of these and by so doing gained the enmity of many who thus lost valuable property. It also resulted in outbreaks among slaves, incipient riots, because this humane tendency in the king emboldened them to claim more than he had intended. It showed that sometimes the indiscriminate franchisement of slaves may be a dangerous thing.

Examinations

The most radical reform instituted at the advice of this Sang Geui was the establishment of a national competitive examination similar to those held in China. In Korea it is called the *kwaga*.

The examination was a sixfold one: (1) heptameter verse, (2) hexameter verse, (3) commentary, (4) historic citation, (5) medicine, (6) divination.

Chinese Favoured

Communication with China seems to have become more frequent and close, for we find that in 960 an envoy went to China carrying as gifts 50,000 pounds of copper and 4,000 pieces of rock crystal used in making spectacles. This was likewise a period of Chinese immigration, encouraged without doubt by the flattering reception given to Sang Geui. The king gave the visitors a hearty welcome, provided them with houses, gave them office and even secured them wives. So far did he go in the way of providing houses that he incurred the resentment of some of his highest officials, one of whom, So P'il, asked the king to take his fine residence from him as a gift. In surprise the king asked him why he wanted to give it up. The answer was, 'It will be seized anyway when I die and I would rather give it up now and spend the rest of my days preparing a little home somewhere for my children.' This threw the king into a rage; but the shot told, for he stopped the form of injustice from that very day.

The following year, 961, a sweeping change was made in the style and colour of official garments. This was also under the direction of Sang Geui. For the highest rank purple was used, and for the second rank red, for the third rank deep red, and for the fourth rank blue.

Incapable King

How far this king had degenerated from the standard set by the founder of the kingdom, less than fifty years before, is apparent from the fact that he was the pliant instrument of anyone who had access to his ear. He believed anybody and everybody. Enemies accused each other before him and he accepted every statement as true. The result was that the prisons were simply bursting with inmates and the executioner's axe was busy night and day. Hundreds of men were executed whose only crime was that they had been accused before the king. Added to this was a prodigal waste of treasure in the building of palaces, the assumption throughout of Chinese clothes and the entertainment of countless 'friends' who came from across the border, on the principle, no doubt, that where the carcass is there will the eagles be gathered together. This state of things continued up to 969, going from bad to worse. That year the king took to himself two Buddhist monks as mentors. He suddenly awoke to the fact that many murders lay at his door and he began to have twinges of conscience. He thought to make it right by a wholesale favouring of Buddhism. He put himself entirely into the hands of the monks and let them manage all the affairs of state to suit themselves. But this, while it may have eased his conscience, brought no betterment to the state. He was imposed upon in the grossest manner and never once guessed it. He lost the respect of all men of sense and reason. His useless reign dragged on till 976 when the country was relieved of the mighty incubus by his death. The prisons were overrun with innocent men, priestcraft had wound its octopus tentacles about every branch of the government. Energy and patriotism had been eradicated; for, the moment a man possessing these traits appeared, jealousy caused him to be accused to the credulous king and he was thrown into prison.

Reform

But now his son, Chu, came to the throne. His posthumous title is Kyong-jong. His first act was to open the prison doors and liberate all who were not condemned felons. This act of mere justice was greeted by applause from the people. It was the signal for a general reform in the methods of administration. The monks were sent back to their monasteries. The competitive examinations were renewed and an impetus was given to the study of the classics. The king in person examined the papers of the candidates. But death put an end to his promising career after six short years and in 982 his younger brother, Ch'i, posthumous title Song-jong, ascended the throne. Fortunately he was of the same mind as his deceased brother and the good work went on unchecked.

He first did away with the senseless festivals described under the reign of Wang Gon, at which all manner of animals were represented. He changed the names of official grades to correspond with those of the Tang dynasty in China. Intercourse with China was revived and frequent envoys passed back and forth. It was in the second year of his reign, namely 983, that the time-honoured custom was instituted of the king plowing a piece of land in person each year. This too was borrowed from China. Confucianism received a great impetus during these days; an envoy to China brought back a picture of the emperor's shrine, of the patron genius of China, of Confucius' shrine, and a history of the seventy-two disciples of the great sage. Financial affairs engaged his attention too, for we find that in this year 984 the legal rate of interest on money was set at ten per cent *per mensem*. The defences of the country were not neglected. A fortress was begun on the banks of the Yalu River but the people of the Yŭ-jin tribe caused the work to be suspended.

Kitan Growing

The Kitan tribe were still in the ascendant and so ominous was the growth of their power that the envoy from China who came to perform the ceremony of investiture of the new king, intimated that China would be glad to join the forces of Koryŭ in an invasion of the Kitan territory. We are not told what reply was given but nothing seems to have come of it. Buddhistic encroachments were checked and a stop was put to the seizure of houses for the purpose of erecting monasteries. Mourning customs were changed; the three years' limit was shortened to 100 days, the one-year limit to thirty days, the nine months' limit to twenty days, the six months' limit to fifteen days and the three months' limit to seven days. Special instructions were given to the governors of the provinces to foster agriculture, and prizes were offered for superior excellence in agricultural methods as proved by their results. The governors were allowed to take their families with them to the provincial capitals. This marks a long step in advance, for it would seem that heretofore the families of provincial governors had been held at the national capital as a guarantee of good behavior on the part of the governors while in the country.

The king caused the erection of great storehouses in the various parts of the country for the storage of rice to be used in time of famine. The students in the Confucian school were encouraged by gifts of clothes and food, and several were sent to China to prosecute their studies. In 987 the soldiers' implements of war were beaten into agricultural implements, especially in the country districts. A second trial was made of liberating slaves but without satisfactory results. It made those that were not freed so arrogant that the attempt was given up. A further invasion was made into the territory of priestcraft by the discontinuance of certain important festivals, but the fact that the law against the killing of any animal in the first, fifth or ninth moons was still in active force shows that Buddhism was still a powerful factor in the national life. Kyöng-ju, the ancient capital of Silla, was made the eastern capital of the kingdom, a merely honourary distinction.

The annals state that this reign beheld the inauguration of the humane custom of remitting the revenues, in part or in whole, in times of famine, also the custom of the king sending medicine to courtiers who might be ill.

The growing power of Kitan in the north was a cause of uneasiness for we find that in 989 the whole north-east border was thoroughly garrisoned. The time was approaching when this half-savage tribe would add another proof that conquest is usually from the cooler to the warmer climate.

During the commotion incident upon the founding of the dynasty and the extinction of the kingdom of Silla, the bureau of history had been largely neglected. Now it was reorganised and the annals of the kingdom were put in proper shape.

The king was apparently trying to steer a middle course between Buddhism and Confucianism, for the pen of the annalist records that no animals were to be killed on the king's birthday, and in the next stroke that wives were to be rewarded for unusual virtue, and again that the king went out of the city to meet an envoy bringing the great Buddhistic work, Tă-jang-gyŭng, from China, and still again that the first ancestral temple was erected. Well would it have been could this equilibrium have been maintained.

One of the sons of Wang Gon was still living. His name was Uk. He was the author of a court scandal which illustrates the lax morals of the time. He formed a liaison with the widow of his younger brother. The king learned of it and visited his anger upon the offender by banishing him. The woman bore a son and then went forth and hanged herself on a willow tree. The nurse brought up the child and taught it the word father. One day the child was brought into the presence of the king, when it rushed forward, caught the king by the garments and cried father. The king was deeply moved and sent the child to its father in banishment. When Uk died the boy was brought back to the capital and given office. He eventually became king.

Quarrel with Kitan

In 993 the cloud in the north began to assume a threatening aspect. A feeble attempt was made to stem the march of the now powerful Kitan tribe, but without avail. The Kitan general, So Son-ryŭng, made this a *casus belli*, and, mustering a strong force, pushed down into Koryŭ territory. The king put Gen. Păk Yang-yu at the head of the Koryŭ forces and himself went with the army as far as P'yŏngyang. At that point news came that the enemy was going around the flank and had already taken one important fortress there. The king hurried back to Song-do. Gen. So Son-ryŭng sent a curt message saying 'Ko-gu-ryŭ once belonged to Kitan. We have come to claim only our own. It remains therefore only for you to surrender and become our vassals.' In answer the king sent Yi Mong-jun to negotiate a peace on the best possible terms. Arriving at the camp of Gen. So he boldly demanded why the northern tribe had presumed to break across the boundary. Gen. So replied that the land was the property of his master and the sooner the king acknowledged it and accepted Kitan as his suzerain the better for all parties. The envoy returned to the capital and a great council of war was held. Some advised to surrender, but some said 'Offer them all the territory north of the Tă-dong River as a compromise measure.' The king chose the latter alternative and began by having the people there throw into the river all grain that they could not carry away, so that it might not fall into the hands of the enemy. The Kitan general was highly pleased with this concession but his pride had a fall when, a few days later, he was defeated by the Koryŭ forces under Gen. Yu Bang. Thereupon he modified his demands to the mere recognition of the suzerainty of Kitan; but this the king was unwilling, under the circumstances, to agree to.

Gen. So was not satisfied with the grade of the general sent to negotiate the treaty and demanded that the prime minister of Koryŭ be sent to do it. A high official was therefore sent but he refused to bow before the Kitan general. The latter said, 'You are from Silla and we are from Ko-gu-ryŭ. You are trespassing on our territory. We are your neighbours. Why do you persist in sending envoys to the court of China? That is the reason we are now at war with you. Restore our land, become our vassals and all will go well.' The envoy refused to agree to this. He said 'We are Ko-gu-ryŭ people. How else could our land be Koryŭ? The capital of Ko-gu-ryŭ was at P'yŏngyang and you formed a small part of that kingdom; so why do you claim that we have usurped the power? Our territory extended far beyond the Yalu River, but the Yŭ-jin people stole it from us. You had better first go and recover that part of Ko-gu-ryŭ which the Yŭ-jin stole and then we will gladly bow to you as suzerain.' What there was in this argument that convinced the hardy warrior of the north we cannot say, but it served its purpose, for he first spread a great feast and afterwards broke camp and marched back to his own country without obtaining the coveted surrender.

China Refuses Assistance

The king, in order to maintain the semblance of good faith, adopted the Kitan calendar. The next step, however, showed the true bent of his mind, for he sent a swift messenger to the court of China with an urgent request for aid against the arrogant people of the north. But the Sung emperor apparently thought he had his own hands full in watching his own borders and declined to send the aid requested. This put an end to the friendship between Koryŭ and the Chinese court, and all communication was broken off. The king of Kitan sent a commissioner to Koryŭ to look after his interests there and when he returned to the north he took a large number of women as a gift from the Koryŭ king to his master.

It was now, near the end of the tenth century, that Koryŭ was first regularly divided into provinces. There were ten of them. Their names and positions were as follows. Kwan-nă, the present Kyŭng-geui; Chung-wŭn, now Chung-ju; Ha-nam, now Kong-ju; Yong-nam, now Sang-ju; Kang-nam, now Chŭn-ju; San-nam, now Chin-ju; Hă-yang, now Na-ju; Sak-pang, now Ch'un-ch'ŭn, Kang-neung and An-byŭn; P'ă-su, now P'yŏngyang; and Kă-sŭng, another name for Song-do. These were rather the provincial centres than the provinces themselves.

In pursuance of the policy adopted in reference to the kingdom of Kitan, ten boys were sent northward to that country to learn its language and marry among its people. The final act of suzerainty was played when in 996 the 'emperor' of Kitan invested the king of Koryŭ with the royal insignia. The end of the reign was approaching, but before it was reached one of the most important events of that century transpired. It occupies little space on the page of history. Many a court intrigue or senseless pageant bulks larger in the annals, but it was one of the most far-reaching in its effects. It was the first coining of money. It was in this same year, 996. These coins were of iron but without the hole which so generally characterizes the 'cash' of today.

In 998 the king died and his nephew, Song, posthumous title Mok-jong, ascended the throne. His first act was to revise the system of taxation, probably by causing a remeasurement of arable land. Officials received their salaries not in money nor in rice, but to each one was assigned a certain tract of land and his salary was the produce from that particular tract. In the third year of his reign, 1000 CE, he received investiture from the Kitan emperor. His fifth year was signalized by a five days' eruption of a volcano on the island of Quelpart. This reign was destined to end in disaster.

The widow of the late king formed a criminal intimacy with one Kim Ji-yang, whom she raised to a high official position. The whole kingdom was scandalized. She had the walls of her palace decorated with sentiments expressive of the epicurean dictum 'Eat, drink and be merry'; and curiously enough expressed the belief that after enjoying all this world had to give they would all become Buddhas in the next. This is probably a fair sample of the Buddhistic teaching of the times, at least this was its legitimate fruit. She and her lover soon began to plot against the young king. The latter was ill at the time but knew well what was going on. He sent for Sun, the illegitimate son of Uk, of whom we spoke in the last chapter, with the intention of nominating him as his successor. At the same time he sent post-haste to the country and summoned Gen. Kang Cho, a faithful and upright man. On his way up to the capital the general was falsely told that it was not the king who had summoned him but the queen dowager's lover. Enraged at being thus played upon, the stern old general marched into the capital and seized the lecherous traitor and gave him his quietus. He then turned upon the king and put him to death as well. He had not looked carefully into the case, but he deemed that the whole court needed a thorough cleaning out. He completed the work by driving out the queen dowager who deserved the block more than any other; and then he seated the above-mentioned Sun on the throne. His posthumous title is Hyön-jong. This was in 1010 CE.

WAR AND PEACE WITH KITAN

The first act of king Hyön-jong after announcing to Kitan his accession to the throne was to raze to the ground the palace of the queen dowager who had dragged the fair fame of Koryŭ in the mire. His next move was to build a double wall about his capital. Evidently coming events were casting ominous shadows before, and he saw the storm brewing.

We should say at this point that during all these reigns the annals make careful note of every eclipse. This is brought prominently to our notice by the statement in the annals that in the sixteenth year of this reign there should have been an eclipse but that it did not take place. This throws some light upon the science of astronomy as practiced in those dark days.

The common people looked upon an eclipse as an omen of evil, but this would indicate that among the educated people, then as today, they were understood to be mere natural phenomena. In 1010 the storm, which had already given sharp premonitions of its coming, broke in all its fury. It must have come sooner or later in any event, but the immediate pretext for it was as follows: Two Koryŭ generals, Ha Kong-jin and Yu Chŭng, who had been placed in charge of the forces in the north, when Gen. Kang-cho was recalled to the capital, took matters into their own hands and looked for no orders from headquarters. The desperate state of things at the capital partly warranted them in this, but they carried it too far. Of their own accord they attacked the eastern Yŭ-jin tribe and though they did not succeed in the attempt they impressed those people so strongly that an embassy came bringing the submission of that tribe. The two generals who seem to have partially lost their balance with the increase of their importance, wantonly killed every member of this embassy. As soon as the young king heard of this he promptly stripped them of their honours and banished them. This, however, did not mend matters with the outraged Yŭ-jin people, and they hastened to inform the Kitan emperor of the whole matter. Thereupon the proclamation went out from the Kitan capital, 'Gen. Kang-cho has killed the king of Koryŭ. We will go and inquire into it.'

As a preliminary, a messenger was sent to Song-do to demand why the king had been put to death. The officials were thrown into a panic and hastened to send and envoy to Kitan to explain matters. He was held a prisoner by the emperor. The king sent again and again, ten envoys in all, but an ominous silence was the only answer. It appeared that something serious was about to happen, but just what it was could not be surmised. In order to be ready for any emergency, the king sent Generals Kang Cho and Yi Hyŭn-un to T'ong-ju (now Sŭn-ch'ŭn) in the north to guard against a sudden surprise.

Kitan Troops Cross the Yalu

Early in December the spell was broken and the watchers by the Yalu hurried in with the news that a cloud of Kitan warriors was already crossing the stream. The invading army 400,000 strong, so say the records, pushed forward and surrounded the Koryŭ forces at Heung-wha camp. When it was found, however, that they would stand their ground and fight, the invaders sent presents of silk and other valuables and advised them to surrender, and said 'We liked the king whom Kang Cho killed, and we are determined to overthrow the murderer. You assist us in this. If not we will destroy you root and branch.' The reply was 'We prefer to die rather than surrender.' Thereupon the enemy sent more costly presents still but the answer was the same. When it became plain that there was to be bloodshed before Koryŭ would come to terms, the Kitan emperor divided his immense army into two divisions, sending 200,000 men to the vicinity of Eui-ju and 200,000 to T'ong-ju. Gen. Kang Cho cunningly disposed his little army between two creeks where he was protected on either flank. It is said that he had a species of battle chariot with swords attached to the axles of the wheels so that when they charged among the ranks of the enemy the latter were mown down. On this account the little Koryŭ army was at first successful. Then Gen. Kang Cho was seized by that common infatuation of fancied security and in the midst of the fighting he sat down in his pride and began playing a game of go-bang. A messenger hurried up with the news that the line of battle had been broken on the west and that the enemy were pouring in. Gen. Kang Cho laughed and said 'Do not come to me with such an insignificant piece of news. Wait till they come in numbers worthy of my sword; then come and tell me.' Soon a messenger came saying that the Kitan forces were approaching in full column. Thereupon Gen. Kang arose and prepared for battle. While doing so the annals say that the spirit of the murdered king appeared before him and chided him for scorning the power of Kitan. He took off his helmet, and, bowing before the apparition, said 'I have committed an offence worthy of death.' The Kitan soldiery rushed in and seized him. They bound him in a cart and took him away.

Nothing now lay between the invading army and universal rapine. The army penetrated far into the territory of Koryŭ, cut off 30,000 heads and ravaged right and left.

When Gen. Kang Cho and Gen. Yi Hyŭn-un were brought before the Kitan emperor the bonds of the former were cut and he was bidden to stand forth. 'Will you become my subject?' 'I am a Koryŭ man. How can I be your subject?' They cut his flesh with knives but he remained firm. When the same question was put to Gen. Yi Hyŭn-un he replied: 'As I now look upon the sun and moon, how can I remember any lesser light?' Such were the words of his apostasy. Kang Cho cried out upon him as a traitor, and then bowed his head to the axe.

P'yŏngyang Besieged

The Kitan army was now in full march on P'yŏngyang, but the broken remnants of the Koryŭ army united at 'Long Neck Pass' and successfully opposed the progress of the invaders. A little diplomacy was now made use of by the Kitan general. He sent a letter to Heung-wha camp, purporting to be from Kang Cho, ordering them to surrender, but the commander, Yang Kyu, replied 'I listen only to the king.'

Kwak-ju (now Kwak-san) and Suk-ju (now Suk Ch'ŭn) fell in quick succession and soon the victorious army of Kitan was thundering at the gates of P'yŏngyang. The general in command was Wŭn Chong-sŭk and his two lieutenants were Chi Ch'oa-mun and Ch'oé Ch'ang. The commander was willing to surrender without a fight and went so far as to write out the surrender, but the other two prevented this by seizing the paper, tearing it up and putting the Kitan messenger to death. The camp of these generals was without the city, but the panic of the people inside increased to such an extent that all the forces entered the city to ensure quiet.

The Kitan General-in-Chief now received from the king an offer of surrender. It caused the greatest satisfaction in the Kitan camp and orders were given that the soldiers should cease ravaging the surrounding country. Ma Po-u was sent as Kitan commissioner in Song-do and was accompanied by an escort of 1,000 men under the command of Gen. Eul Neum.

We can see how little connection there was between the capital and the army in the field by the fact that this submission on the part of the king did not lead to the surrender of P'yŏngyang nor to a cessation of hostilities by the generals who commanded the forces there. When a second messenger was sent into the city to ask why the former one did not return he too was put to death.

Gen. Eul Neum was ordered to reduce P'yŏngyang and he approached to attack it but was driven back with a loss of 3,000 men. This attempt failing, the conquerors decided to lay siege to the town. When the inmates saw this they knew that the end was near. A plan was made whereby a part of the troops should make a sally from the West Gate and another part from the East Gate and together they hoped to dislodge the enemy. But one of the generals, instead of following out the plan, improved the opportunity to make good his escape. The other party was therefore in a trap and had to surrender. But still two generals held the city.

Meanwhile a band of 1,000 soldiers under Gen. Yang Kyu attacked Kwak-ju by night, and put the Kitan garrison to the sword, and took 7,000 people away to Tong-bu for safety.

Seige Raised

When the Kitan forces found they were likely to have difficulty in bringing P'yŏngyang to terms they gave it up and marched away eastward. Thereupon the general Chi Ch'oa-mun hastened to Song-do and announced that he had fled from P'yŏngyang. The 'residency' of Ma Po-u seems to have been a short-lived one and terminated when it was found that the submission of the king amounted to little when the armies would not surrender. Courtiers urged an immediate surrender but Gen. Kang Kam-Ch'an said 'If we could put them off a while and gain time they would be gradually worn out. The king should move south out of harm's way for a time.' So that very night the king and queen and a large number of officials together with 5,000 troops moved southward to Chŭk-sŭng. The king's southward flight was by no means an easy one. The very first night out from the capital the house where he slept was attacked by a band of traitors and malcontents. The king escaped to the mountains where he was attended by the faithful Gen. Chi. From this retreat he recalled the two generals who had been banished for attacking Yŭ-jin without orders, and restored them to their positions. Escorted by Generals Chi, Ch'o and Chu, the king slowly retreated toward Wang-ju. All his numerous escort had left him excepting his two wives, two palace women and two intimate friends. Gen. Chi kept a sharp lookout for the bands of robbers who were roaming about the country. Once when hard pressed by these irresponsible gentry, Gen. Chi spirited the king away under cover of night and concealed him in To-bong monastery in Yang-ju a little to the northeast of the present Seoul, and the robbers were thrown completely off the scent.

Gen. Ha Kong-jin told the king that the Kitan forces had invaded Koryŭ for the purpose of punishing Gen. Kang Bho, and as this had been accomplished all difficulty between Koryŭ and Kitan could be easily settled by a letter from the king to his northern suzerain. The letter was written and sent by the hand of a trusty man. It said that the king had left Song-do for an expedition into the country to quell certain disturbances there. When the messenger was asked how far the king had gone he answered that he had gone several thousand *li*. This seemed plausible to the Kitan court and soon its army was working its way slowly back to the boundary, the first stop being made at Ch'ang-wha.

A Rebel Governor

This retreat was more with a view to obtaining a wintering place than with a desire to favour Koryŭ, for no sooner had the next season, 1011, come than the Kitan army marched straight down through the peninsula and entered the capital and burned the palaces and most of the common houses. The king was in Kwang-ju but, learning of this disaster, he hurried still further south with his two wives to Ch'ŭn-an in the present Ch'ung-ch'ŭng Province. From there he continued south to Chŭn-ju where he was treated very cavalierly by the governor who met him in common clothes and without the ceremony befitting a royal visitor. In fact this governor had determined to put the king out of the way. To this end he hired three men to go by night and assassinate him. But the door was guarded by Gen. Chi who bolted it firmly and then mounted the roof and cried loudly to all who were loyal to the king to rally round him. The next day the governor was summoned before the king. Some of the generals were clamorous for his death but Gen. Chi who was as wise as he was faithful vetoed this, for the king was not in a position to face the opposition that the execution of the governor would arouse in the province. It will be remembered that Wang Gon had left command that as the south was disaffected none of his descendants should marry among its people. This shows that the king when he went south found it unwise to exercise all the prerogatives of royalty. So the governor was left intact and the king moved further south to Na-ju.

Meanwhile the Kitan forces were not having it all their own way in the north. Gen. Kim Suk-heung of Kwi-ju attacked a powerful force of the enemy and secured a signal victory. It is said that he put 10,000 men to death. Then Gen. Yang Kyu made a dash at the enemy at Mu-ro-da near Eui-ju and killed 2,000 and recovered 3,000 prisoners. Also at Yi-su there was a battle in which 2,500 Kitan men were killed and 1,000 captives rescued. At Yo-ri-ch'ŭn also 1,000 more were killed. These three desperate engagements occurred on the same day.

Gen. Ha Kong-jin was at this time a hostage in the Kitan capital, and he managed to send a letter to the king informing him that the forces of Kitan were slowly retreating. This made it possible for the king to start on his way back to the capital. The first stage was to Chŭn-ju.

The retreating forces of Kitan were again engaged at A-jin but as heavy reinforcements arrived at the moment, the Koryŭ generals, Yang Kyu and Kim Suk-heng, lost the day and fell upon the field of battle. This victory, however, did not stop the retreat of the invading army. There had been very heavy rains, and many horses had perished and many soldiers were practically without arms. Gen. Chon Song, who assumed command after the death of the two generals at K-jŭn, hung on the flanks of the retreating enemy and when half of them had crossed the Yalu he fell upon the remainder and many of them were cut down and many more were drowned in midstream. When it became known that all the Kitan forces were across the border it took but a few days to re-man the fortresses which had been deserted.

The king now hastened northward stopping for a time at Kong-ju where the governor gave him his three daughters to wife. By the first he begat two sons both of whom became kings of Koryŭ, and by the second he begat another who also became king. He was soon on the road again, and ere long he reentered the gates of his capital which had undergone much hardship during his absence. His first act was to give presents to all the generals and to order that all the bones of the soldiers who had fallen be interred. He followed this up by dispatching an envoy to the Kitan thanking them for recalling their troops. He banished the governor of Chŭn-ju who had attempted his life. He repaired the wall of the capital and rebuilt the palace.

Gen. Ha Executed

Gen. Ha was still in the hands of the Kitan but he was extremely anxious to return to Koryŭ. He therefore feigned to be quite satisfied there and gradually gained the entire confidence of his captors. When he deemed that it was safe he proposed that he be sent back to Koryŭ to spy out the condition of the land and report on the number of soldiers. The emperor consented but changed his mind when he heard that the king had returned to Song-do. Instead of sending Gen. Ha back to Koryŭ he sent him to Yun-gyŭng to live and gave him a woman of high position as his wife. Even then the general did not give up hope of escaping and was soon busy on a new plan. He purchased fleet horses and had them placed at stated intervals along the road toward Koryŭ with trusty grooms in charge of each. Someone, however, told the emperor of this and, calling the exile, he questioned him about it. Gen. Ha confessed that his life in exile was intolerable. When the emperor had offered him every inducement to transfer his allegiance and all to no avail, he commanded the executioner to put an end to the interview. When news reached Song-do that Gen. Ha had preferred death to disloyalty, the king hastened to give office to the patriot's son.

The work of reconstruction was now commenced, in 1012. Kyöng-ju was no longer called the eastern capital but was changed back to a mere prefecture. The twelve provinces were reconstructed into five and there were seventy-five prefectures in all. This plan however was abandoned two years later. Now that Koryŭ had regained control of her own territory, the Yŭ-jin tribe thought best to cultivate her good will and so sent frequent envoys with gifts of horses and other valuables. But when the Emperor of Kitan, angry because the king refused on the plea of ill health to go to Kitan and do obeisance, sent an army and seized six of the northern districts this side the Yalu, the Yŭ-jin turned about and ravaged the northeast boundary. The next year the Yŭ-jin joined Kitan and crossed the Yalu but were speedily driven back by Gen. Kim Sang-wi.

In 1014 the king came to the conclusion that he had made a mistake in casting off the friendship of China and sent an envoy to make explanations; but the Emperor Chin-jong (Sang dynasty) was angry because he had been so long neglected and would have nothing to do with the repentant Koryŭ.

Military and Civil Factions

In the autumn the Kitan army was again forced back across the border. The Koryŭ army had now grown to such proportions that the question of revenue became a very serious one and the officials found it necessary to suggest a change. They had been accustomed to 'squeeze' a good proportion of the soldiers' pay and now that there was danger of further change which would be only in the officials' favour, the soldiers raised a disturbance, forced the palace gates, killed two of the leading officials, and compelled the king to banish others. They saw to it that the military officials took precedence of civil officials. From that time on there was great friction between the military and civil factions, each trying to drive the other to the wall.

The next year, 1015, the Kitan people bridged the Yalu, built a wall at each end and successfully defended it from capture; but when they attempted to harry the adjoining country they were speedily driven back. The military faction had now obtained complete control at the capital. Swarms of incompetent men were foisted into office and things were going from bad to worse.

The king was much dissatisfied at this condition of affairs and at someone's advice decided to sever the knot which he could not untie. He summoned all the leaders of the military faction to a great feast, and, when he had gotten them all intoxicated, had them cut down by men who had lain concealed in an adjoining chamber. In this way nineteen men were put out of the way and the military faction was driven to the wall.

Kitan Invasion

Year by year the northern people tried to make headway against Koryŭ. The Sung dynasty was again and again appealed to but without success. Koryŭ was advised to make peace with Kitan on the best terms possible. The Kitan generals, Yu Pyul, Hăng Byŭn and Ya-yul Se-chang, made raid after raid into Koryŭ territory with varying success. In 1016 Kitan scored a decisive victory at Kwak-ju where the Koryŭ forces were cut to pieces. Winter however sent them back to their northern haunts. The next year they came again and in the following year, 1018, Gen. So Son-ryŭng came with 100,000 men. The Koryŭ army was by this time in good order again and showed an aggregate of 200,000 men. They were led by General Kang Kam-ch'an. When the battle was fought the latter used a new form of strategem. He caused a heavy dam to be constructed across a wooded valley and when a considerable body of water had accumulated behind it he drew the enemy into the valley below and then had the dam torn up; the escaping water rushed down the valley and swept away hundreds of the enemy and threw the rest into such a panic that they fell an easy prey to the superior numbers of the Koryŭ army. This was followed by two more victories for the Koryŭ arms.

The next year, again, the infatuated northmen flung themselves against the Koryŭ rock. Under Gen. So Son-ryŭng they advanced upon Song-do. The Koryŭ generals went out thirty miles and brought into the capital the people in the suburbs. Gen. So tried a ruse to throw the Koryŭ generals off their guard. He sent a letter saying that he had decided not to continue the march but to retire to Kitan; but he secretly threw out a strong force toward Song-do. They found every point disputed and were obliged to withdraw to Yŭng-byŭn. Like most soldiers the Koryŭ forces fought best when on the offensive and the moment the enemy took this backward step Gen. Kang Kam-ch'an was upon them, flank and rear. The invaders were driven out of Yŭng-byŭn but made a stand at Kwi-ju. At first the fight was an even one but when a south wind sprang up which lent force to the Koryŭ arrows and drove dust into the eyes of the enemy the latter turned and fled, with the exulting Koryŭ troops in full pursuit. Across the Sŭk-ch'ŭn brook they floundered and across the fields which they left carpeted with Kitan dead. All their plunder, arms and camp equipage fell into Koryŭ hands and Gen. So Son-ryŭng with a few thousand weary followers finally succeeded in getting across the Yalu. This was the greatest disaster that Kitan suffered at any time from her southern neighbour.

Gen. So received a cool welcome from his master, while Gen. Kang, returning in triumph to Song-do with Kitan heads and limitless plunder, was met by the king in person and given a flattering ovation. His Majesty with his own hands presented him with eight golden flowers. The name of the meeting place was changed to Heung-eui-yŭk, 'Place of Lofty Righteousness'. When Gen. Kang retired the following year he received six honourary titles and the revenue from 300 houses. He was a man of small stature and ill-favoured and did not dress in a manner befitting his position, but he was called the 'Pillar of Koryŭ'. Many towns in the north had been laid waste during the war and so the people were moved and given houses and land. The records say that an envoy came with greetings from the kingdom of Ch'ŭl-ri. One also came from Tă-sik in western China and another from the kingdom of Pul-lă. Several of the Mal-gal tribes also sent envoys; the kingdom of T'am-na was again heard from and the Kol-bu tribe in the north sent envoys.

Buddhism Versus Confucianism

In 1020 Koryŭ sent an envoy to make friends again with her old time enemy Kitan and was successful. The ambition of the then Emperor of Kitan had apparently sought some new channel. Buddhism, too, came in for its share of attention. We read that the king sent to Kyöng-ju, the ancient capital of Silla, to procure a bone of Buddha which was preserved there as a relic. Every important matter was referred in prayer to the Buddhistic deities. As yet Confucianism had succeeded in keeping pace with Buddhism. In 1024 the king decreed that the candidates in the national examinations should come according to population; three men from a 1,000-house town, two from a 500-house town and one each from smaller places. Several examinations were held in succession and only those who excelled in them all received promotion. The great struggle between Buddhism and Confucianism, which now began, arrayed the great class of monks on the side of the former and the whole official class on the side of the latter. The former worked upon the superstitions of the king and had continual access to him while the latter could appeal to him only on the side of general common sense and reason. Moreover Buddhism had this in its favour that as a rule each man worked for the system rather than for himself, always presenting a solid front to the opposition. The other party was itself a conglomerate of interests, each man working mainly for himself and joining with others only when his own interests demanded. This marked division of parties was strikingly illustrated when, in 1026, in the face of vehement expostulations on the part of the officials, the king spent a large amount of treasure in the repairing of monasteries. The kingdom of Kitan received a heavy blow when in 1029 one of her generals, Tă Yŭn-im, revolted and formed the sporadic kingdom of Heung-yo. Having accomplished this he sent to the king of Koryŭ saying 'We have founded a new kingdom and you must send troops to aid us.' The Koryŭ officials advised that advantage be taken of this schism in Kitan to recover the territory beyond the Yalu which originally belonged to Ko-gu-ryŭ and to which Koryŭ therefore had some remote title. Neither plan was adopted. It seemed good to keep friendly with Kitan until such time as her power for taking revenge should be past, so envoys were sent as usual, but were intercepted and held by the new king of Heung-yo. This policy turned out to be a wise one, for soon the news came that Kitan had destroyed the parvenu.

Now that the fortunes of Koryŭ were manifestly in the ascendant, many people in the north sent and swore allegiance to her, thus following the example of a certain Kitan envoy who at this time transferred his citizenship voluntarily from Kitan to Koryŭ.

The 'Great Wall' of Koryŭ

The king died and his son Heum, posthumous title Tŭk-jong, came to the throne in 1032. He married his own sister. All friendly relations with Kitan were broken off, because the bridge across the Yalu was not destroyed. It did not seem a friendly act to leave this standing menace to the peace of Koryŭ. In view of this the king ordered a wall to be built across the entire peninsula from the Yalu River to the Japan Sea. It was nearly 1,000 *li* [one li equals one-third of a mile] long. This would seem almost incredible were it not that the facts are given in such detail. The wall was twenty-five *cha* high and the same in breadth and stretched from Ko-gung-nă Fortress, near Eui-ju on the Yalu, to Yöng-heung near the Japan Sea. The Kitan people tried to hinder this work but without avail. This period marks the acme of Koryŭ's power and wealth. She had reached her zenith within a century and a quarter of her birth and now for three centuries she was destined to decline.

The younger brother, Hyöng, of this King Tŭk-jong, succeeded him in 1035, after a short reign of three years. He continued the work of making impregnable the defences of the north. He built a wall from Song-ryŭng Pass in the west to the borders of the Yŭ-jin tribe in the north-east. He also built a Fortress Chă-jŭn, now Ch'ang-sŭng. His reign beheld the riveting of Buddhistic chains upon the kingdom. Those who could read the signs of the times surmised this when, in 1036, the king decreed that, if a man had four sons, one of them must become a monk. Because of the Buddhistic canon against the spilling of blood the death penalty was commuted to banishment. Another Buddhistic anniversary was instituted. The king also inaugurated the custom of having boys go about the streets bearing Buddhistic books upon their backs from which the monks read aloud as they passed along. This was for the purpose of securing blessings for the people.

Primogeniture

In order to counteract the tendency toward luxury, the king forbade the use of silk and gold and went so far as to burn up the whole stock of silk held by the merchants. He made a new law of primogeniture. The first son is to succeed. If he dies, the son of the first son succeeds. If there is no grandson the second son succeeds. If there is no son by the wife the son by a concubine succeeds. If there is none then a daughter succeeds. The Yŭ-jin tribe came with rich gifts and promised faithfully to refrain from raiding the frontier again. In 1047 the king was succeeded by his younger brother, Whi, posthumous title Mun-jong, who was destined to sit upon the throne for thirty-seven years. After announcing to his suzerain his accession, he followed the custom of his house and married his sister.

This monarch at first showed a blending of Buddhistic and Confucian influences, for the annals state that in his second year he fed 10,000 monks in the palace and gave them lodging there, and that shortly after this he built a Temple to Heaven before the palace. The Yŭ-jin tribe broke their promise and made a descent upon the border fortresses but were driven back; and not only so, but the Koryŭ forces followed them to their haunts and burned their villages to the ground.

In 1053 the system of taxation was overhauled and a new schedule of weights was made. The king sent a letter to Kitan complaining that the bridge across the Yalu still stood, that a wall had been built to secure it and that a horse relay system had been established, with this bridge as one of its termini. It seemed, in the words of the letter, that 'Kitan was the silkworm and Koryŭ was the mulberry leaf'. The king was anxious to attempt an embassy to China and for that purpose suggested that a boat be built on the island of Quelpart but the officials dissuaded him from the attempt.

Japanese Envoys

The year 1056 was signalized by the arrival of an envoy from Japan. It is probable that the strong Buddhistic tendency which had developed in Japan had tempted the Japanese to send and secure further instruction in that cult and to secure relics and paraphernalia. The envoy may have asked that Buddhist teachers be sent, but the records say nothing to this effect.

Buddhism Takes Hold

Buddhism was making steady advances. A large quantity of metal intended for the manufacture of arms was taken by order of the king and made into nails for use in building monasteries. He took away houses from many wealthy people, among them some of his own relatives, and gave them to the monks. The law requiring that of four sons one must become a monk was now revised so as to read that one of every three should don the cowl. Nearly every house furnished its monk. The king said 'From the very first our kings have encouraged Buddhism and each generation has paid attention to the building of monasteries. By so doing many blessings have been received. Now that I have become king I find that many evils are oppressing the state because of the neglect of the important precept. I will now mend this breach in our conduct and restore to the country her former prosperity.' So he built monasteries in various places. The officials all used their influence against this but the monks carried the day. A Buddhist book called *Tal-jang-gyŭng* was sent by Kitan as a gift to Koryŭ.

This period was not without some hopeful signs. A law was passed that no man should be punished before being tried before three judges. The government built a fleet of 106 sailing vessels to carry the government rice from one port to another. The boats made six trips a year.

But the advances, or rather retrogressions, in a Buddhistic line were still more marked. In 1065 the king's son Ku cut his hair and became a monk. A law was promulgated that no beast should be killed in the land for three years. A monastery was being built in Song-do containing 2,800 *kan*, each *kan* being eight feet square. It took twelve years to complete it. When it became ready for occupancy there was a magnificent festival at which all monks within a radius of many miles were present. The feasting lasted five days. There was an awning of silk, covering a passageway from the palace to this monastery. Mountains and trees were represented by lanterns massed together. The king dressed in the robes of a high priest. In this monastery was a pagoda on which 140 pounds of gold and 427 pounds of silver were lavished.

EVER-CHANGING ALLIANCES

Revenue and Mathematics

It is evident that population and revenue are proportionate. Not often is the question of population touched upon in the Korean annals but some light is thrown upon it by the statement that at this time the revenue from the north, from the most distant places only, was 49,000 bags of rice. From this we must infer that the north was fairly well populated.

An interesting point in connection with the mathematical knowledge of the time is brought out in the statement that the system of land tax was changed and was collected at a certain rate per each square of thirty-three paces; but if the field was large the tax was a certain amount for each tract forty-seven paces square. The square of thirty-three is 1,089 and the square of forty-seven is 2,209, which is the nearest possible to twice the square of thirty-three. It would seem then that they had some notion of the properties of geometrical figures.

It was about this time that Kitan changed its name to Yo. She at once sent an envoy announcing the fact. These were the golden days of Koryŭ's relations. The Yŭ-jin tribe of To-ryŭng-ko-do-wha came and swore allegiance as also did the Chang-man and Tu-hul tribes. A few years later a Japanese ruler named Sal-ma sent gifts to the Koryŭ court as also did the people of Tsushima.

During the latter years of this reign the Kitan people were induced to break down the bridge across the Yalu but it was done only by sending an abject letter in which the Koryŭ king said 'As all the world is yours and all the people in the world belong to you, you have no need of a bridge to bind us to you.'

Friends with China Again

In 1077 an envoy came from the Emperor of China (Sung dynasty) asking for aid against the Kitan. The king might well have turned and answered that as the emperor had remained deaf to Koryŭ's entreaties for help so now Koryŭ would decline to respond. But he did nothing of the kind; this opportunity to reestablish friendly relations with China was hailed with delight by all classes. The king, though ill, was carried on his bed outside the city walls to meet this welcome messenger. The latter was treated royally and was loaded with so many gifts that he could not take them back with him. He had no intention, however, of leaving them entirely, for he sold them and took the money instead. This sort of thrift was something new to the Koreans and they showed their disgust by ridiculing him; and when he left they spat upon the ground in token of their contempt. We are not told that Koryŭ gave the aid requested. And yet the friendly relations were continued, as is seen from the fact that in 1079 the emperor sent physicians and medicines to Koryŭ. We have here the first definite mention of gold mining in the statement that the people of Hong-wŭn dug 100 ounces of gold and 150 ounces of silver, which they sent to the king. He graciously gave it back to them.

In 1084 the king died and his adopted son Hun, posthumous title Sun-jong, came to the throne; but he died almost immediately and was succeeded the same year by his younger brother Un, posthumous title Sŭn-jong. When the messenger announcing this arrived at the gates of the Kitan capital he was refused entrance, for they said there must be some underlying cause for the sudden death of King Sun-jong.

Confucianism Wanes

Under the new king, Buddhism continued its rapid advance. In the first year of his reign he instituted a Buddhist examination to take the place of the ordinary examination which was at bottom Confucian; and so Buddhism scored a decided victory over her rival. It was a blow from which Confucianism recovered only by the extinction of the dynasty. These examinations the king attended in person, a Buddhist book being carried before him. He sent the prince to China to learn more about the tenets of the popular faith and when he returned the king went out to welcome him home. The young man brought back 1,000 volumes of Buddhistic books. Later the king secured 4,000 volumes more from the same source. The records distinctly state that he sent also to Japan to secure still other Buddhistic books. This is a strong indication that Japan did not obtain her Buddhism largely from Korea. It proves at least that she had a more direct channel for the procuring of Buddhist literature than by way of Korea, otherwise Koryŭ would hardly have applied to her for books. The king married his own sister. The bridge across the Yalu had been destroyed but it would seem that it had been again built, for now in 1088 the records say it was finally destroyed.

King Sŭn-jong could not do enough for Buddhism. A vast amount of government rice was turned from its legitimate uses and found its way into the storerooms of monasteries. The king constructed a thirteen-story pagoda in the palace. His mother made frequent visits to one of the monasteries.

The only act of this king which was not with special reference to Buddhism was the stationing at Eui-ju of a large number of war chariots to be used in defence of the frontier.

Han-yang Made Secondary Capital

In 1095 the king was succeeded by his son Uk, posthumous title Hön-jong, who was only eleven years old. His uncle Ong become regent but proved unfaithful and in the following year drove the boy from the throne and proclaimed himself king. His title was Suk-jong. The most important events of his reign were in connection with the founding of a second capital as

Han-yang, the present Seoul. The monk Tosun who, it will be remembered, had taught the young Wang-gön the science of war, had also left a prophecy to the effect that after 160 years it would be well for the kingdom if the site of the capital be changed. The preliminary arrangements were made early in this reign but it was not until the year 1104 that a palace was actually constructed there, nor was the royal residence changed either at this time or at any later period, for any considerable length of time. A few important laws were promulgated; that if relatives intermarried they could not receive official position; that the nomination of an heir to the throne should be made only after consultation with the court of the northern suzerain; that candidates who failed to pass the government examinations should be solaced by receiving military rank.

It is said that in 1100 copper cash had begun to circulate for the first time with freedom among the people. Buddhism also made material advances during this reign and riveted its fetters more firmly upon the body politic. On the whole it was a very clean reign, when we remember that a usurper was on the throne.

In 1106 Suk-jong's son U, posthumous title Ye-jong, came to the throne. At the very first he was confronted by a new problem. The people had yet to learn that the coinage of money is a purely government monopoly. The readiness with which cash circulated tempted some to attempt to counterfeit it. The king consequently promulgated a law inflicting a heavy penalty upon this offense and at the same time made a law against the adulteration of food.

Having, in his third year, married a near relative he took as a teacher a monk named Un-jin, another indication of the steady progress of that cult. The talk about the change of site for the capital resulted in the building of a palace at P'yŏngyang and several royal progresses to each of the proposed sites.

The tribe of Yŭ-jin had repeatedly promised to remain peaceful and had as often broken their word; so now when they began to grow restless again, the king decided to make an end of the matter. He sent a strong force into their territory, killed 4,800 men and took several thousand prisoners. The territory was divided into four administrative districts.

In 1115 the king developed a fad. He became an enthusiastic botanist. He ransacked the kingdom for rare and beautiful plants and sent them to China in exchange for many kinds that were not indigenous.

Beginnings of the Kin Empire

We have now arrived at the threshold of events which were destined to result in the founding of a great dynasty. In order to explain we must go back a few years. Early in this dynasty a Koryŭ monk from P'yŏngyang, named Keum-jun, had fled, for some reason not stated, to the town of A-ji-go among the Yŭ-jin tribe. He had there married a Yŭ-jin woman and gotten a son whom he named Ko-eul. He in turn begot Whal-ra, and to him were born many sons, the eldest of whom was Hyo-ri-bal and the second Yong-ga. The latter was unusually bright and popular and eventually became chief; but on his death the son of his brother Hyo-ri-bal, named O-a-sok, took his place. O-a-sok died and his younger brother, A-gol-t'a, became chief. Yŭ-jin was at this time a small weak tribe under the sway of the Ki-tan court, but now the masterly genius of A-gol-t'a had come to her help, matters were destined to assume a different complexion.

It was now in 1114 that the little tribe of Yŭ-jin broke off its allegiance to Kitan and prepared to carve out a career for herself under her great leader. Soon an envoy came in haste from the capital of Kitan commanding the king to stand ready to drive back the Yŭ-jin tribe if they attempted to escape into his territory, for the emperor of Kitan was about to chastise his recalcitrant vassal.

The next year A-gol-t'a with sublime presumption proclaimed himself emperor and named his kingdom Kin. At the same time he changed his own name to Min.

The Kitan emperor sent again demanding a contingent of Koryŭ troops. After anxious consultation it was decided to keep the soldiers near home and guard the interests of Koryŭ. In the war between Kitan and Kin the former were severely handled and again appealed to Koryŭ for help, but now with no hope of success.

The next year, 1116, a Koryŭ envoy Yun Eun-sun was sent to the Kitan court but he did not return, so a second one was dispatched to learn the cause. The fact is, the first envoy had fallen into the hands of a new power named Wŭn which had been set up in eastern Kitan by a man named Ko Yŏng-ch'ang. War was still raging between Kitan and Kin and the whole country was in a state of turmoil and confusion. The second envoy from Koryŭ fell into the hands of the Wŭn people but got out of the difficulty by promptly stating that he was accredited to them by the king of Koryŭ; and he forthwith laid out his present. This made the upstart 'emperor' of Wŭn wild with delight and, loading the envoy with rich presents, he sent him back home. Instead of going back to the king, however, the envoy returned secretly to his own home, and it was only by accident that the king learned of his return. When he did learn of it he sent for the man and inflicted summary punishment. Of course the Wŭn people liberated the other envoy and sent him home. Him also the king punished for having saved his life by seemingly offering allegiance to Wŭn.

The emperor of China sent an envoy to Koryŭ with gifts of musical instruments and took advantage of the occasion to ask the Koryŭ king about the Kitan people. The king answered, 'Of all the savage tribes they are the worst.' When this reply reached the Chinese court some of the courtiers said that the king of Koryŭ was trying to keep China from knowing Kitan, since there was treasure there which Koryŭ wanted to secure for herself. The emperor therefore sent and made an alliance with Kitan, which, as the sequel shows, cost him dear.

Kitan was being hard pressed by Kin, and Gen. Ya Ryul-lyŭng wanted to escape and find asylum somewhere, so the king sent him a verbal invitation to come to Koryŭ. He replied that he could not do so without a written invitation. The Koryŭ statesmen feared that this covered some kind of trickery and the written invitation was not sent.

Koryŭ desired to put out a feeler to see how she stood with the Kin power so she sent a message saying 'The district of P'o-ju is rightfully Koryŭ territory and we should be pleased to have it turned over to us.' The answer was given without an hour's delay 'Certainly, take it and do with it as you wish.' Evidently the great Kin leader did not intend to let a single district stand between him and the goodwill of a power which might cause him serious trouble while he was prosecuting his designs upon China.

The year ended with a great feast at the capital of Koryŭ at which dancing girls from all parts of the country congregated.

The records say that they came 'in clouds' which indicates the social status of the country. Buddhism had her representative in every home, but no severe asceticism would seem to have characterized the people, if this report is true.

The year 1117 beheld repeated triumphs of the Kin leader over the Kitan forces, the flight of the Kitan general Ya Ryul-lyŭng by boat, the burning of the Kitan fleet and the cession to Koryŭ of two more districts, thus placing her border again at the Yalu River. But this concession was of design for it was followed by a letter from the Kin court which read as follows: 'The elder brother, the Emperor of the Great Kin, to the younger brother, the king of Koryŭ; we were a small, weak tribe and were badly treated by the Kitan power but now we are about to destroy it. The King of Koryŭ must now make with us a firm treaty which shall be binding to the ten thousandth generation.'

This met with an almost universal negative among the wise heads of Koryŭ, but one voice was heard saying 'They may be in a position to do us great harm and we should comply with this demand.' The latter opinion did not prevail. Three years later another envoy came from the king of Kin with gifts but the accompanying letter was couched in low language which was construed into an insult and was answered in the same tone. The king then hastened to repair the fortresses in the north and to increase the height of the wall stretching across the country; but the Kin emperor sent and forbade it. When he received as answer the question 'What affair is it of yours?' he kept his temper and did not press the demand for he was anxious just then to be on good terms with his southern neighbour.

We must not imagine that these years were barren of events of importance within the bounds of Koryŭ herself. Splendid monasteries were built, notably the beautiful An-wha monastery; embassies and gifts were received from China; the king made trips to P'yŏngyang and Han-yang. In spite of the height to which Buddhism had climbed, we read in the annals that the king frequented the society of dancing girls to such an extent that he drew down upon himself the censure of one of his highest officials, whom he consequently banished.

In 1123 the king's son Hă, posthumous title In-jong, came to the throne. An official, Yi Ja-gyŭm, who had risen to the highest position under the former king seemed to think himself in a sense on an equality with the young king now on the throne, and wanted to have him bow to him, but the other officials interfered and prevented it. In order to make his position the more secure, and to strengthen his influence over the king, Yi Ja-gyŭm bestowed upon him his four daughters to wife. Naturally he incurred the bitter enmity of the other officials, who sought means for destroying him, but without success. As a last resort they sent a band of soldiers to the palace to kill him. But he escaped to his private house, taking the king with him. From that place he governed the land as he wished. Finding the king an incumbrance he tried to do away with him by the use of poisoned bread, but someone warned the king, and instead of eating the bread he threw it out of the window and the magpies, which soon discovered it, fell dead on the spot. Thereupon the king sent a secret message to one of his generals and soon the traitor was travelling southward into exile and all his connections and followers were put where they could do no more harm.

Kitan and Sung Dynasty Fall

It was in the third year of this king, 1124, that the Kin armies finally overthrew the Kitan power. The false report came to Koryŭ that China had defeated the Kin forces and that the leader of the defeated power was coming to find asylum in Koryŭ. The king was advised by some to take this opportunity of dealing Kin a staggering blow, but the more cautious advised delay until the report should be authenticated. This was fortunate, for the report proved false.

It was in 1126 that the northern Sung dynasty came to an end at the hands of the all-conquering Kin. The records state that Kin leaders carried the last emperor of the Sung dynasty away and set up one Chang Pang-ch'ang as king in his stead, and changed the name of the dynasty to Ch'o. When this had been effected the Kin emperor sent Gen. Ya Ryul Ka-geum to Koryŭ bearing his commands to the king, but what those commands were the records do not tell.

The influence which priestcraft had exercised in Koryŭ was well illustrated by a monk Myo-chung of P'yŏngyang who told the King that there was no more 'king Spirit' in the soil of Song-do, but if he should move the capital to P'yŏngyang the Kitan, Kin and Sung would all become subject to him. The king believed every word of this and ordered a palace to be built there for his occupancy. A year or so later, after sending the Kin court his abject submission, he essayed to move to the northern city by boat, but a fresh breeze sprang up and he quickly changed his mind and hurried back to Song-do. The coastwise trade must have been of considerable importance, for we read that the water on the bar at Hong-ju harbor, was too shallow for boats of large burden to cross, so the king put several thousand men to work to deepen the channel; but to no effect.

The fight between Confucianism and Buddhism went steadily on. The king was the puppet of the latter but could not always carry out his plans. He wanted to take away the support of Confucian schools and turn over the funds to the monks, but this called out such a storm of remonstrances that he hastened to recall the order. He had not forgotten the flattering words of the monk Myo-chung, and now in 1130 he took occasion to visit the city of P'yŏngyang. The tricky monk had made preparation for his coming. Hollow loaves of bread were prepared with holes in their sides after the style of a jack-o'-lantern. Oil was placed inside and as the king approached the town at dusk these were floated down the stream, and the oil on the water, shining in the light of the setting sun, reflected all the hues of the rainbow. The monk told the king that this was the dragon's breath. This was to convince the king of the truth of his former statement. But the king's attendants were sceptical and sent messengers who returned with the bread floats, thus unmasking the trickster. They demanded the head of the monk but the king did not consent.

Rebellion Quelled

Foiled in this the ambitious monk laid new plans. In 1135 they were ready to be put in execution. Together with a fellow traitor, Cho Kwang, he massed soldiers at P'yŏngyang and set up a kingdom of his own which he named Ta-wi. He called the army the 'Celestial Army,' perhaps to keep them in good humor. The government forces easily overcame these insurrectionary forces and Cho Kwang, finding that the end was approaching, tried to buy pardon by cutting off the head of the monk and bringing it to the capital. The king forgave him, but no sooner had he re-entered the gates of P'yŏngyang than he raised the standard of revolt again. The royal forces laid siege to the city, and having broken down a portion of the wall affected an entrance. Cho Kwang, seeing that there was no longer any chance of safety, set fire to his house and perished in the flames.

We find in the records the curious statement that the law against murder was revised, making that crime a greater one than the killing of a cow. The following year there was a Buddhistic festival at which 30,000 monks were present.

In the year 1145 occurred an event of great importance. A century and a quarter had now passed since the kingdom of Silla had fallen and as yet the annals of Silla, Ko-gu-ryŭ and Păk-je had not been worked up into a proper history. This year it was done and the great work entitled *Sam-guk-sa*, or *History of the Three Kingdoms*, was the result. This work which, though rare, exists today, is the thesaurus of ancient Korean history, and it is the basis upon which all subsequent histories of ancient Korea are founded. Its compiler, Kim Pu-sik, is one of the celebrated literary men of Korea and may truly be called the father of Korean history.

An Abject King

In-jong was succeeded in 1147 by his son Hyön, posthumous title Eui-jong. Never before had a king given himself over so abjectly to the priesthood. The people were thoroughly discontented with his course, but he would listen to no remonstrances. It would have been better had he been a more consistent Buddhist but his drinking, gambling and licentiousness gave the lie to his religious pretentions and left the impression that he was in reality only the tool of the priesthood. It is said that his visits to a certain monastery were so frequent that an awning had to be erected from the palace to its gates, and if at any time the king was not to be found they looked for him in this monastery. He was an object of ridicule to the whole people. A diviner told him that if he built a palace at Păk-ju (now Pă-ch'ŭn) in Whang-hă Province, in seven years he would overcome both Kitan and Kin. The king was simple enough to follow his advice. He wasted the public treasure on the wildest debaucheries, gave high positions to monks and surrounded himself with a vile set of men who debauched the palace women.

In 1165 numbers of the Kin people crossed the Yalu and settled at In-ju and Chŭng-ju. The magistrates raised a force of soldiers on their own account without royal authority and drove out the intruders and burned their houses. The Kin emperor made the king restore them to their places but the magistrates again drove them out; so the Emperor sent a body of troops and seized sixteen of the country officials.

The officials desired to stop the king's frequent visits to his favourite monastery. One day as he was passing along his covered passageway they made his horse rear violently and at the same time one of them let fall an arrow before him. The king was terrified, supposing that someone had shot at him, so he returned to the palace in haste and barred the gates. He charged a slave of his brother's with having shot the arrow and after wringing a false confession from him by torture put him to death.

A Good Governor for Quelpart

In 1168 Ch'oé Ch'ŭk-kyŭng became prefect of T'am-na (Quelpart). He was well liked by the people and when he was removed and another man put in his place they rose in revolt, drove out the successor and said they would have no governor but

Ch'oé. So the King was obliged to reinstate him. These people of Quelpart were very unruly. It was only during the reign of this king's father that the first prefect had been sent to that island.

The king sent a commission to Dagelet island off the east coast to find out whether it was habitable. They brought back an adverse report.

Besides his partiality to Buddhism the king added another burden to those which the people already carried. He made the eunuchs his instruments to exact money from the people, and to such as supplied him with the most money from this illegal practice he gave rank and honours. The king was continually feasting, but none of the military men enjoyed his favour or shared his hospitality. Matters came to a crisis when in 1170 one of the military officials was struck by a civil official of a lower grade in the presence of the king while at a monastery outside the city. The matter was hushed up for the moment but when the company separated some of the generals assembled the palace guards and seized and killed the two leading civil officials. One, Han Roe, escaped and hid behind the king's bed. In spite of this the generals entered and dragged him away to his death. Then they began to slaughter the civil officials and eunuchs indiscriminately.

The records say that the dead bodies were piled 'mountains high'. The military officials had a sign by which they might be distinguished. The right shoulder was left bare and they wore a headdress called the *pok-tu*. Whoever was found lacking these two signs was cut down. The king was in mortal fear and tried to propitiate the leading general by the gift of a beautiful sword. He accepted it but the work of death went on. They took the king back to the capital and, arriving at the palace, cut down ten leading men at that point. Then they went to the palace of the crown prince and killed ten more. Proclamation was made in the main street 'Kill any official wearing the garments of the civil rank'. This was the sign for a general slaughter and fifty more of the officials were murdered. After this, twenty eunuchs were beheaded and their heads were set upon pikes.

Though the king was badly frightened he continued his evil course of life without abatement. The generals wanted to kill him but were dissuaded. The persecution of the civil officials continued but there was some discrimination, for two of them who were better than the rest were spared and protected. A civil official, returning from China, learned of this *emeute* and, gathering forces in the country, approached the capital; but at a certain pass an unfavourable omen was seen in the shape of a tiger sitting in the road. The omen was true, for the improvised army was defeated by the insurrectionists. One Chöng Chung-bu was the leading spirit in this business and he now proceeded to pull down all the houses of the civil officials, turning a deaf ear to the expostulations of those who pitied the widows and orphans. From this time dates the custom of destroying the house of any official or gentleman who is guilty of any serious crime against the king.

The King Banished

Gen. Chöng came to the conclusion that the king was a hopeless case and so he banished him to Kö-je in Island, Kyŭng-sang Province, and the Crown Prince to the island of Chin-do, and made way with a large number of the king's relatives and hangers-on. He then put the king's younger brother Ho on the throne. His posthumous title is Myŭng-jong. This was in 1171.

Then all the offices were filled by military officials, Gen. Im Keuk-ch'ung becoming prime minister. Mun Keup-kyŭm was one of the civil officials who were spared, and he now feigned to be well content with the condition of things and gave his daughter to the son of one of the generals in marriage. An envoy was sent to the Kin court saying that as the king was old and sick his brother had been given the reins of power.

One of the generals, Yi Ko, desired to affect a revolution and, gathering his friends about him, promised them high honours in case the attempt should succeed. Thereupon he took with him to a feast a number of his followers with swords hidden in their sleeves. Gen. Ch'oa Wŭn, however, suspected something and communicated his suspicions to Gen. Yi Eui-bang who managed to get Gen. Yi Ko out into the anteroom and there felled him to the ground with an iron mace and dispatched him. His followers were also seized and killed.

The Emperor Suspicious

The emperor suspected that the deposed king had been forcibly ejected and so sent a letter severely blaming his successor. An envoy was dispatched to the Kin court to explain matters. He talked well but the emperor still suspected something and refused to answer the king's letter. The envoy thereupon sat down and deliberately began to starve himself to death. This secured the desired answer and the envoy returned to Song-do. The emperor sent a commission to enquire into the matter. The commissioner was feasted at the capital and told that the deposed king was old and sick and had gone away to a distant part of the country and could not be produced.

The ill will between the military and the monks was well illustrated when the palace caught fire. General Chöng saw many monks running toward the burning buildings, but rather than have them enter he locked the gates and let the buildings burn to the ground.

The remnant of the civil officers were ever on the lookout for opportunities to get the upper hand again and drive out the military party. To this end Kim Po-dang sent letters to prefects far and wide and a time for a rising was agreed upon. The banished king was put in the van of the army thus improvised and they advanced as far as Kyöng-ju. But the plan miscarried and Kim, its originator, was seized by the people and sent to Song-do where he was put to death. Before dying he exclaimed 'I was in league with all the civil nobles'. This was probably not true, but it caused a fresh outbreak of the military party upon the civil nobles, and scores of them were killed. At last a reaction set in and the military leaders, feeling that they had gone too far, tried to make amends by giving their daughters to the sons of the civil officials in marriage.

Attempted revolution

At this point occurred one of the most revolting events that blot the pages of Korean history. Gen. Chöng, hearing that the banished king had come as far as Kyöng-ju sent Gen. Yi Eui-mun to put him out of the way. After the leader and 200 members of the ex-king's guard had been treacherously killed the ex-king himself was spirited away to a neighbouring monastery. He was taken out to the brink of a pond behind this monastery and there Gen. Yi, who was a man of immense stature, seized him in his arms and crushed his ribs, killing him instantly. The body was wrapped in blankets, placed in two kettles, which were placed mouth to mouth, and thrown into the pond. When this monster, Gen. Yi, returned to Song-do he was loaded with honours. Later a monk, who was a good swimmer, raised the body and gave it decent burial.

In spite of the overwhelming power exercised by the military party, the king was devoted to Buddhism. The monks were very anxious to kill Gen. Yi, who had taken such an active part in deposing the late king; so they massed in front of the palace and set fire to it by first firing the adjoining houses. Gen. Yi made a sudden sally with a strong guard and killed 100 of the monks. He followed this up by demolishing five monasteries whose sacred vessels and other utensils he confiscated.

TURMOIL AND STRIFE

Cho Wi-jong was a P'yŏngyang man with a towering ambition, and he now deemed the time ripe to put the wheels in motion. He therefore drew about him a strong body of troops. All the districts about P'yŏngyang joined him excepting Yŭn-ju, which remained loyal to the king. The people of that place were afraid of the rebel but the loyal prefect Hyŭn Tŭk-su forged a letter purporting to be from the royal army *en route* for P'yŏngyang. This gave the people courage to hold out.

Cho and his troops marched toward Song-do and encamped not far to the west of the town. Gen. Yi Eui-bang, having first seized and killed all the P'yŭng-an officials who happened to be in the capital, marched out against the rebels. At the first attack the seditious force broke and fled. Gen. Yi chased them as far as the Ta-dong River. He crossed that river and lay siege to P'yŏngyang; but winter was coming on and he was obliged to retire to Song-do. Cho then made two or three attempts to overthrow the loyal town of Yŭn-ju, but without success.

Gen. Yi was a ruthless man, who had no love of humanity in him, and would kill his best friend if it served his purpose. For this reason Gen. Chöng did not dare to associate with him, but threw up his commission and went into retirement. His son got a priest to dog the footsteps of Gen. Yi and wait for a chance to kill him. This he finally accomplished and Gen. Yi and many of his relatives were killed; and the queen, who was his daughter, was driven away.

Cannibalism

As Cho Wi-jong, the P'yŏngyang traitor, was gradually losing power he desired to get help from the Kin emperor. For this purpose he sent two envoys, but one of them killed the other on the way and then fled to Song-do. Cho sent another, but him the Kin emperor seized and sent a prisoner to the Koryŭ capital. In the spring the royal forces besieged Cho in P'yŏngyang again and famine within the walls became so great that men ate each other. Many of the townspeople came out by stealth and as they were well received by the besieging force, well-nigh all the civilians in the city came over the walls by night. When the city fell, Cho was killed and his wife and children were sent to Song-do where they were hung in the centre of the city.

Anarchy

The rebel forces were scattered but reunited in various places and terrorized the whole north, so that envoys to the Kin court had to go a roundabout way to avoid them. The whole country in fact was in a state of anarchy. In the south whole sections of the country were disaffected toward the government and bands of men roamed the country. There was a rising also in

Whang-hă Province. In P'yŏngyang the people rose and drove out the governor. The king was forced to begin the correction of abuses. He sent all about gathering information as to how the people were governed and as a consequence 800 officials were cashiered. But the attempt at renovation came too late. In the west the bands of robbers looted right and left and could not be apprehended. The capital itself swarmed with thieves. The ancestral temple itself was robbed of its utensils. But all this time the king kept up a round of carousals and debaucheries at which he himself played the buffoon, and danced for the delectation of his guests, and that too at a monastery. A sacred place truly!

In the twelfth year of the reign, 1182, we find an interesting application of what goes in these days under the name of 'faith cure'. A priest claimed to be able to cure any disease. Being called before the king he said, 'If anyone drinks water in which I have washed my hands he will be immediately cured.' He further explained 'After drinking the water, pray earnestly to Buddha. Then rise and say 'I am cured', and if you really believe you are cured, you will be so.' Crowds of people applied to him for treatment. He seduced many of the women who came to him.

Gen. Yi Eui-mun was now court favourite and he usurped all the leading offices and acted as pander-in-general to the king by seeking out and forcibly carrying to the palace young and handsome girls. This seemed intolerable to such loyal men as Gen. Ch'oé Chung-heun, and he, in company with his brother, surrounded the palace, killed Yi Eui-mun and many others of his ilk, chased away many illegitimate sons of the king, who had become monks, and would not let them enter the palace again. This all happened in 1196, and two years later the reformer continued the good work by deposing the old and indolent king, banishing the crown prince to Kang-wha and putting the king's brother Mun on the throne. His posthumous title is Sin-jong. The banishing of the crown prince and his wife was affected in a very heartless manner. They were ordered out of the palace at a moment's notice and, coming forth entirely unprepared for the journey, were mounted on horses in a cold rain and hurried away to Kang-wha. A terrible storm raged the day the King was deposed, as if in sympathy with the throes through the country was passing.

The Ta-nă Well

There was a saying current among the people which shows at once how superstitious they were and to what an extent the eunuchs were wont to abuse their power. They said 'If the King uses water from the Ta-nă Wall many eunuchs will arise and will cause the government to be administered badly;' so the well was filled up. Another instance shows what a terrible temptation there was for the people to abuse their power. This same reformer Ch'oé Chung-heun, though himself a man of perfect uprightness, had a brother who now took advantage of his position to force the king to take his daughter as queen. To do this the real queen had to be banished. As it happened, the king was deeply attached to her, but he was in no position to refuse to do the bidding of the powerful courtier. After a tearful parting she went into exile.

The Queen Restored

This was as yet unknown to the reformer, but when he learned of it his indignation was deep and fierce. Cloaking his feelings, he called his brother to a feast and there reminded him that they were not of a high enough family to furnish a queen, and he charged him to give up the attempt. The next day, the villain changed his mind again. His mother expostulated with him and he felled her to the floor. Gen. Ch'oé was told of this and, surrounding himself with a strong bodyguard, he proceeded to the palace gate. When his niece was brought in her chair and was about to enter to become queen, the faithful old general disputed the passage and a fight ensued between his men and his brother's. The former were successful and the wretch betook himself to flight, but was pursued, taken and killed by the general himself. The rightful queen was restored to her station.

Slaves Revolt

The six years of this king's reign were one long scene of turmoil and strife. In the first place the slaves revolted. They said 'The high men are not made so by the decree of heaven. Great men are those who do well. Let us fight for our rights; Gen. Ch'oé is from as low a grade as ourselves. Let us become high men too.' They rendezvoused at Heung-guk monastery and decided as a preliminary measure to demand from their masters the deeds of themselves (for slaves as well as houses were deeded property) and to burn them. They were betrayed to Gen. Ch'oé who trapped 100 of them, tied stones about their necks and drowned them in the river. The south was overrun by marauding parties whom the king bought off by gifts of food, clothes and land. In Chin-ju the governor's servants locked him in his private dungeon, gathered a band of men and put to death all who would not join their standard. It is said that 6,400 men were killed because of refusal to join them. The same scenes were enacted in various places, notably in Quelpart and Kong-ju.

In the midst of these scenes the king died and was succeeded in 1205 by his son Tok, posthumous title Heui-jong.

THE MONGOL INVASION

The Mongol invasion of the Koryŏ dynasty aligned with the predominance of military power in Korea. This was unprecedented, and also the only time that the military order gained the upper hand over the civil order. Despite the Mongols being ever-victorious in military campaigns, they never could claim complete victory over Korea. Koryŏ was not completely occupied or colonized by Mongols; however, it was forced to provide tremendous amounts of tribute throughout the Yuan period, and often came under political pressure and manipulation from the Yuan court. Mongol intervention continued to the end. There was also a brief period during which Koryŏ was trapped between the Yuan and Ming, and had constantly to switch sides with their alliance in order to survive.

Unfortunately, Koryŏ never had wise and thoughtful kings all through this period. However, it was also true that Koryŏ kings never had real power to implement policies without permission or intervention from the Yuan emperors. Most Koryŏ crown princes lived as hostages in Beijing in their early life and were obliged to take Mongol princesses as their primary consorts. Mongols also constantly manipulated Koryŏ thrones with random abdications and enthronements, sometimes pitting father and son against each other. The Koryŏ dynasty ended soon after the Mongol Yuan collapsed in China. Homer Hulbert (whose text continues in this section) provided great details about major events during the Koryŏ period, for readers who seek the big picture and historical patterns. However, his excessive references to numerous names and similar events can be overwhelming.

THE MONGOLS

We have now arrived at the threshold of events which were destined to make Asia one great battlefield and to cause the sovereigns of Europe to tremble on their thrones.

The Mongols lived north of Yŭ-jin and were in a sense connected with them. Their first great chief was Ya-sok-hă (Yusuka) who first led the revolt which separated the Mongol power from the Yŭ-jin. He together with Keui-ak-on conquered forty of the northern tribes in quick succession and brought them all under his flag. His son's name was Chŭl-mok-jin, the great Genghis Khan. It was now in the second year of Heui-jong, in 1206, that the great Genghis proclaimed himself emperor and named his empire Mong.

Meanwhile Ch'oé Chung-heun was not proof against the seductions of ambition and power, and we next find him seizing the people's houses and building himself a magnificent residence adjoining the palace. People said of him that he buried a boy or a girl under each corner post.

When the spring of 1212 opened, an envoy was sent to the Kin court but was intercepted by Mongol videttes who had by this time worked their way southward to a point that commanded the road between Koryŭ and Kin. The Kin people recovered the body and sent it back to Koryŭ.

Gen. Ch'oé had acquired so much power that he was in reality the ruler of the land, holding much the same position that the Shogun of Japan is said to have occupied. He may not inappropriately be styled the Shogun of Koryŭ. For this reason the king desired to get him out of the way. To this end he put upon his track a number of monks, but as they began by attacking his servant he quietly slipped into a chest and they could not find him. His bodyguard became aware of his predicament and forced the palace gates, killing right left; and they would have killed the king had not the wily old general stepped out of his hiding place and prevented it. The latter banished the king to Kang-wha and the crown prince to Chemulpo and set upon the throne one Chong, whose posthumous title is Kang-jong.

The only event recorded of this reign is the arrival of an envoy from the Kin court, who wanted to enter the palace by the central or royal gate. He insisted upon it until he was asked the question 'If you enter by the royal gate, by what gate would your master enter should he come here?' This silenced him.

Kang-jong was succeeded in 1214 by his son Chin, posthumous title Kang-jang. This was destined to be the longest and by far the most eventful reign of the dynasty for it lasted forty-five years and witnessed the great Mongol invasion.

Kin Weakens

The Kin power was now trembling under the Mongol onslaught and envoys came demanding aid from Koryŭ in the shape of rice and horses. The king ostensibly refused but allowed the envoys to purchase rice and carry it away with them.

Again a dark cloud hung over Koryŭ's northern border. It was not the Mongols as yet, but the remnant of the Kitan forces who were unable to withstand the Mongols and so had fled south into Koryŭ territory. At first the Koryŭ forces were able to keep them in check but as they came in ever increasing numbers they broke down all opposition and were soon ravaging Whang-hă Province, making P'yŏngyang their headquarters. The lack of Koryŭ soldiers was so evident that men of all classes, even the monks, became soldiers. It was of no avail. They were cut down like stubble and Whang-ju fell into Kitan hands. The enemy was soon only eighty *li* from the capital. Consternation reigned in the city and the people all procured swords or other weapons and manned the walls.

To this outward danger was added the terror of civil strife for the priests took this inopportune moment to attack the old general, Ch'oé, who still ruled with a high hand. He turned on them however and cut down 300. He then instituted an inquisition and as a result 800 more were killed.

Such then was the desperate position of Koryŭ; a powerful enemy at her door, the south rife with rebellion, and in the capital itself 'mountains of dead and rivers of blood'. Victorious Kitan came sweeping down on Song-do, but for some reason, perhaps because they had heard that the town was well defended, they made a detour, appearing next on the banks of the Im-jin River halfway between Song-do and the present capital. There they suffered defeat at the hands of the Koryŭ forces as they did also later at the site of the present capital. In view of these defeats the Kitan army retired to Tă-băk San. Now another cause of anxiety appeared in the shape of the Yŭ-jin allies of the Mongols who crossed the Yalu and took Eui-ju. But Koryŭ, wide awake to the danger, threw upon them a well-equipped force which destroyed 500 of them, captured many more and drove the remaining 300 across the river. The king now built a royal residence at Pă-gak San to the east of Song-do, for he had been told that by so doing he would be able to hold the north in check.

Mongol Allies

Myŭn Ku-ha of east Yŭ-jin, being defeated by the Mongols, came in his flight towards the Yalu, but the Koryŭ general, Chŭng Kong-su, caught him and sent him safely to the Mongol headquarters. This pleased the Mongols hugely and they said 'We must make a treaty of friendship.' We must remember that the Mongols were at war with Kitan and had driven her army across into Koryŭ, but at first did not pursue them. Now, however, an army of 10,000 men under Generals T'ap Chin and Ch'al Cha, were sent to complete the destruction of the Kitan power. They were joined by Yŭ-jin allies to the number of 20,000 men under Gen. Wan-an Cha-yŭn. As these allies were advancing against the doomed army of Kitan, the remnant of which, 50,000 strong, was massed at Kang-dong, a great snowstorm came on and provisions ran low. Koryŭ was asked to supply the deficiency which she did to the extent of 1,000 bags of rice. This still more helped her into the good graces of the Mongols. But the records state that the Mongols were so little beyond the condition of the savage that there could be little real friendship between them and the people of Koryŭ. The latter showed it too plainly and the Mongols of course resented it.

In this army that was marching to the annihilation of Kitan there was a contingent of Koryŭ forces under Gen. Kim Ch'ui-ryo who is described as being a giant in size with a beard that reached his knees. He was a favourite with the Mongol generals and was treated handsomely by them.

The siege of Kang-dong was prosecuted vigorously and soon the greatest distress prevailed within the walls. The leader finally gave up hope and hanged himself, and the 50,000 men came out and surrendered. Gen. T'ap reviewed them, took off the heads of 100 of the leaders and released the remainder. The Mongol leader wished to make a visit to Song-do to see the king but he could not leave his army, so he sent an envoy instead. He gave the Koryŭ generals rich presents and released 700 Koryŭ captives that had been previously taken. Many Kitan captives were put into the hands of the Koryŭ generals as a result of the decisive termination of the war against Kitan and many of the heretofore inaccessible parts of the north were opened up, and they were called the 'Kitan District'.

Ere long the Mongol envoy approached Song-do and the king sent out a messenger to meet him, but this did not satisfy him, for he exclaimed 'Why did not the king come out to meet me?' It took some persuasion to induce him not to turn back. When he had audience with the king he wore the heavy fur clothing of his native country with a fur headdress, and carried a sword and a bow. Approaching the king he seized his hand and showed him the letter from the Mongol emperor, Genghis Khan. The king turned pale and was exceedingly embarrassed at this familiarity, and the officials asked each other how the presence of this barbarian could be endured. They induced him to retire and assume Koryŭ garments, after which he reappeared and the king presented him with gifts of gold, silver, silk, and linen.

Gen. Cho Ch'ung accompanied the retiring Mongol and Yŭ-jin allies as far as the Yalu where they bade him an affectionate adieu and declared that he was a man of whom Koryŭ should be proud. The Mongol general, Hap Chin, left forty men at Euiju to learn the Koryŭ language and told them to stay there till he returned. Gen. Cho then returned to P'yŏngyang where he was lionized and fêted. The old man Ch'oé Chung-heun feared that Gen. Cho would attempt to throw him down from his high position and thought it would be better to have him nearby, where he could watch him; so he forged a letter purporting to be from the king, ordering him to come down to the capital. He obeyed.

Mongol Demands

It seemed at this time that the relations of Koryŭ and the Mongols would remain friendly, but if Koryŭ thought this she was destined to be rudely awakened. The Mongol and Yŭ-jin allies sent to Myŭng-sŭng and said 'Koryŭ must send an envoy and do obeisance each year.' This was said in so offensive a way that it seemed to be an attempt to provoke war. We are not told what answer was given but it sufficed for the time to secure peace.

The great Ch'oé Chung-heun who had carried things with such a high hand now fell ill and died. This caused more commotion than the death of several kings. He was buried with royal honours. He left many sons, of whom U and Hyang were first and second. Hyang was a bold and powerful man, and before the father died he warned U against him. U succeeded to his father's position which, as we have seen, corresponded closely with that of the Shogun of Japan.

A serious rebellion broke out in the north under two leaders, Han Sun and Ta Chi, the cause being the illegal exactions of the prefects. When the king found that it could not be put down by peaceful means he sent Gen. Kim Ch'ui-ro to put it down by force. The east Yŭ-jin leader, Myŭn Ku-ha, at first sided with the rebels but later changed his mind, invited Han Sun and Ta Chi to a feast, got them intoxicated, assassinated them, put their heads in a box and sent it to the king, thereby earning the goodwill of the latter. The king then reformed the abuses in the rebellious section and peace was at last secured.

The Mongols were not to be content with an empty friendship, and in 1221 they sent a demand for revenue, consisting of 10,000 pounds of cotton, 3,000 rolls of fine silk, 2,000 pieces of gauze, 100,000 sheets of paper of the largest size. The envoy who brought this extraordinary letter was provided commodious quarters and excellent food but he expressed his dissatisfaction at everything by shooting arrows into the house posts, and by acting in a very boorish manner generally. The only man who could do anything with him was Kim Heui-jo who charged him with killing a man in Eui-ji, and threatened to have him imprisoned. Thus meeting bluster with bluster he made the brutal northerner listen to reason. When the envoy was about to go to an audience with his weapons in hand, this same Kim made him lay them aside. Other Mongol and Yo-jin messengers came and Kim managed them all so well that no trouble arose.

It was becoming apparent that the Mongols were likely at any time to make a descent upon Koryŭ; so, in the following year, 1222, a wall was built near the Yalu river, extending from Eui-ju to Wha-ju. It is said that this was completed in the marvelously short space of forty days, a feat which shows not only how great a power Koryŭ could exert when necessary but how important she deemed it that this wall should be built.

Japanese Pirates

The year 1223 CE marks the beginning of that long series of depredations which Japanese freebooters inflicted upon Koryŭ between 1200 and 1400. In this year they landed on the coast of Kyŭng-sang Province and ravaged the district of Keum-ju. With the opening of the next year, a Mongol envoy came modifying the demand for tribute to sea otter skins only. The Kin dynasty was now tottering to its fall but was destined to cling to life for another ten years. This year saw it nearly fall before the Mongol power. Koryŭ therefore discarded the Kin calendar. The friendship between the Mongols and Koryŭ was destined to be rudely broken in the year 1225, and through no fault of the latter except the inability to keep order in her own territory. The Mongol envoy, returning to the north, was set upon by a Koryŭ highwayman and was robbed of the gifts which he was carrying home. Thus all friendly relations were ruptured and another step was taken toward the final catastrophe. This year also witnessed another Japanese raid in the south.

The Yŭ-jin who had now assumed the Mongol clothes, and were in reality an integral part of the Mongol power, made a descent upon Koryŭ in 1226 in the vicinity of Eui-ju. The prefect deemed it too pressing a matter to wait till word could be received from Song-do, so he sent 1,000 men immediately against the raiders and drove them back. The king forgave the irregularity but refused to reward him.

Ch'oé U who, as we know, was the prime minister, was duped by a diviner into believing that he was to become king someday, and he foolishly divulged the secret to a certain Kim, and soon it became common property. As punishment for this, as well as to get himself out of trouble, Ch'oé U had both Kim and the diviner drowned.

The depredations of the Japanese were without the cognizance of the Japanese government and were against its wish. This appears from the fact that when in 1227 an envoy, Pak In, was sent to Japan to remonstrate against them, the government of that country acquiesced and arrested and killed a number of the corsairs.

Both this year and the next Yŭ-jin bands ravaged the northern part of Koryŭ, but at the same time asked that a treaty be concluded. The ink was hardly dry on this before it was broken by the very ones who advocated it.

A Korean 'Shogun'

Ch'oé U followed in his father's steps and having established himself in the viceroyship began to abuse the people, stealing houses and lands from them wherewith to build himself a princely mansion, 200 paces long. In the court of it he had mock battles and the soldiers played at ball. The expense of this was borne by the people, whose faces were already being ground to furnish the regular revenue. His younger brother, Hyang, who long since been had banished, attempted to raise an insurrection in favour of the exiled king; but Ch'oé U sent a strong force and chased his brother until he was run to earth in a cave among the mountains where he was killed.

Mongols Cross the Yalu

It was now the year 1231, the year which saw the outbreak which had been threatening ever since Genghis Khan came to the chieftainship of the Mongol armies. As the spring opened a powerful Mongol army moved southward across the Yalu under the leadership of Sal Ye-t'ap and took the fortress of Hamsin near Eui-ju. They followed this up by storming Ch'ŭl-ju which ended only after the prefect had set fire to his house and destroyed his whole family and he and his associates had cut their own throats.

The king did not intend to submit without a struggle. He sent Generals Pak Sö and Kim Kyöng-sol at the head of a large army to operate against the invaders. They rendezvoused with all their forces at Ku-ju, the four gates of which were strongly barricaded. The Mongols commenced the attack at the south gate. The Koryŭ soldiers made five brilliant sallies and forced the enemy to retire. The honours of this victory fell to Gen. Kim who pursued the enemy some distance and then returned to the town in triumph. The Mongols, who seem to have been independent of any base of supplies and made the country through which they passed supply them, now left this town untaken and the Koryŭ army undefeated in their rear, and marched boldly southward, taking Kwak-ju and Sŭn-ju. From this point the Mongol general Sal Ye-t'ap sent a letter to the king saying 'Let us make peace. We have now taken your country as far as Han-sin and if you do not come to terms with us we will draw reinforcements from Yŭ-jin and crush you.' The messenger who conveyed this very candid letter got only as far as P'yŭng-ju where he was seized by the people and imprisoned. While waiting for an answer, the invaders tried another attack on Ku-ju but with no better success. Not only so, but they were badly defeated at Au-puk fortress.

The king now reinforced the army in the north and at the same time feasted 30,000 monks at the capital in order to influence the celestial powers to bring about a cessation of war.

But at the same time the Mongol forces were reinforced by Yŭ-jin troops and with high spirits crossed the Ta-dong river and swept down to P'yŭng-ju to wreak their vengeance on that place where even yet the Mongol messenger with the letter for the king was languishing in durance vile. By a night attack they took the place, burned it to the ground, killed the prefect and even destroyed every dog and other domestic animal in the place. Then they advanced toward Song-do and soon appeared beneath its walls. There the Mongol generals P'o-do, Chŭk-kŭ and Tang-go went into camp. They supplied their army by foraging all through the surrounding country, in which operation thousands of people were killed, their houses destroyed, and their goods confiscated, especially all kinds of food. The people in the capital were in the greatest distress. Ch'oé U, the viceroy, stationed all the best troops about his own house and left the inferior troops to guard the palace.

Mongols Leave Song-do Untaken

The Mongol general Sal Ye-t'ap was now in the north. The king had already sent one messenger to ask for terms of peace and had received the following answer: 'I am emperor. If you wish to fight it out then come on and fight. If not then surrender, and be quick about it, too.' The king now sent another messenger on a similar errand. He returned with two Mongol commissioners and three more soon followed. They were immediately admitted to an audience and a conference followed, after which the king sent rich presents to Gen. Sal Ye-t'ap who seems now to have joined the main army before Song-do, and also to the other generals. What the result of the conference was is, for some reason, not stated in the records, but that it was not entirely satisfactory to the Mongols, or if satisfactory not sufficiently so to make them forego the pleasure of plundering, is seen from their next move, for they left Song-do and went southward to the centre of the peninsula, the rich province of Ch'ung-ch'ŭng.

The cowardly prime minister showed his colours by sending a man to find a retreat for him on the island of Kang-wha, but the messenger fell into the hands of Mongol foragers.

Gen. Sal Ye-t'ap had gone north and joined another division of the Mongol army and again he attacked Ku-ju. He made engines of war called *ta-p'o-ch'a*, a sort of catapult, with which to reduce this town, but the magistrate, Pak Sö also made similar instruments which hurled huge stones, and the besiegers were compelled to retire to a distance and take refuge behind various kinds of defences. The Mongols made three attempts to deceive the prefect by forged letters purporting to be from the king and saying, 'I have surrendered and therefore you must submit,' but Pak Sö was not to be caught by so simple a trick. The besiegers then tried huge scaling ladders, but these were cut down by the defenders as fast as they were put in place. An aged Mongol general, who made a circuit of the town and marked the splendid state of defence into which the place had been put, declared that he had never seen a place so well defended.

So the little town stood and the great Mongol general was forced to seek other fields for the display of his prowess. He sent a letter to the king finding fault because of the death of the first Mongol messenger and modestly suggesting that peace could be secured if he would surrender and give 20,000 horse loads of clothing, 10,000 pieces of purple silk, 20,000 sea otter skins, 20,000 horses, 1,000 boys, 1,000 girls and 1,000,000 soldiers, with food, to help conquer Japan. In addition to this the king must go to the Mongol court and do obeisance. These were the terms upon which Koryŭ could secure peace.

The King Surrenders

With the beginning of the next year, 1232, the king sent two generals bearing a letter of surrender. With it he sent seventy pounds of gold, thirteen pounds of silver, 1,000 coats, and 170 horses. He moreover stated that the killing of the Mongol messenger was not the work of the Koryŭ government but of a band of insurgents and robbers. The officials had to give their garments in order to make up the number that was sent. Each prefect along the route was charged with the duty of seeing that the Mongols were in no way molested.

But Pak Sö the prefect of Ku-Ju was an obstinate man and would not give up his fortress even when he knew the king had surrendered. It was only after a great deal of argument and expostulation that he at last capitulated. The Koryŭ people wanted to kill him for his obstinacy but the Mongols said 'He is your greatest man and you should prize him highly.'

So ended the first act of the tragedy, but it was not to be the last. A Mongol residency was established at Song-do and Mongol governors were stationed at important centres throughout the country. The Mongol resident insisted upon entering the palace by the middle gate which the king alone used, but it was shut and barred and he was not able to carry his point. When the tribute above mentioned reached Gen. Sal Ye-t'ap he expressed the greatest dissatisfaction with it because it fell so far short of what was demanded and he imprisoned the messenger who brought it. The king sent an envoy to the Mongol capital saluting the emperor as suzerain for the first time.

REBELLION AGAINST THE MONGOLS

That neither the Koryŭ king nor any of the officials believed that the end of the trouble had come is evident. No sooner had the tumult of war subsided than the question arose in the Koryŭ councils as to the moving of the court. Some objections were made, but Ch'oé U silenced them by killing off a few of the objectors. As for the king, he could not make up his mind to go; but the viceroy showed no hesitation. Seizing the government carts he loaded his household effects upon them and moved to the island of Kang-wha. He also urged the people to do likewise, and put up placards threatening with death anyone who should speak against removing. Meanwhile the people throughout the country were rising in revolt against the Mongol governors and were driving them out. This was sure to call down upon the troubled land another invasion, and the king at last made up his mind to follow the example of his viceroy and move to Kang-wha. A palace had been prepared for him there and on the appointed day a start was made from the capital. It happened to be in the midst of the rainy season when the roads are well-nigh impassable. The whole cavalcade soon found itself mired, and torrents of rain added materially to the discomfort. Even ladies of noble rank were seen wading with bared limbs in the mud and carrying bundles on their heads. The wailing and crying of this forlorn multitude was audible for a long distance. Gen. Kim Chung-gwi was left to guard the capital. When the king at last arrived on the island he found that the palace was not ready for occupancy and he was obliged to live in a common house while the officials shifted for themselves. Messengers were immediately sent in all directions ordering the people to leave the mainland and seek refuge on the islands.

The common people in Song-do were in utter confusion. Anarchy stared them in the face. A slave by the name of Yi T'ong gathered about him a band of slaves and raised an insurrection. The general who had been placed in charge was driven out, the monks were summoned to help in the sack of the town and all the government buildings were soon looted. It is hardly complimentary to Buddhism that her monks were invited by this seditious rabble to help in these lawless acts but it is probably a true picture of the times. When this came to the ears of the king he sent Gen. Yi Cha-sung to put down the insurrection. The slaves barricaded the road but the general dispersed them and at night gained admittance to the city by feigning to be a deserter. Once within, he caught the slave leader Yi T'ong and the rest soon dispersed.

When the news of this exodus from the capital and the driving out of the Mongol governors reached the Mongol capital it caused a sensation. The emperor, in a white heat, sent a messenger post-haste to Song-do and behind him came a powerful army. The demand was 'Why have you changed the capital? Why have our people been driven out?' The king replied that the capital was changed because all the people were running away, but he affirmed that although he had removed to Kang-wha his friendly feelings toward the Mongols had not changed. To this the Mongols made the only answer that was to be expected from them. They fell upon the northern towns and put them to indiscriminate slaughter. Men, women and children fell beneath their swords. Gen. Sal Ye-t'ap himself came to attack Cho-im fortress. In that place there was a notable archer. He shot with unerring skill and every arrow found its victim. Aided by this man the garrison offered such a stubborn resistance that the Mongols at last fell back in disorder. It is said that Gen. Sal Ye-t'ap himself was one of the victims of this man's superb marksmanship. The king offered him official position but he would not accept it.

The spring of 1233 found the emperor's anger somewhat abated and instead of sending another army he sent another envoy with four formulated charges. (1) No Koryŭ envoy had come to do obeisance. (2) Highwaymen had killed a Mongol envoy. (3) The king had run away from his capital. (4) The king had given false figures in the census of Koryŭ. We are not told whether these were answered but we may infer that they were, and in the humblest tone.

Popular Insurrections

It would be singular indeed if, in such lawless times, there were not many insurrections in the country. A considerable insurrection was gotten up in Kyŭng-sang Province but was put down with a heavy hand, for the records say that after the battle between the rebels and the loyal troops the road for six miles was lined with dead. In P'yŏngyang likewise there was a rising led by one Pil Hyŭn-bo. The King sent Gen. Chŏng I alone to settle the difficulty. He had already been a P'yŏngyang prefect and had put down one insurrection. He was feared throughout the whole section. As he approached the northern city his servant besought him not to enter it, but he replied that such were the king's orders. So he went to his death, for the insurrectionists, failing to win him over to their side, gave him his quietus. The viceroy then sent 3,000 picked troops to the rebellious city. They took the rebel leader, cut him in two and sent the fragments of his body to the king. The second in command named Hong Pok-wŭn, fled to the Mongols, by whom he was warmly welcomed.

He became their guide in many subsequent expeditions. These renegades were a source of constant trouble between Koryŭ and the Mongols; so much so that the King took pains to show favour to the parents and relatives of those who had fled to the Mongol flag. This same year a second wall was built about Kang-wha. The king sent asking the Mongols to recall the rest of their troops, and it was done.

With the opening of the following year, 1234, great numbers of people were summoned to help in the building of a palace on Kang-wha. At this time the utmost favour was shown to Buddhism. Sacrifices were offered on all the mountains and beside the streams with the hope of enlisting the sympathy of the gods. The viceroy also looked out for himself, for we are told, probably with some exaggeration, that he built himself a house twenty *li* in circumference. It was in this same year that the Kin dynasty became extinct.

Mongol Occupation

With the opening of the next year the real occupation of the land by the Mongols commenced. The north was systematically occupied, scores of prefects being seized. The king of Kang-wha meanwhile was trying to secure a cessation of these hostilities by turning sun worshipper, for every morning from seven to twelve the officials spent their time worshipping that very useful, but hardly divine, luminary. The year following increased the hopelessness of Koryŭ's position a hundredfold, for the Mongols established seventeen permanent camps in P'yŭng-an and Whang-hă Provinces. They came as far south as Han-yang, the present Seoul. They then proceeded southward to the very extremity of the peninsula, and camps were established through all that portion of the land. The only reverse the Mongols met in this triumphal march was at the hands of Son Mun-ju the prefect of Chuk-ju, now Chuk-san, who had learned the tactics of the Mongols while serving in the north. Every day he foretold successfully at what point the enemy would make the next attack. People said he was inspired.

It would seem that the Mongols, however, did not remain long in the south, for we read that when the standard of revolt was raised the following year at Na-ju, the Koryŭ forces, sent by the king, speedily overcame them. This would hardly have been likely had the Mongols been in force in that vicinity.

We must remember that the Mongols were continental people and knew nothing of the sea. Even the narrow strip of water between Kang-wha and the mainland daunted them. And so it was that the king from his island retreat defied the tremendous Mongol power.

By 1238, when the Mongols again flooded the country with their soldiery, the people had mostly found refuge among the mountains and on the thousands of islands which lie off the western coast of Korea. It would be impossible for anyone to imagine the suffering and distress entailed by these invasions. The records say that the people simply left their houses and fields and fled to these places of refuge. What did these hundreds of thousands of people live on as they fled, and after they reached their places of retreat? What breaking of old bonds of friendship and kinship, what rending of family ties and uprooting of ancient landmarks! It is a marvel that the land ever recovered from the shock. These Mongols were fiercer and more ruthless than the Japanese who overran the country three centuries later and they were far more numerous, besides. Plunder being their main motive, their marauding bands covered a much greater territory and mowed a much wider swath than did the soldiers of the great Hideyoshi, who kept to comparatively narrow lines of march. Nor did these Mongols meet the opposition which the Japanese met. The Mongols made a clean sweep of the country, and never again do we read of those splendid armies of 200,000 or 300,000 men which Koryŭ was once able to put into the field, even when groaning under the weight of a corrupt court and a rampant priesthood. It is from these days that dates that utter prostration of Koryŭ's power which left her an easy prey to every Japanese freebooter who had 100 good swords at his back.

After ravaging to their hearts' content the Mongols withdrew in 1236 to their own territory but sent a messenger ordering the king to go to Peking and bow before the Mongol emperor. He refused, but sent instead a relative by the name of Chŭn with a letter asking the emperor to excuse him from attempting the difficult journey to the Mongol court. Again the next year the same demand was made, but this time the king simply declined to go. The Mongols then modified their demand and ordered the King to come out from his island retreat and return to Song-do. This the king had no intention of doing; but the next year he sent another relation named Sun as a hostage to the Mongol court asserting that this was his son. The emperor believed this and married Sun to one of his own near relatives.

Gayuk Khan

The Mongol Emperor Ogdai died in 1242 and the queen dowager took charge of affairs during an interval of four years, until 1246, when Gayuk became emperor. This brought peace to troubled Koryŭ for a period of five or six years. During this time, all that was left of her resources was used up in sending five or six embassies to the Mongol court each year. The moment the pressure of war was raised the king followed once more the bent of his inclinations, and while the country was in the very lowest depths of distress he feasted royally in his island retreat, while the viceroy vied with him in the splendour of his entertainments. It is said that at one feast 1300 musicians performed. Meantime the people were slowly returning to their homes.

Gayuk Khan came to the Mongol throne in 1246, and it was the signal for the renewal of hostilities against Koryŭ. At first 400 men came, ostensibly to catch sea otter but in reality to spy out the country and learn the mountain passes of the north. The king was not expecting a renewal of hostilities, or else was too much taken up with his feasting to attend to the defences of the north; so the people fled in panic before this handful of invaders. Many of them took refuge on Wi-do Island off P'yŭng-an Province and there engaged in agriculture. They built a great dam across an estuary of the sea and reclaimed a large tract of cultivable land, but they suffered badly from lack of wells.

In 1249 Gayuk died and the regency again devolved upon the queen dowager. Peace again reigned for a time, broken only by a single attempted invasion by the Yŭ-jin people, which was unsuccessful. The king began the erection of a new palace at Song-do in order to make it appear that he intended to obey the standing injunction of his suzerain to go back to the capital.

Mangu Khan

The Mongol regency ended in 1251 and Mangu Khan became emperor. An envoy was immediately despatched to inquire whether the king had yet obeyed this command, but as the answer was unsatisfactory the Koryŭ envoy who appeared at the emperor's court the following year was thrown into prison and a last envoy was sent with instructions to settle the question definitely. If the king would come out and return to his capital the people might remain on Kang-wha, but if the king refused, the envoy was to return with all haste to the Emperor and war would be declared at once. A certain Korean, hearing about these instructions, hastened forward and informed the king and urged that he go out and meet the envoy. To this the king did not assent. When the envoy arrived the king set a great feast for him, in the midst of which the Mongol arose and, assuming a terrible aspect, demanded loudly why the king did not leave the island and return to Song-do. Without waiting for an answer to the question he strode out of the hall and posted back to the north. The people were in dismay and said to each other, 'This means war again.'

Great Invasion of 1253

When the lengthening vernal sun of 1253 had melted the northern snows this prophetic word was verified. The renegade Koryŭ general, Hong Pok-wŭn, told the emperor that the king had triple-walled the island of Kang-wha and would not move therefrom. War, ever welcome to these first Mongol emperors, was now afoot. The first detachment of 10,000 troops was led by the emperor's brother Song-ju. With many allies from the Yŭ-jin and other tribes he crossed the Yalu. Then the Mongol general, A Mo-gan, and the renegade Hong crossed and advanced as far as the Ta-dong River. Following these came Gen. Ya Gol-dă with sixteen chieftains in his train and with a formidable array of troops.

The envoy Sun who, we will remember, had married a Mongol princess, now wrote an urgent letter to the king saying 'The emperor is angry because you persist in disobeying him and he is sending seventeen kings against you. But he says that if you will leave the island and follow out his commands he will even now recall the army. You have now an opportunity of giving your country a lasting peace. If you leave the island, send your son to the emperor and receive the Mongol envoy well, it will be a blessing to the kingdom of Koryŭ. If you will not do this, I beg of you to put all my family to death.'

Beneath this last appeal lay a terrible threat and the king realized it. A great council was convened and the universal voice was in favour of compliance; but a single voice was raised in opposition. It said 'How much treasure have we squandered on this insatiable barbarian, and how many good men have gone as envoys and never returned. Let the king go out now from this place of safety and when we behold him a corpse our condition will be enviable indeed!' This word startles the assembly. Cowards that they are, they rise to their feet and with one voice applaud the stirring words and charge the king to stay in his island fortress and still defy the savage of the north.

Gen. Ya Gol-dă now sent a messenger to the king purporting to be from the emperor saying 'I have begun from the rising sun and I will conquer to its going down. All people rejoice but you, who do not listen. I now send Gen. Ya Gol-dă. If you receive him well, I will leave you in peace; if not, I will never forgive the offense.' Immediately putting his troops in motion the redoubtable general approached the strongest fortress in Whang-ha Province. It was surrounded by almost perpendicular precipices. The commandant laughed at the Mongols and defied them, and feasted in their sight. But the Mongols, directing all their energy at a single point, soon battered down a portion of the wall, set fire to the buildings with fire arrows, and with scaling ladders effected an entrance. The commandant hanged himself, and 4,700 of the garrison were put to the sword. All children above ten years old were killed and all the women were ravished.

Gen. Ya Gol-dă, being at To-san in Whang-ha Province, received a plaintive letter from the king asking him to retire from the country. He told the bearer of this missive 'The emperor says the king is too old to bow. I am going to find out whether this is true. I will give him just six days to get here.' The messenger argued the dangerous condition of the road and said it could not be done in that time. Then the Mongol forces turned eastward and began to destroy the fortresses and loot the storehouses, at the same time sending to the king saying 'If every prefect in the land will send in a written surrender I will retire.' This was impossible in the present state of turmoil, and it probably was a mere pleasantry on the part of the Mongols.

Siege of Ch'un-ch'ŭn

The town of Ch'un-ch'ŭn was a rather formidable place and its siege and fall offer some interesting indications of the method of Mongol warfare. First a double fence or stockade was built around the town and outside this a bank six feet high and a ditch correspondingly deep. Ere long the supply of water in the town gave out and the people killed their cattle and drank the blood. The distress was terrible. Cho Hyo-ip, a leading man, seeing that there was no escape, first burned up his family and then killed himself. The prefect fought until he was exhausted and then threw himself into a burning house and perished. A party of the strongest of the remaining soldiers made a fierce attack upon one portion of the stockade and succeeded in breaking through, but they could not force the bank and trench beyond. The enemy entered, razed the town and burned the grain, and the women were carried away. During this time the king was using the only means left for turning the tide of war. He was worshipping every spirit that he could think of, and before every large boulder. He raised all his ancestors several rounds in the ladder of apotheosis; but it all seemed to have little effect upon the progress of events. Another renegade, Yi Hyŭn, arose in the north and forced many districts into his following.

In the course of time Gen. Ya Gol-dă arrived before the town of Ch'ung-ju in Ch'ung-ch'ŭng Province, but being unable to reduce it without a regular siege, he left his main army there and came north to the vicinity of Kang-wha. He then announced, 'If the king will come out and meet me here I will take my forces back across the Yalu.' With this message he sent ten Mongol generals to the king. The latter complied, and with a heavy guard came across the straits and met Ya Gol-dă at Seung-ch'ŭn-bu. Gen. Mong Go-dă was present with Ya Gol-dă at the interview which followed. The Mongol general said 'After we crossed the Yalu into Koryŭ, thousands of your people fell every day. Why should you think only of your own comfort while your people are dying thus by tens of thousands? If you had consented to come out sooner, many lives would have been saved. We now ought to make a firm treaty.' He added that Mongol prefects must be placed in each district and that a force of 10,000 in all must be quartered upon Koryŭ. To this the king replied that with such conditions it would be extremely difficult for him to return to Song-do. In spite of this the Mongol leader placed one of his men in each of the prefectures. The only question which was discussed in the royal councils was how to get rid of the Mongols. One man dared to suggest that the crown prince be sent to intercede with the emperor. The king flew into a rage at this but soon he was so far mollified as to consent to sending his second son, Chang, with rich gifts to the Mongol court, a course of procedure which once more drained the royal coffers to the last farthing.

The king had promised the Mongols to go back to Song-do 'gradually' as fast as preparations could be made, and also to destroy the palaces in Kang-wha. The Mongols kept their word and retired but as they went they plundered and ravaged. When they had gone the king caught the renegade Yi Hyŭn and killed him and his son, and banished all his adherents. This was a dangerous course, for this man had acted as guide to the Mongols and the latter were more than likely to resent his death. So it turned out, for an envoy came post from the Mongol court complaining that only the king alone had come out from Kang-wha, and that a man who had helped the Mongols had been slain for it. Whether the king answered these complaints satisfactorily we do not know, but soon the emperor developed a new plan. He sent Gen. Cha Ra-dă with 5,000 troops to become governor-general of Koryŭ.

A Ferocious Governor-General

The emperor little knew what sort of a man he was letting loose upon Koryŭ. No sooner had this beast in human shape crossed the frontier than he began a systematic course of extermination. He killed right and left, every living thing. The king hastened to remonstrate but he answered 'Unless all the people have their hair cut I shall continue to kill.' The records say that he carried into captivity the enormous number of 206,800 souls, both men and women, and that of the dead he left behind no estimate was ever made. When the emperor heard of this, even his fierce heart was touched, and the next year, 1255, he recalled the monster. The latter obeyed but on his way north he built fortified camps along the way, for future use.

In spite of the thanks which the Koryŭ king sent to the emperor for this deliverance, the latter allowed this same general to come back with a powerful force, and accompanied by the same former envoy, Sun, who had married the Mongol princess. The king had to go out and meet them and waste his remaining treasure in useless presents. So thoroughly was his exchequer depleted that his own table was but ill supplied.

The two countries were now nominally at peace, but as Gen. Cha seemed bent on fighting, there seemed to be nothing to do but to fight. Some of his soldiers were roughly handled at Chung-ju where 1,000 were killed. Again in the east a large detachment of his troops were heavily defeated.

At last Gen. Cha came, in his sanguinary wanderings, to the vicinity of Kang-wha and displayed his banners in sight of that island, to the great uneasiness of its occupants. Sun, the renegade, was now a Mongol general and was as bitter against Koryŭ; as any of the northern savages.

The king, in despair, sent Kim Su-gan to the emperor to make a last appeal to his clemency, but the emperor replied, 'I cannot recall my troops, for your king will not come out from his retreat'. To this the envoy made the beautiful reply, 'The frightened quarry will not come forth from its hole till the hunter has departed. The flower cannot spring from the frozen sod'.

Upon hearing this the emperor immediately gave orders for the recall of the ruthless Gen. Cha.

A New Viceroy

Ch'oé Hang, the son of Ch'oé U, had held the position of viceroy for eight years. His course had been one of utter selfishness and oppression. Many honourable men had met their death at his hands. He now died, leaving a son, Ch'oé Chung, a young man of considerable power. When the viceroy died his retainers did not announce the fact until the household had been put in readiness for any emergency and a strong armed guard had been stationed at every approach. We can argue from this fact that the viceroyalty was anything but pleasing to the king and that in case the viceroy died the king would be glad of an opportunity to abolish the office altogether. Subsequent events proved the truth of this supposition. When everything was in readiness the death was announced and the young man Ch'oé Chung was put forward as viceroy. The king was obliged to confirm him in the office. He had no power to refuse. Ch'oé Jung was a son by a concubine and from this time the annals contain no mention of men's birth on the mother's side. This was because Ch'oé Jung killed everybody who was heard speaking slightingly of his birth. If anyone had a spite against another he could always effectually vent it by charging him with having said that Ch'oé Chung was of common birth.

Disaster and distress followed each other thick and fast in these days. An insurrection arose in Kang-wŭn Province under the leadership of one An Yul, but was put down. A famine wasted the country and the poor were fed out of the government supplies. The Mongols though nominally at peace with Koryŭ seemed to consider the territory as their legitimate foraging ground, and now they came walking through the land, coming even to the gates of Song-do. The king sent Gen. Yi Eung and feasted the unwelcome guests in the hope of inducing them to leave the unhappy country. It was a vain hope. They turned southward and continued their thieving across the Han River even to Chik-san. The king feasted them again and asked them to desist. The leader replied that he would do so if the king would come out of Kang-wha and send the Crown Prince to the Mongol court. As this leader was that same Gen. Cha who had once been recalled by the emperor for cruelty, we may easily understand how anxious the king was to be rid of him, at any cost. He therefore consented to the conditions, and Gen. Cha retired as far as Yŭn-ju and ordered all the detachments of his army to desist from plundering. The king kept his word, in part at least, for he sent not the Crown Prince but his second son together with Ch'oé Chung.

Viceroy Overthrown

Ch'oé Chung used his wits for the purpose of personal emolument and his credulity also led him into all kinds of difficulties. His grand mistake was in casting off an aged slave, Kim In-jun, who had served his father and grandfather faithfully and deserved better treatment at the young man's hands. The worm, thus trodden upon, turned and bit to the bone. It was as follows. The aged servant, gaining access to the king, told him that the young viceroy was dead and in a moment secured another man as leader of the soldiers. Clad with his new power the vengeful old man caught and killed some of the most intimate friends of the viceroy and in the early morning gained access to the viceroy's house and hunted him from room to room. He found him hidden in a disused chimney flue from which he was speedily drawn forth and dispatched. When the old slave announced this to the king the latter said, 'You have done me a great favour', and could hardly refrain from tears. The king then destroyed the picture of Ch'oé Chung-heun who had founded the viceroyalty, and distributed the ill-gotten wealth of the Ch'oé family among the people. It is said that even the lowest citizen received at least three bags of rice or other grain. At the same time all Ch'oé's following were banished.

Mongol Ravages

The year 1258 had now come, the last that the aged King Ko-jang was destined to see. In this year the Mongols came again as usual. They began by building and garrisoning a fortress at Eui-ju. Then Gen. Cha Ra-dă with a small body of 1,000 troops came southwards as far as Su-an in Whang-hă Province. It shows how utterly shorn of power Koryŭ was, that this general should dare to penetrate so far into the land with only 1,000 men at his back. Hearing of this the aged king decided to try a little artifice. He came out of Kang-wha, across the straits to Tong-jin on the opposite bank, in order to make it appear that he had complied with the emperor's command. Gen. Cha demanded that the crown prince also come out. He made a line of camps all the way from Song-do to Tong-jin and settled down as if he intended to stay and see his orders obeyed. The king had retired to the island again upon the near approach of the Mongols and now the latter redoubled their demands and ravaged more remorselessly than ever. They swarmed all about Kang-wha and nothing but a narrow strip of water lay between the king and that more than half savage army. The water proved, however, an effective barrier. All this time another Mongol force under Gen. San Gil-dă was wasting the northern and eastern districts, The people of Wha-ju and of fourteen other towns, led by one Sin Chip-pyŭng sought refuge on Cho-do island but finding this insecure, moved to another; but some Koryŭ renegades led Mongol troops there and overthrew the little colony.

The king now altered his tactics. Sending an envoy to China he said 'I have desired to obey the emperor but hitherto I have been prevented by the powerful officials. Now that the viceroy has been put out of the way I will go back to Song-do and do as you shall direct. But we are surrounded by your soldiery and it is hard to move. We are like mice when the cat is about. Let them be ordered back home and I will do as you direct.'

Meanwhile two traitors in the north had overpowered the Koryŭ general and had gone over to the enemy. The whole north was therefore without a single defence and was being held by these two traitors under Mongol orders. Such was the unhappy condition of affairs when the year 1258 came to a close.

KUBLAI KHAN AND THE INVASION OF JAPAN

The year 1259 opened with the sending of an envoy to China but he was waylaid, robbed, and killed by Koryŭ ruffians; thus Koryŭ was ever discredited in the eyes of China. The Mongols now began to make fields about P'yŏngyang with the intention of making that city a permanent Mongol centre. They repaired the walls of the town and constructed new war boats on the river.

The king came to the decision that there was no possibility of ridding himself of this incubus but by sending the crown prince to China. When Gen. Cha Ra-dă heard of this he was highly pleased. Of course it would appear that he had brought about this happy result. This was in the third moon and Gen. Cha expected the arrival of the prince the following month. When he heard that he was not to start till the fourth moon he was angry; the king therefore hurried the preparations and sent the prince off in the third moon. The escort consisted of forty men, and there were 300 horse-loads of gifts. In good time all arrived at the court of the Mongol emperor. Gen. Cha however did not enjoy his triumph, for at this very time he sickened and died.

When the prince arrived at the Chinese court the emperor was away on a campaign against the Sung Empire in the south; so he announced himself to the official in charge at the capital, Song Kil. The latter asked if the king had as yet gone back to Song-do, to which the prince replied in the negative, but added that the king would go as soon as possible if the emperor demanded it. Song Kil rejoined 'How can we recall the soldiers so long as the king does not leave Kang-wha?' The prince replied 'Gen. Cha said that if I came the troops would be recalled. If they are not recalled the people will have no hope except in flight.' When Song Kil heard this he countermanded an order which had been given for additional troops to be sent into the peninsula. Word was sent, instead, ordering the destruction of the palaces on Kang-wha. The order was obeyed and it is said that the fall of the buildings sounded like distant thunder. But the aged king who had suffered so many vicissitudes of fortune was not to survive this great shame, and in the summer of 1259 he passed away.

The Regency

Koryŭ was now without a king and the crown prince was far away in China. It was decided to form a regency to act until the return of the prince. At first it was conferred upon the second son of the deceased king but the officials, remembering that the dying king had said 'Put my grandson in as regent until the prince returns', made the change, and the crown prince's son, Sun, became regent pending his father's return.

As the Mongol troops continued their depredations in the north an envoy was again dispatched to the emperor's court. As the latter was still away campaigning in the south the envoy made bold to follow him up. He passed Chŭk-san and finally found the emperor at Hyŭp-ju and delivered his message. The emperor said 'If you profess to be friendly with me why are you always talking about my troops being in the way? Yet since the crown prince has come to China I am willing to show you this favour'. He thereupon sent an order for the retirement of all Mongol troops from Korea.

Some busybody told the emperor that Koryŭ had no desire to hold faith with China and in consequence an envoy came in haste to Song-do demanding why the people who had fled to the islands did not return to their homes. The reply was that the detention of the prince in China was a cause of uneasiness and that even if he returned it would take at least three years to get the people back to their homes; how much less could it be done with the prince in China. This then became the standing complaint of the Mongols, that the Korean people would not come back to the mainland.

By this time the uncertainty of affairs and the fact that the central government was weak and the Mongols still numerous caused great instability in the north. The people were easily induced to revolt on the slightest provocation. It became a regular custom for the people, if they did not like their prefect, to kill him and transfer their allegiance to the Mongols. The central government did not dare to punish them, for this would provoke the Mongols, and reprisals would be in order. At the same time there was trouble in the south, for pirates from both Japan and the Sung kingdom of southern China kept ravaging the island of Quelpart. An official was sent from Song-do to take in hand the defence of the island but the people found him worse than the pirates had been.

The Prince Finds Kublai Khan

It was in 1260 that the crown prince followed the emperor southward, but soon after reaching the emperor's camp the latter died in the town of Hap-ju and Gen. A-ri Pal-ga took the reins of power arbitrarily. The prince knew that the great general Hol-p'il-ryŭl (Kublai) would doubtless become emperor in spite of this seditious movement on the part of A-ri Pal-ga; so he secretly effected his escape from the latter's camp and struck directly across the country to Kang-nam where he found Hol-p'il-ryŭl in charge of an army, and, informing him of the emperor's decease, they both hastened toward Peking. It was not till the crown prince returned to Peking that he learned of his father's death and he hastened to assume the mourner's garb.

The emperor, Kublai Khan, sent him back to Koryŭ with great honour, believing that, as he was to become king of Koryŭ, the vassal power would thus become more closely united to China. Two Mongol generals came with him as escort. These were Sok Yi-kă and Kang Wha-sang. On the way these generals were told by a Koryŭ renegade that the crown prince would change the capital to Quelpart. They asked the prince to face this man and deny the charge but he assumed a royal attitude and exclaimed 'I would cut off my hair and become a slave before I would meet the villain'. The generals were ashamed to press the matter. As they approached Kang-wha the prince's son, the acting king came with a great retinue to meet them at Che-jung Harbor, where they all took boats and crossed to the island. As the Mongol generals strongly urged the king to go back to Song-do, the latter sent many of the officials back there in order to make it appear as if he would follow shortly. All Mongol soldiers were now recalled from Koryŭ and all their prefects as well. The emperor likewise gave the king a present of seals, clothing, bows, arrows, silks, and other articles of value. The king so far conceded to the wishes of his suzerain as to remove from Kang-wha to Tong-jin on the adjacent mainland, from which, however, it was but half an hour's sail across to the island again. In addition to this the king sent the heir apparent to China with gifts, of which, in view of the depletion of Koryŭ's treasury, the officials gave the greater part out of their private means. The main request preferred at Kublai's court was that he would not listen longer to the representations of Koryŭ renegades whose one object was to stir up strife and keep the countries at war with each other. The emperor assented to this.

In 1261 the emperor made a requisition upon Koryŭ for a large amount of copper and lead. The king did not have the copper and yet did not dare to refuse; so he sent to A-t'o in China and bought copper and delivered it as ordered, but told how he had procured it. The emperor charged him with lying and claimed that he was remiss in her duties as a vassal. He moreover ordered that the king take a census of Koryŭ, establish a horse relay system, train soldiers, and prepare provisions for an army. The king was unable to comply and an estrangement grew up between him and the emperor which was unfortunate for both. Hong Tagu, a Koryŭ renegade, took advantage of this to charge the Koryŭ prince, who was then in Peking, with having insulted the Mongol crown prince. The emperor believed the charge and cut off the Koryŭ prince's revenues and treated him with marked coldness. Hong also poisoned the emperor toward Koryŭ by intimating that she would soon attempt to throw off the yoke of China. But by the following year the relations seem to have become cordial again, for when the king asked that the tribute be remitted on the ground of the heavy expense of rebuilding palaces at Songdo, the emperor not only consented but sent a present of 500 sheep. Koryŭ was also fortunate in the sending of an envoy to Japan, for he returned with a large amount of rice and cloth from Tsushima, which had been stolen by Japanese corsairs.

The King Goes to China

In 1263 the king was ordered to repair to Peking. A long discussion followed, some of the courtiers advising one thing and some another. The monks at this time said, in effect, 'I told you so', for they had long ago promised the king that if he would favour them he would not be called to Peking. But go he did, leaving his son to administer the kingdom in his absence. Sun, whom we will remember as the Koryŭ gentleman who had married a Mongol princess and who was thoroughly Mongolized, told the emperor that there were 38,000 troops in Koryŭ and that someone should go and bring them to China where they could act as allies for the Mongols in their conquests. To this Yi

Chang-yung, who was in the king's retinue, answered. 'Formerly we had that number of soldiers but many have died and few are left. If the emperor cannot believe this let him send Sun with me to Koryŭ and we will review all the troops and learn the truth.' This was a telling blow, for Sun knew that if he once crossed into Koryŭ territory his life would not be worth an hour's ransom; so he discreetly held his peace. The king came back to Song-do in December of the same year.

In 1264 the Japanese pirates made another descent upon the shores of southern Koryŭ but were driven away by the royal forces under Gen. An Hong.

Chinese Envoys to Japan

In 1265 the seed was sown that led to the attempted invasion of Japan by the Mongols. A Koryŭ citizen, Cho I, found his way to Peking and there, having gained the ear of the emperor, told him that the Mongol power ought to secure the vassalage of Japan. The emperor listened favourable and determined to make advances in that direction. He therefore appointed Heuk Chŭk and Eun Hong as envoys to Japan and ordered them to go by way of Koryŭ and take with them to Japan a Koryŭ envoy as well. Arriving in Koryŭ they delivered this message to the king and two officials, Son Kun-bi and Kim Ch'an were appointed to accompany them to Japan. They proceeded by the way of Kö-je Harbor in Kyŭng-sang Province but were driven back by a fierce storm and the king sent the Mongol envoys back to Peking. The emperor was ill satisfied with the outcome of the adventure and sent Heuk Chŭk with a letter to the king ordering him to forward the Mongol envoy to Japan. The message which he was to deliver to the ruler of Japan said 'The Mongol power is kindly disposed toward you and desires to open friendly intercourse with you. She does not desire your submission but if you accept her patronage the great Mongol empire will cover the earth.' The king forwarded the message with the envoys to Japan, and informed the emperor of the fact.

Meanwhile the emperor was being worked upon by designing men who were seeking to injure Koryŭ. They succeeded so well in their designs that he sent an envoy bearing a list of specified charges against the king. (1) You have enticed Mongol people to Koryŭ. (2) You did not feed our troops when they were in Koryŭ. (3) You persistently refuse to come back to the capital. (4) When our envoy went to Koryŭ you had a spy watch him. (5) Your tribute has not been at all equal to the demand we made. (6) You brought it about that the Japanese did not accept our offer. The emperor's suspicions continued to increase until finally he sent a general, U-ya Son-dal, to demand that Yi Chang-yong and Kim Chun, two of the most influential officials of Koryŭ, together with the father and son of the latter, be brought to Peking. Kim Chun, on learning of this, advised that the envoy be promptly killed and that the king remain in some island, out of harm's way. But the king knew that such a course would be suicidal and firmly refused. So Kim Chun himself put Gen. U-ya Son-dal to death and then announced the fact to the court. The king and court were dumbfounded at his temerity but dared not lay hands on him, though they all felt sure they would suffer for his rash act. Fortunately for them, however, other events of great importance were happening which distracted the attention of the emperor and secured immunity from punishment. These events we must now relate.

The Mongol and Koryŭ envoys, upon reaching the Japanese capital, were treated with marked disrespect. They were not allowed to enter the gates, but were lodged at a place called T'ă-jă-bu, outside the west gate of the city. There they remained five months, and their entertainment was of the poorest quality. And at last they were dismissed without receiving any answer either to the emperor or to the king.

Kubali Khan's Message to Japan

Kublai Khan was not the kind of a man to relish this sort of treatment and when he heard the story he sent a messenger straight to Koryŭ telling the king 'I have decided to invade Japan. You must immediately begin the building of one thousand boats. You must furnish four thousand bags of rice and a contingent of 40,000 troops.' The king replied that this was beyond his power, for so many of the people had run away that workmen could not be secured in sufficient numbers. The emperor, however, was resolute and soon sent an envoy to see if his orders were being carried out, and to make a survey of the straits between Koryŭ and Japan, in the vicinity of Heuk-san Island. The emperor could scarcely believe that the Japanese would dare to treat his envoy so disrespectfully as had been reported and he suspected that it was some sort of ruse that the king of Koryŭ had been playing on him; so he decided to send his envoy Heuk Chŭk once more to Japan. This time also he was accompanied by a Koryŭ envoy, Sim Sa-jŭn.

Meantime Kim Chun finding that his foul murder of the Mongol envoy went unpunished, became prouder and more headstrong. His son stole two boatloads of vegetables intended for the king's own table. This roused the ire of the king. Kim

Chun might kill all the Mongol envoys he wished but when it came to stealing from the king's table something must be done. There was only one official, Im Yun, who hated Kim Chun worse than he feared him and the king selected this man for the work in hand. Sending away all the other officials to a neighbouring monastery to sacrifice to Buddha for his health, he summoned Kim Chun and, when he had him at his mercy, let Im Yun fall upon him with a club and take his life. Kim Chun's brother likewise fell the same day and the household of the offender was broken up. The usual impotence of the king was illustrated here by the very trick to which he was forced in order to rid himself of his traitorous subject.

The spring of 1268 opened, and still the envoys had not returned from Japan. The Koryŭ people managed to capture some Japanese from Tsushima who had come near the Korean coast. They were sent to Peking together with an envoy. The emperor was delighted, showed the captives all over the palace and reviewed the army before them. After showing them all the grandeur of the Mongol court, he sent them back to tell their king about it and to urge him to make friends with the great Yuan empire. This same year the crown prince went to the Mongol court.

Revolution

Im Yun, whom the king had used as an instrument for the removal of the obnoxious Kim Chun, did not intend to go without his reward. He began to plan how he might become a kingmaker himself. He desired to depose the king and put another in his place who would be quite subservient to himself. To this end he began to banish those who might oppose him in this scheme, and at last when he had cleared the way and deemed the time ripe, he surrounded himself with a powerful guard and called all the officials to a council. He told them that the king desired to kill him, but rather than die tamely he was resolved to do something desperate. He asked them if they agreed, but no man dared to open his mouth. Then putting on his armour he led the way to the palace and proclaimed Chang as king. This Chang was a distant relative of the king. He also made all the officials bow to him. The records say that this deed was accompanied by a tremendous storm of rain in which the deposed king was driven forth on foot. Im Yun and his lewd followers then proceeded to loot the palace.

The parvenu Chang, at the instance of Im Yun, sent an envoy to the Mongol court saying that the king had handed over the reins of government to him. The king's son, who had gone but lately to the Chinese court, was now on his way home. He arrived at night on the farther bank of the Yalu River and was there met by a secret messenger who had crossed in the dark to tell him that Chang had usurped the throne and that soldiers had been stationed at Eui-ju to kill him when he arrived. So the prince turned and hastened back to the emperor and a letter was immediately dispatched demanding the reinstatement of the rightful sovereign. After two such appeals had remained unanswered the emperor threatened to send an army to enforce the demand. The officials thereupon became afraid and reluctantly put the rightful king back upon his throne.

The King Goes to China

The emperor then ordered both the king and the man who had deposed him to go to China in order that the matter might be investigated. The king went but Im Yun refused and sent his son instead. The emperor ordered the king to write out the cause of the trouble but the latter feared that if he did so it would make trouble for him when he went back, for Im Yun was a powerful and unscrupulous man. He therefore told the emperor that he was troubled with a lame hand that prevented his writing. Later however, in private, he made the matter bare before the emperor and as a consequence Im Yun's son was thrown into prison. Before returning to Koryŭ the king asked the emperor to bestow upon his son, the crown prince, the hand of one of the Mongol princesses, to give him a Mongol escort back to Koryŭ, to place a Mongol governor at P'yŏngyang and to return to the control of Koryŭ the northern districts of the peninsula. The emperor consented to all but the last of these requests. When the king came back to Song-do, Im Yun attempted to oppose him but was speedily put down and decapitated.

Arriving at the capital the king went into camp outside the walls to await the completion of the palace which was in course of construction. The troops oppressed the people, and when the king ordered them to disband they marched out in a body and went by boat to Chŭl-la Province and began to act in a rebellious manner. A royal army, sent against them, chased them into the island of Chin-do where they forced the people to join their standards. Mongol and Koryŭ troops were sent against them, but the people hated the Mongols so heartily that this rather added to the difficulty than otherwise, and the disaffection, spreading with increased rapidity, began to assume serious proportions. The emperor learned of this and, believing that the king was hardly equal to the task of managing the affairs of the government, sent a commissioner to assume control at Song-do.

Preparations to Invade Japan

Matters stood thus when in 1270 the emperor determined to send another envoy to Japan. Cho Yong-p'il and Hong Ta-gu were appointed to this important mission and they were joined in Koryŭ by the representative of that country, by name Yang Yun-so. This embassy was charged with the somewhat dangerous task of demanding the submission of Japan. The emperor did not anticipate success in this, as is shown by the fact that he had rice fields made in Pong-san, Koryŭ, to raise rice for an army of invasion which he intended to launch upon Japan. For this work he ordered the king to furnish 6000 plows and oxen, as well as seed grain. The king protested that this was quite beyond his power, but as the emperor insisted he sent through the country and by force or persuasion obtained a fraction of the number demanded. The emperor aided by sending 10,000 pieces of silk. The Koryŭ army had dwindled to such a point that butchers and slaves were enrolled in the lists. The rebel army had been driven out of Chin-do, but a remnant had crossed over to Quelpart where the kingdom of T'am-na still flourished. Many of these rebels had been captured on Chin-do and had been taken as captives to China. Now at the request of the king they were sent back to Song-do for punishment. A curious complication arose in connection with this. These rebels, when they first went to Kang-wha had stolen the wives of many of the officials there and had carried them south. These women accompanied their newly acquired husbands to China; but now that they were all returned to Song-do many of them again met their former husbands. Some were received back gladly while others were not wanted, owing to new arrangements which were quite satisfactory. But the king commanded that all officials who found their former wives should take them back.

The emperor, influenced by evil-minded men who exaggerated the wealth of the peninsula, demanded that Koryŭ send a large amount of timber to China, but the king answered that he could not accomplish impossibilities. The commissioner who had been sent was a capable man and was well liked by the people in spite of his Mongol nationality. The commissioner fell ill and was fast approaching his end. The king sent him some medicine but he refused to take it, saying that if he took it and yet died the emperor might charge the king with having made away with him by poison. So the disease ran its course and the commissioner expired amid the lamentations of the people. Their appreciation of this Mongol's kindness shows how badly they were accustomed to being governed. Their high appreciation of his mild and just government overcame even their prejudice against his birth.

Kublai Proclaims the Yuan Empire

It was in this same year that Kublai Khan proclaimed the name of his empire Yuan.

When the Mongol and Koryŭ envoys returned from Japan they were accompanied by a Japanese envoy. The king hurried them on to Peking where they were received by the emperor with great delight, who hoped that he had now gained his point. But he did not relax his preparations for an invasion, for he commanded the king to hasten the construction of boats and the collection of provisions. Everything however was hindered by the rebels on Quelpart who built there a strong fortress and made it a centre from which to harry the southern islands and even parts of the mainland. The exchequer was exhausted and the people could not endure further taxation. Many of them fled from their homes to escape the exactions of the government. It is said that one day the king himself had to get along without any side dishes or condiments.

The land seemed doomed to misfortune. A marauding party of Japanese landed at Keum-ju and the people, in fear of their lives, treated them well and gave them whatever they asked for. This the renegade Hong Ta-gu told the emperor with embellishments of his own and averred that Koryŭ was making friends with Japan with a view to an invasion of China. The action of the people of Keum-ju made this seem probable. This fed the emperor's suspicions of Koryŭ's bad faith and added materially to the overwhelming difficulties under which the land was already staggering.

The matter of the Quelpart rebels came to an issue when they began ravaging the coast of Chŭl-la Province, burning at one place between twenty and thirty ships and carrying away a number of Mongol soldiers as prisoners. The following spring a strong body of Mongol and Koryŭ troops crossed to Quelpart, overthrew the stronghold of the rebels and placed there a garrison of 500 Mongol and 1000 Koryŭ troops.

Koreans Build Boats for the Mongols

The eventful year 1273 opened with a vigorous demand on the part of the emperor that the king prepare 300 vessels, for which he was to supply not only the labour but the materials as well. At the same time the vanguard of the army of invasion, 5,000 strong, came to Koryŭ, perhaps to see that the commands of the emperor were promptly complied with. They brought 33,000 pieces of silk to use in purchasing supplies for their maintenance. Silk was the very last thing that the poverty-stricken people of Koryŭ wanted, but it was forced upon them and they had to buy whether they wished or not. The king in attempted obedience to the emperor's demands assembled 3,500 carpenters and other artisans necessary to the building of the boats, and the work was begun.

The Mongol governor who had been placed at P'yŏngyang was a man of dark and fierce aspect and he was universally feared and hated. He also demanded the society of the fair sex and seized women right and left. Famine stared the capital in the face and the emperor was obliged to send 20,000 bags of rice to relieve the distress. In spite of the inauspiciousness of the times the crown prince who had been plighted to a Mongol princess was sent to Peking where the nuptials were celebrated. No sooner had this been done than the emperor sent to Koryŭ the main body of the army which was to cross the straits and attack Japan. It consisted of 25,000 men. Thus slightingly did the great conqueror gauge the prowess of the Island Empire.

King Wŭn-jong died while the prince was in China and the emperor hastened to confer upon the latter the insignia of royalty and send him back to take charge of affairs at home. This prince's name was Ko, posthumous title Ch'ung-ryŭl. The princess, his wife, did not accompany him to Koryŭ at first but waited to follow at leisure. When the young king arrived at Song-do has first act was to send an escort to bring his Mongol queen to him.

The Expedition Sets Sail

The events above recorded had followed thick and fast upon each other and now the great and long contemplated invasion of Japan was about to become an accomplished fact. The entire army of invasion rendezvoused on the southeastern coast of

Korea, opposite the islands of Japan. It consisted of 25,000 Mongol troops under Generals Hol Ton, Hong Ta-gu and Yu Pok-hyöng; and 15,000 Koryŭ troops under Gen. Kim Pang-gyŭng. The flotilla that was to carry this army across the straits consisted of 900 boats. Sailing from the shores of Korea the fleet made for the island of Iki near the mainland of Japan. Entering the harbor of Sam-nang they found a small garrison stationed there. Generals Kim and Hong attacked and routed this outpost, returning to the fleet, it is said, with 1000 heads. From this point they approached the mainland, landing at several points for the purpose of making a general advance into the country. The Japanese however attacked them briskly and checked the advance, but were themselves checked by a Koryŭ General, Pak, whom the Mongols praised highly for his valour.

It was a foregone conclusion that the allied Koryŭ and Mongol forces must retire sooner or later. Forty thousand men could do nothing on the Japanese mainland. So they retired slowly back to their boats. Nature aided the Japanese, for a storm arose which wrecked many of the boats and many more were scattered, so that the total loss to the allied forces was something over 13000. The scattered remnants of the fleet rendezvoused as best they could at the harbor of Hap and from there made their way back to Koryŭ. So ended the first attempt to subdue the Land of the Rising Sun.

The King's Mongol Queen

Meanwhile events were not at a standstill in the peninsula. The king went as far as P'yŏngyang to meet his bride. Escorting her back to the capital he gave her a palace of her own, fitted up according to her fancy. The records say that she had sheep skins hanging in the doorways. This would probably be in accord with Mongol ideas. The former queen was lowered to the position of second wife or concubine. The Mongolizing tendency had now gone so far that the king ordered the officials to adopt the Mongol coiffure. The order was not obeyed until after long and heated debate, but at last the conservatives were voted down and all submitted to the new style. At the same time the Mongol dress was also adopted.

An amusing incident is reported as having occurred about this time. A courtier named Pa-gyu observed to the king, 'The male population of the country has been decimated but there are still plenty of women. For this reason it is that the Mongols take so many of them. There is danger that the pure Koryŭ stock will become vitiated by the intermixture of wild blood. The king should let each man take several wives and should remove the restrictions under which the sons of concubines labour.' When the news of this came to the ears of the women they were up in arms, as least the married portion; and each one read to her spouse such a lecture that the subject was soon dropped as being too warm to handle. When the king passed through the streets with Pa-gyu in his retinue the women would point to the latter and say 'There goes the man who would make concubines of us all.'

Another Envoy to Japan

In spite of the failure of the plan of invasion, the emperor could not believe that Japan was serious in daring to oppose his will and so sent another envoy demanding that the Japanese sovereign come to Peking and do obeisance. We may well imagine with what ridicule this proposition must have been received in the capital of the hardy islanders.

THE ZENITH OF MONGOL INFLUENCE

The sporting proclivities of the Mongol queen of Koryŭ were an object of wonder and disgust to the people, for she was accustomed to accompany the king in his expeditions and was as good a horseman as any in the rout. It may well be imagined that the finances of the country were in bad shape, and it was found necessary to reconstruct the revenue laws to meet the constantly recurring deficit. For the first time in the history a general tax was levied on all the people, high and low alike. Hitherto taxes had been levied only on the better class of people. This tax was called the *hop'o* which means 'house linen,' for the tax was levied in linen cloth. This shows that although coin circulated, barter was as yet the main method of interchange of commodities.

The custom of dressing in white must be a fairly ancient one for we learn that at this time the government ordered the use of blue instead of white, as blue is the colour that corresponds to east. The birth of a son to the king's Mongol consort was the signal for great rejoicings and festivities. Everyone offered congratulations, even the discarded queen.

A Jealous Queen

It is said that the king paid some attention to this former queen and that it aroused the fierce jealousy of the Mongol queen. She declared that she would write and complain to the emperor that she was being ill-treated. She was dissuaded from this by the earnest entreaties of the officials. At the same time a further concession was made to the Mongolizing tendency by changing the names of official grades to those in use among the Mongols.

The emperor had not given up his plan of subduing Japan, and for this purpose he began the preparation of boats in the south of Korea, calling upon the Koreans to supply all the requisites. But this was not the only use to which he put his Koryŭ vassal, for he also demanded women and pearls; the former were taken from the men and the latter from the women; and both were sent to the Mongol court.

A Thrifty Queen

The Mongol queen of Koryŭ was a thrifty woman and let no small scruples stand in the way of the procuring of pin-money. She took a golden pagoda from one of the monasteries and melted it down. The bullion found a ready market. She also went into the ginseng raising business on her own account, taking people's fields by force and marketed the crop of ginseng in Nanking, where it brought a good price. She thus turned an 'honest' penny. But it all went against the aristocratic tendencies of the king. That the queen was not without a touch of superstition is shown by the fact that she desisted from accompanying the king to the grave of Wang Gon when told that the spirit of the founder of the dynasty was a strong one and that if she went she might be attacked by some dangerous disease.

When someone hinted to the queen that the former queen was plotting against her life she promptly had her seized and put to the torture, and it would have cost her her life had not the officials interfered and won the inquisitors over to clemency. But her oppression of the people went on unchecked and she sequestered so much of their property that hundreds of people were driven into actual mendicancy.

Even when news of her mother's death reached her she stopped feasting but a short time, to shed a few conventional tears, and then resumed her revels. This was perhaps her greatest offence in the eyes of the people of Koryŭ. But her affection for her husband was very real for we learn that when he was taken sick and she was told that it was on account of her lavish use of money, she stopped building, sent away her falcons and restored a gold pagoda to the monastery from which she had taken it. She had ideas of her own as to the proper treatment of women by the sterner sex, for when the king preceded her in one of the processions she turned back and refused to go. The king went back to pacify her but she struck him with a rod and gave him a round scolding. She was meanwhile doing a stroke of business in sea otter skins. She kept a large number of men hunting these valuable animals, but when she found they were 'squeezing' half the catch she imprisoned the offenders.

Mongol Influence at Its Zenith

It was not till 1279 that all the officials, high and low, military and civil, had adopted the Mongol coiffure and dress. It was now that the Mongol influence was at its zenith in the peninsula. In this year the whole royal family made a journey to Peking and it was the signal for a grand festival at that capital. It put an end once for all to the suspicions entertained by the emperor relative to the loyalty of the king of Koryŭ. The busybodies therefore found their occupation gone. On their return the queen resumed building operations, seized over 300 of the people's houses and had 1,000 men at work erecting a palace.

Second Invasion Planned

Meanwhile what of the Mongol envoy who had been sent to Japan with his daring demand that the Japanese sovereign go to Peking and do obeisance? He had been promptly killed, as might have been anticipated. When the king sent word to Peking that the emperor's envoy had been killed, another invasion was immediately decided upon; and the king was charged with the duty of preparing 900 vessels to transport a great army of invasion across the straits. The king was hardly prepared for such an undertaking. He was spending his time in revelry and debauchery. He called to Song-do all the courtesans, sorceresses, and female slaves and had them join in singing obscene songs for the delectation of his guests. His manner of life was in no sense worthy of his position. It is not surprising therefore that famine found its way to Koryŭ the following year, and the emperor had to give aid to the extent of 20,000 bags of rice.

The king wanted to lead the army of invasion, and so the emperor called him to Peking to discuss the matter. But Hong Ta-gu talked the emperor over and secured the post of General-in-Chief himself. He raised 40,000 regular troops and another general raised 100,000 more among the vassal tribes. The king advised that only the men from the dependent tribes be sent, but that their number be increased. To this the emperor did not consent, and soon the king came back to his capital where he went to work preparing the 900 boats, 15,000 sailors and 10,000 bags of rice, together with many other things that would be needed. The emperor sent Hong to superintend these preparations and the king, being thrown completely into the shade, could do nothing but obey orders. Hong was so obnoxious to the king that he requested the emperor to remove him and let

Gen. Kim Pang-gyŭng superintend the work of preparation. To this consent was given.

It was in the next year, 1282, that all the troops rendezvoused at Hap-p'o, now Ch'ang-wŭn, and prepared to embark. The king went down from the capital to review the whole array. There were 1,000 boats in all. Of Koryŭ soldiers there were 20,070, of Mongols there were 50,000. The soldiers from the dependent tribes, of which there were 100,000, had not yet arrived. It is hard to say just who these 100,000 men were. The records say they were from Kang-nam but they are also designated by another character in the records which would imply a different origin.

The Expedition Sets Sail

Then the whole flotilla sailed away to the conquest of Japan. They made for Tă-myŭng Harbor where the first engagement with the Japanese took place. At first the invaders were victorious and 300 Japanese fell, but when the latter were reinforced the Mongols drew back with great loss. The allied forces then went into camp where it is said that 3000 of the Mongols died of fever. Gen. Hong was very anxious to retreat, but Gen. Kim said, 'We started out with three month's rations and we have as yet been out but one month. We cannot go back now. When the 100,000 contingent arrives we will attack the Japanese again.' Soon the reinforcements came.

Terrible Catastrophe

The invading army now pulled itself together and sailed for the mainland of Japan. As they approached it a storm arose from the west and all the boats made for the entrance of the harbor together. As it happened the tide was running in very strong and the boats were carried along irresistibly in its grip. As they converged to a focus at the mouth of the harbor a terrible catastrophe occurred. The boats were jammed in the offing and the bodies of men and the broken timbers of the vessels were heaped together in a solid mass, so that, the records tell us, a person could walk across from one point of land to the other on the solid mass of wreckage. The wrecked vessels contained the 100,000 men from the dependent tribes, and all of them perished thus horribly, excepting a few who managed to get ashore. These afterwards told their story as follows: 'We fled to the mountains and lay hidden there two months, but the Japanese came out and attacked us. Being in a starving condition, we surrendered, and those of us who were in fair condition were made slaves and the rest were butchered.'

In that great catastrophe 8,000 Koryŭ soldiers perished, but the remaining Koryŭ and Mongol forces, beholding the miserable end of the main body of the invading army, turned their prows homeward and furled their sails only when they entered a Koryŭ harbor.

New Preparations

At first the emperor was determined to continue the attempt to subdue the Japanese, and immediately sent and ordered the king to prepare more boats and to furnish 3,000 pounds of a substance called in the records *tak soé*. The character *tak* means a kind of wood from whose pulp paper is made, and the character for *soé* means metal, especially such as is used in making money. Some have conjectured that this refers to paper money, others that it simply meant some metal.

A Koryŭ citizen, Yu Ju, advised the emperor to use only Koryŭ troops and the men from Kang-nam in his next invasion of Japan and to provide in advance 200,000 bags of rice in the peninsula. The emperor thereupon ordered the king to lay aside 40,000 bags with this end in view. The king answered that if all his officials could get but 10,000 bags, this greater number was surely out of the question. So he was told to set aside as many as he could.

The Plan Given Up

The following year, 1283, changed the emperor's purpose. He had time to hear the whole story of the sufferings of his army in the last invasion; the impossibility of squeezing anything more out of Koryŭ and the delicate condition of home affairs united in causing him to give up the project of conquering Japan, and he countermanded the order for the building of boats and the storing of grain.

The record of the next few years is hardly worth writing. The royal family went to Peking with 1,200 men as escort and remained there six months. Returning, they spent their time in trampling down good rice fields in the pleasures of the chase and in seeking ways and means of making government monopolies of various important commodities, especially salt. On a single hunting expedition 1,500 soldiers accompanied the royal party afield. The queen developed a strange propensity for catching young women and sending them to her people in Peking. A law was promulgated that before a young man married he must notify the government. This was done for the purpose of finding out where marriageable girls lived so that they could be the more easily seized and sent to China. One official cut off his daughter's hair when he found that she was to be sent to China. The king banished him for this and beat the girl severely. It is said that these girls upon arriving in China became wives, not concubines.

Famine in China

In 1289 a famine in China resulted in a demand for 100,000 bags of rice from Koryŭ. The king was at his wits end but by great exertion and self-sacrifice on the part of the officials 60,000 bags were collected. They were sent by boat, but 6000 were destroyed in a storm and 300 men were lost.

But now in 1290 a new element of danger appeared in the shape of the wild tribe of T'ap-dan across the northern border who began to ravage the outlying Koryŭ towns. When they had penetrated the country as far as Kil-ju the king sent an army against them, but more than 20,000 came swarming down from the north and seized two districts in Ham-gyŭng Province. They ate the flesh of men and dried the flesh of women for future consumption. The Koryŭ troops held them in check at first. The emperor sent 13,000 troops to reinforce the Koryŭ army. In spite of this, however, the king felt obliged to take refuge in Kang-wha for fear of surprise. The following year the T'ap-dan savages came as far south as Kyŭng-geui Province and all the officials and many of the people fled before them.

It was a literary man of Wŭn-ju who was destined to be the first to bring them to a halt. Wŭn Ch'ung-gap gathered about him all the strong men of the neighbourhood and drove back the van of the invading force. Then the great body of the savage horde came and surrounded the town. Wŭn killed the messengers they sent demanding surrender, and sent back the heads as answer. A desperate attack was made but the little garrison held firm till by a lucky chance a rumour of some kind caused a panic among the attacking forces and in the stampede that followed every man's sword was at his neighbour's throat. While this was going on Wŭn and his fellows made a sudden sally and captured the savage chief To Cha-do, and sixty of his attendants were cut down. The rabble then took to their heels and from that day never dared to attack any considerable town.

The spell of terror which had held the people of Koryŭ was now broken and they found no more difficulty in keeping these savages at arm's length. Ten thousand Mongol troops arrived and began a campaign against these freebooters and in Ch'ung-ch'ŭng Province had a splendid victory over them, leaving, it is said, a line of thirty *li* of dead as they pursued the flying enemy. When the Mongol troops went back home, their general told the emperor that the war had destroyed the crops of Koryŭ and that 100,000 bags of rice must be sent. The emperor consented, but when the rice arrived the officials and men of influence divided the rice among themselves, while the people went without.

A Son's Rebuke

All this time the crown prince was suffering a lively feeling of disgust at the sporting propensities of his father, and now that he was about to return from Peking he wrote his father a very sarcastic letter saying, 'As all the public money has been used up in hunting tournaments you must not lay an extra expense upon the treasury by coming out to meet me.' The king was ashamed and angry but went as far as P'yŭng-ju to meet his son and took advantage of the occasion to hunt along the way.

That Kublai Khan harbored no ill will against the Japanese on account of his failure to conquer them is shown by his sending back to their country several Japanese whom the Koreans had caught and carried to Peking. Two Koryŭ men carried them back to Japan; but the Japanese did not return the courtesy, for the two Koryŭ messengers were never seen again.

Timur Khan Makes Changes

The king and queen were both in China when the emperor Kublai died and they took part in the funeral rites, although the Mongol law forbade any outsider to participate in them. Timur Khan succeeded Kublai. He apparently had no intention of invading Japan, for of 100,000 bags of rice which had been stored in Koryŭ for that purpose, he sent 50,000 to the north to relieve a famine-stricken district. He also gave back to Koryŭ the island of Quelpart which had been in Mongol hands since the time when the Mongol and Koryŭ soldiers had put down the rebellion. From this time dates the use of the name Ché-ju, which means 'District across the water,' and by which the island has ever since been known.

The King Abdicates

The king had now completed his cycle of sixty-one years and the soothsayers were appealed to to read the future. They said evils were in store and he was advised to give amnesty to all but capital criminals, repair the tombs of celebrated men, give rice to the poor, and remit three years' revenue. But grey hairs had not brought wisdom to the king. His time was spent in frivolity and sensuality. The crown prince looked with unfriendly eye on these unseemly revels and when, in the following year, 1297, his mother, the Mongol princess, died, he claimed that her death was due to one of the favourite concubines, and as a consequence the suspected woman was killed. The prince had married a Mongol princess in China and now at her summons he went back to China. The old man, bereft of both wife and concubine, wrote the emperor that he wished to surrender the reins of power into the hands of his son.

The emperor consented and in the following year the prince was invested with the royal insignia, while his father was honoured with the title 'High King'. The new queen was a Mongol and as she came to the Koryŭ capital a new palace was constructed for her. But her royal husband saw fit to follow the example of his forebears and take to himself a concubine. The queen, by her frequent exhibitions of jealousy, lost what little love her lord had ever felt for her. She was not long in letting the state of affairs be known at Peking and soon an imperial mandate arrived consigning the concubine and her father to prison. Then another came remanding both to China. Then a high monk came to mediate between the king and queen. This proved ineffectual and the emperor commanded both king and queen to appear before him in Peking. It was done and the royal seals were put back into the hands of the aged king. The prince and his unhappy queen were kept in China ten years.

The close of the century beheld an old dotard on the throne of Koryŭ, so incapable of performing the duties of his high office that the emperor was obliged to send a man to act as viceroy while the old man spent his time trifling with mountebanks and courtesans. The records state that he had lost all semblance to a king.

A New Slave Law

The viceroy whom the emperor had sent was named Whal-yi Gil-sa, and one of his first proposals was to do away with slavery;

but objection was raised that then a slave might become an official and use his influence to wreak vengeance upon his former master. So a law was made that only the eighth generation of a manumitted slave could hold office.

In 1301 an envoy was sent to Peking to make the audacious proposal that the crown prince's wife should be made the wife of a Korean official named Chong. This was because the Koryŭ officials believed she had been criminally intimate with him and they were anxious to get the prince back on the throne. An official originated the scheme of having this Chong take the prince's wife and ascend the throne himself, but the emperor ordered him thrown into prison. When this had been done the aged king sent an envoy pleading that the prince be sent back to him. As this was not granted the king himself went to Peking where he lodged at first at his son's house, but after a quarrel with him moved to the house of the discarded princess, his daughter-in-law. The emperor tried to mediate between father and son but without effect. Then he tried to send the old man back to Koryŭ; but rather than go back the aged king took medicine to make himself ill and so incapable of travel. He was fearful that he would be assassinated on the way by his son's orders.

Ch'ung-sŭn Ascends the Throne

The emperor died in 1308 and was succeeded by Guluk Khan. This young man was the friend of the prince, and as a consequence the old king was thrown into prison, his nearest friends killed or banished and the young man was raised to a high position under the Chinese government and his friends, to the number of 180, were made officials. But it was the old man that the emperor finally sent back to Koryŭ to rule at the same time he making the prince king of Mukden. Though so far away from the capital of Koryŭ the prince was the one who really ruled Koryŭ, so the records say. The father soon died and the prince immediately proceeded to Song-do and assumed the throne in this same year 1308. His posthumous title was Ch'ung-sŭn.

He had been kept out of his own so long that he now proceeded to make up for lost time, and vied with his father's record in revelry and debauchery. It is said that a courtier took an axe and went to the palace, where he asked the king to decapitate him as the sight of these excesses made him hate life. The king was ashamed, though we are not told that he mended his ways.

A Kingless Country

In his second year he revived the government salt monopoly and put the money into his private purse. Heretofore it had been divided between certain monasteries and officials. The Mongol empress made him furnish large quantities of timber from Păk-tu Mountain, floating it down the Yalu. It was used in the building of monasteries. The whole expense was borne by the king. The latter was now spending most of his time in Peking. The Koryŭ officials earnestly desired him to come back to Song-do, but he refused. There was a constant flow of eunuchs and courtesans from Koryŭ to Peking and it would be difficult to imagine a more desperate condition of affairs in the king-deserted country. How it was being governed we do not know. It was probably governing itself. The rural districts, which had been laid waste by the Mongol armies and which had been deserted by their occupants, were probably being gradually occupied again and the less they heard of Song-do the better they liked it.

In the third year of his reign the king killed his son because some busybodies told him that the young man was conspiring to drive him from the throne. This shows the depths to which the court had sunk, when kings were not sure but that their own sons were their worst enemies. Orders kept coming from Peking to make certain eunuchs Princes. These orders could not be disregarded. These eunuchs had doubtless been in Peking and were known to be devoted to Mongol interests. All this time the king was in Peking where his presence began to be something of a bore. The mother of the emperor urged him to go back to Koryŭ. He promised to go in the following autumn, but when the time came he changed his mind and abdicated in favour of his second son.

The new king, named To, posthumous title Ch'ung-suk, came to the throne in 1314. One of his first acts was to take a thorough census of the people. Unfortunately the result is not recorded. The revenue laws were also changed and a new measurement of the fields was ordered with a view to a more effective collection of the revenue. The king likewise had ambitions along religious lines, for he sent 150 pounds of silver to Nanking to purchase books; and 10,800 were secured. The emperor also gave 4,070 volumes. These were doubtless Buddhist books and it is more than likely that many of the books in the Sanskrit or Thibetan character, still found in the monasteries in Korea, are copies of the works introduced into Koryŭ during these times.

King of Mukden

The king who had abdicated was sent back with his son, though he had abdicated solely for the purpose of being able to live permanently in Peking. He spent his time in attending Buddhist festivals, but when he saw into what ruins the palaces in Song-do had fallen he said, 'If my father had feasted less I should have had better palaces.' He soon returned to China where he devoted himself to letters. The emperor offered to make him his prime minister but he declined the honour. He mourned over the lack of letters in Koryŭ and came to realize that it was Buddhism that had proved the curse of the dynasty. He accepted the post of King of Mukden and later became Prime Minister to the emperor.

The young king went to Peking in 1317 to marry a Mongol Princess, and like his father was very loath to come back. We infer that the position of king in Song-do was so hedged about by priestcraft that it was much pleasanter for the king to reside at the Chinese court. Koryŭ must have been exceedingly poor after the desperate struggles she had been through and life in Peking with his hand in the imperial exchequer must have had its attractions.

At the end of a year however the king and his bride came back to Song-do. The records say that in order to induce him to come they had to bribe the soothsayers to tell him that if he did not come he would be involved in war. As soon as he arrived he began to search for unmarried women to send to Peking. He had turned pander to the Mongol court. The men of the upper classes hid their daughters and denied their existence for fear they would be seized and sent to Peking. He himself put in practice the principles he had imbibed at the Mongol court, and spent his days in hunting and his nights in high revelry.

King's Father Banished

The king's father who had been made king of Mukden, made a trip into southern China, or at least as far south as Chŭl-gang and Po-ta San where he engaged in Buddhist worship. Two years later he asked permission to repeat the visit and the emperor consented. But he was suddenly called back to Peking and ordered to go straight to Koryŭ. He refused and the emperor compelled him to cut his hair and to become a monk. He was banished to T'o-bŭn or San-sa-gyŭl in the extreme north. This was because one of the Peking eunuchs, who had formerly been a Koryŭ man and hated the king, told the emperor that the ex-king had on foot a scheme to raise a revolt in China.

At this time there was silver money in Koryŭ in the form of little bottle-shaped pieces of silver, but it was much adulterated by an alloy of copper. The king gave thirty of these bottles and the officials contributed a number more; and with them a silver image of Confucius was made, indicating a slight reaction against Buddhism.

In 1322 the emperor, being deceived by the lying representations of the king's cousin who wished to secure the throne of Koryŭ, ordered the king to Peking. The latter was glad to go, but was obliged to get away secretly by night for fear of being prevented by his officials. When he got to Peking the emperor took away his royal seal and ordered him to remain there, which he doubtless was nothing loath to do. The officials of Koryŭ joined in a letter begging the emperor to send him back, but without success, till in 1324 the emperor died and his successor proclaimed a general amnesty, of which the aged ex-king took advantage to return to Peking from his place of banishment in the north.

The king and queen returned to Koryŭ in the following year. No sooner were they settled in their palace again than they went on a pleasure trip to the Han River; but the trip ended disastrously for while away on the journey the Queen was confined and died in giving birth to a son. This shows to what extremes the passion for the chase led the court.

BEGINNING OF THE END OF THE KORYŬ DYNASTY

With the year 1329 begins a series of events that almost baffles description. The worst excesses of Rome in her decline could not have shown more horrible scenes than those which made the Koryŭ dynasty a byword for succeeding generations.

Horrible Excesses

The king's cousin, who was king of Mukden, was always slandering him to the emperor, for he was itching for the crown of Koryŭ himself. Meanwhile the king was building 'mountains' and pleasure houses without end and his hunters were his favourites by day and the courtesans his boon companions by night. His son was in Peking learning the ways of the Mongol court and preparing to prove as abandoned a character as his father. In 1331, at the request of the king, the emperor made the young man king. The cares of office seem to have interfered with his debaucheries. The prince's name was Ch'ung, posthumous title Ch'ung-hyé. He was sent to Song-do and his father called to Peking. This was well, for the young man hated his father intensely. No sooner had he assumed the reins of power then he ran to ten times the excess of riot that even his father had done. The whole of his newly acquired power was applied to the gratification of his depraved appetites and within a year so outrageous were his excesses that the emperor had to recall him in disgrace to Peking and send back the father to administer the government. This added fuel to the son's hatred of his father.

The reinstated king continued his old courses and added to his former record another desperate crime, in that he frequently stopped a marriage ceremony and forcibly carried away the bride to become a member of his harem. It was a marvel that the people did not rise and drive such a villain from the country. When he made a trip to Peking in 1336 the emperor made him carry his son back to Koryŭ. He was such a desperate scapegrace that Peking itself was not large enough to hold him.

The following year the emperor promulgated a singular order and one whose cause it is difficult to imagine. It was to the effect that all swords, bows, and other martial implements be put away from all Koryŭ houses and that no one be allowed to ride a horse; but all must go afoot. This may have been a precautionary measure to prevent the acquiring of skill in the use of weapons or in horsemanship, so as to render less probable the future use of such acquirements in an attack upon China.

At last, in 1340, the king died and it looked as if the desperate character who for one short year had played fast and loose with Koryŭ royalty would become king. A courtier, Cho Chŭk, surrounded the palace with soldiers with a view to assassinating the young man who had not yet received investiture from the emperor, and at the same time a message was sent to the deceased king's cousin, the king of Mukden, summoning him to Song-do. The young prince, bad as he was, had a considerable following, and a desperate fight ensued in which he was wounded in the shoulder. But Cho Chŭk's forces were routed and he himself caught and beheaded.

The emperor learning of this through the prince's enemies, called him to Peking and took him to task for killing Cho Chŭk, the friend of the king of Mukden; but the facts soon came out, and the prince was exonerated and sent back to Song-do, having been invested with the royal insignia. Unlike his father and grandfather, he did not marry a Mongol princess but took as his queen a Koryŭ woman. He likewise took a large number of concubines. Not content with this he had illicit commerce with two of his father's wives. The almost incredible statement is made in the records that on one occasion, feigning drunkenness, he entered the harem of his dead father and had the women seized and violated them. They tried to escape to China but he prevented them from securing horses for the purpose.

General Suffering

His profligate life was the curse of the country. Nothing was too horrible, too unnatural, too beastly for him to do, if it afforded him amusement. He sent 20,000 pieces of cloth together with gold and silver to purchase many things of foreign manufacture, but what these were we are not informed. One of his amusements was the throwing of wooden balls at a mark, but when this lost piquancy he substituted men for the target and frequently engaged in this truly inhumane pastime. General distress prevailed. Many died of starvation and many ran away to distant places and many became monks in order to escape the king's tyranny. Sons cut off their hair and sold it in order to secure food for aged parents. The prisons were full to overflowing. Suicide was a thing of daily occurrence.

Taxes Increased

The king sent to Kang-neung to levy a tax on ginseng, but as none could be found the messenger levied on the well-to-do gentlemen of the place and this was so successful that the king widened the scope of his operations and made it as hard to live in the country as at the capital. Everything that could possibly be taxed was put on the roll of his exactions. No form of industry but was crushed to the ground by his unmitigated greed. When amusements failed he tried all sorts of experiments to awaken new sensations. He would go out and beat the drum, to the sound of which the workmen were building the palace. This building had iron doors, windows and roof. If the king's pander heard of a beautiful slave anywhere she was seized and brought to this palace which was also her prison and where she spent her time in weaving in company with many other women who had been similarly 'honoured'. Often by night the king would wander about the city and enter any man's house and violate any of its inmates.

When this all came to the ears of the emperor he was furious. An envoy was sent to Song-do with orders to bring the wretch bound to Peking. The king came out to meet this envoy but the Mongol raised his foot and gave the wretch a kick that sent him sprawling on the ground. He was then bound and locked up and after things had been put in some sort of shape in the capital the king was carried away to Peking to answer to the emperor. Many of the king's intimates were killed and many fled for their lives. A hundred and twenty concubines were liberated and sent to their homes.

When the king was brought before the emperor the latter exclaimed 'So you call yourself a king. You were set over the

Koryŭ people but you tore off all their flesh. If your blood should become food for all the dogs in the world justice would still be unsatisfied. But I do not care to kill any man. I will send you to a place from which you will not soon return.' So he was placed on a bier, the symbol of humiliation, and sent away to Ké-yang 'twenty thousand *li* away,' so the records say. No man went with him save his bearers. They carried him from village to village like a dead man. He died on the journey at Ak-yang before reaching his place of exile. When the people of Koryŭ heard of this there was general rejoicing; and a proverb was made which runs, *Aya mangoji*. The *Aya* refers to Ak-yang where he died and *mangoji*, freely translated, means 'damned'.

A General Cleaning Out

The heir to the throne of Koryŭ was a lad of eight years. The emperor asked him, 'Will you be like your father or like your mother?' The lad replied, 'Like my mother,' and thereupon he was proclaimed king of Koryŭ. His posthumous title is Ch'ung-mok. Orders were sent to Song-do to discharge all the servants and officials of the late king, and to put an end to all the evils which had been fastened upon the people. The iron palace was turned into a school. The examination laws were changed. Heretofore the examination had been simply with a view to ascertaining the candidate's knowledge of the classics. Now it was made to include an exegesis of obscure passages and exercises in penmanship. This was followed by an essay on 'What is the most important question of the time.' The emperor also ordered the establishment of a new department, to be called the Bureau of General Oversight.

The empress of China at this time seems to have been a Koryŭ woman and her relatives, who abounded in the Koryŭ capital, expected to have their own way in all matters. This new department, however, arrested and imprisoned many of them and a number died in consequence. The empress therefore sent a swift messenger demanding the reasons for this. The reasons seem to have been good, for the matter was dropped. Of course the young king was not of an age to guide the affairs of state in person. We are left in ignorance as to what form of regency administered the government for him.

In 1348 the boy king died and the question as to succession arose. The king's younger brother Chi was in Koryŭ at the time; but Keui, the son of Ch'ung-suk, the twenty-seventh monarch of the line, was in China. The Koryŭ officials asked that Keui be made king, probably because he was of a proper age to assume the responsibilities of royalty; but the emperor refused, and the following year, 1349, Chi was made king at the age of twelve, posthumous title Ch'ung-jong. Keui, the unsuccessful candidate, was married to a Mongol princess, perhaps as a consolation for his disappointment.

Beginning of Japanese Depredations

With the year 1350 begins a series of Japanese depredations on the coasts of Koryŭ which were destined to cover a period of half a century and which, in their wantonness and brutality, remind us strongly of similar expeditions of the Norse Vikings on the shores of western Europe. In the second year of the young king these corsairs came, but were driven off with a loss of 300 men. Soon, as if in revenge, over 100 Japanese boats were beached on the shores of Kyŭng-sang Province; the government rice was seized and many villages wantonly burned.

That same year a kingdom called Ul-lam sent an envoy with gifts to the king of Koryŭ.

In 1351 again the Japanese corsairs came and ravaged the islands off Chul-la Province.

The emperor, for some reason not stated, decided to make Keui, his son-in-law, king of Koryŭ. He was therefore proclaimed king at the Mongol court and started for Song-do. This was the distinct wish of the Koryŭ officials and of course the boy upon the throne was helpless. He fled to Kang-wha and the next year was killed by poison, but by whose hand administered or at whose instigation is neither known nor recorded. This new king's posthumous title is Kong-min.

The Japanese cared for none of these changes but steadily pursued their ravages, gradually creeping up the western coast.

A Koryŭ man, Yi Săk, who had studied profoundly and had passed the civil examinations in China, now returned to Koryŭ and memorialized the king in reference to five special points, to wit, (1) The necessity of having definite boundaries for the fields. (2) Defence against the Japanese corsairs. (3) Making of implements of war. (4) The fostering of study and learning. (5) The evils of Buddhism.

Omens of the Fall of the Dynasty

All during this reign, so say the records, there were signs and omens of the fall of the dynasty. There were earthquakes, eclipses and comets; worms ate the leaves of the pine trees in the capital, and as the pine tree was the emblem of the dynasty this was ominous; red and black ants had war among themselves; a well in the capital became boiling hot; there was a shower of blood; for many days a fog like red fire hung over the land;

black spots were seen on the sun; there was a shower of white horse hair three inches long; hail fell of the size of a man's hand; there was a tremendous avalanche at Puk-san, near the present Seoul. These *ex post facto* prophecies show the luxuriance of the oriental imagination.

In spite of the Confucian tendency which had manifested itself Buddhism had no intention of letting go its hold on the government, and we find that in his second year the king took a Buddhist high priest as his teacher, and thus the direction was given to his reign that tended to hasten it toward its fall. He also conferred high positions upon Buddhist monks and so alienated the good will of all the other officials. This hostile feeling took definite shape when Cho Il-si surrounded the palace with a band of soldiers, killed many of the leaders of the party in power together with many of the relatives of the Mongol empress, and announced himself prime minister. To screen himself he told the king that it was not he who had caused the execution, but two other men; and he even went to the extreme of putting to death two of his confiding friends in order to give colour to this statement. But Cho Il-si had overestimated his strength and the king, by secret negotiations, was soon able to decorate the end of a pole with his head. Twelve of his accomplices were also killed.

As the Mongol empress was a Koryŭ woman, the maternal grandmother of the crown prince of China was of course a Koryŭ woman. She was living in state in Song-do when her grandson came from Peking to make her a visit. It is said that in the festivities which graced this unusual occasion 5,100 pieces of silk were used in making artificial flowers. Such a feast had never before been seen at the capital of Koryŭ, however frequent they may have been at Peking.

Trouble in China

The records state that in 1355 there was a great rebellion in China. We must remember that between the years 1341 and 1368 affairs were in a chaotic state in China. The last Mongol emperor, Tohan Timur, came to the throne in 1333 and gave himself up to licentiousness and luxury. No attention was paid to the filling of offices according to the time-honoured law of literary merit, but the best positions were given to Mongols by pure favouritism. This caused widespread dissatisfaction among the Chinese and from that time the doom of the Mongol dynasty was sealed.

In 1355 the low-born but brilliant leader Chu Yuan-chang, at the head of the insurrectionary army, crossed the Yang-tse River and took Nanking. This was the great rebellion spoken of in the Koryŭ annals and soon an envoy arrived from Peking demanding aid in the shape of soldiers. Twenty-three thousand men were sent on this forlorn hope. In 1356 a Mongol envoy brought incense to be burned in all the Koryŭ monasteries, doubtless with a view to securing supernatural aid against the rising Ming power.

At the same time great uneasiness was again caused by raids of the Japanese, which increased in frequency and extent. One gang of robbers alone carried out of Kyŭng-sang Province, at one time, 200 boatloads of rice. This year also saw the Ming forces pressing on toward Peking and driving the Mongols back step by step. As the fortunes of the Mongols waned the loyalty of Koryŭ waned accordingly. For the mass of the Koryŭ people, the Mongol yoke had never been less than galling, and they hailed the signs of the times which pointed toward her overthrow.

This tendency to restlessness under the Mongol yoke was shown when the Mongol envoy was carrying the incense about the country to various monasteries. Everywhere he treated the people like abject slaves and trampled on their prejudices and rights. When he came to Chul-la Province the governor promptly threw him into prison and put his son to death. The Mongols in Peking were of course too busy with their own troubles to attempt to chastise Koryŭ for this; and this very impunity added impetus to the anti-Mongol feeling.

Yi Whan-jo Appears on the Stage

In this same year, 1356, we see the first rising of the cloud that was soon to spread over the country and, breaking, clean the land of the corruption which had so long been festering at her core. This event was the coming to the capital of the father of the man who founded the present dynasty, on the ruins of Koryŭ. This man was Yi Cha-ch'un whose posthumous title, given after the founding of this dynasty, was Whan-jo. As his son founded this dynasty it will be fitting to inquire briefly into his antecedents.

His great-grandfather was Yi An-sa, a Koryŭ official who died in 1274, and who was afterwards given the title Mok-jo. His son was Yi Hăng-yi, born in Tŭk-wun in Ham-gyŭng Province, who was compelled by the Mongols to take office under them while they held possession of the north. His posthumous title is Ik-jo. His son was Yi Ch'un, born in Ham-heung in Ham-kyŭng Province, who held rank under Koryŭ between 1340 and 1345. His posthumous title is To-jo. His son was Yi Cha-Ch'un of whom we are now speaking. He was born in 1315 and at the time of which we are writing he was made prefect of his native place, Sang-sŭng, in Ham-gyŭng Province. This part of Koryŭ had been held by the Mongols during the whole period of their occupation of Koryŭ until their loosening grasp let it fall back into the hands of Koryŭ and the king hastened to reorganise his government there.

The relatives of the Mongol empress still nursed the delusion that they could do as they pleased in Koryŭ, secure in the possession of such powerful friends at Peking. But they soon discovered their mistake, for their misdeeds met the same punishment as did those of others. Infuriated at this they planned an insurrection. They thought this newly acquired district of Sang-sŭng would be the most likely to co-operate with them in this scheme; so they opened negotiations with its people. The king therefore summoned Yi Whan-jo to Song-do and warned him against these traitors. Foiled here, the empress' relatives appealed to the country to rise in defence of the Mongol supremacy, which was being thus rudely flouted.

Mongol Power Opposed

They learned what Koryŭ thought of Mongol supremacy when they were incontinently seized and put to death and their property confiscated. The next step was the sending back to China of the Mongol 'resident'. This was followed by an expedition into trans-Yalu territory which seized all the land there which formerly belonged to Koryŭ. Fearing, however, that he was going a little too fast, the king sent an envoy to Peking to tell the emperor that the local governor of the north was responsible for these reprisals and not the central Koryŭ government. Troops were nevertheless stationed in each of these newly acquired districts and fields were cultivated to provide for their maintenance.

Not long after this the important question of coinage came up. We have already seen that the medium in Koryŭ was little bottle-shaped pieces, but as these were each a pound in weight they could be used only for large transactions. Each one of them was worth 100 pieces of linen. It was decided to change to a system of regular coinage, and so the silver was coined into 'dollars' each worth eight pieces of five-strand linen. It is probable that in all small transactions barter was the common method of exchange although there may have been a metal medium of exchange as far back as the days of ancient Chosŭn, 1,000 years before Christ.

A New Capital

The question again came up as to the advisability of moving the capital to Han-yang, the present Seoul. Enquiry was made at the ancestral temple but what answer the spirits made, if any, we are not told. All dishes and implements as well as tile were made black because the peninsula is nearly surrounded by water and black is the colour that corresponds to water according to Chinese and Korean notions. Black was substituted for the prevailing colour in dress which was at that time blue-green, and men, women, and monks all donned the sable attire.

It was at length decided to change the capital to the other site and palaces were ordered built there. They were, so some say, probably outside the present south gate of Seoul.

It is said that in order to decide about the removal of the capital the king had recourse to that form of divination which consisted in making scrawls at random with a pen and then examining them to see what Chinese characters the marks most resembled. At first they did not favour a change, but after several trials the favourable response was obtained.

Alarming Japanese Raids

The year 1359 beheld a recurrence of the dreaded Japanese incursions. At this time the robbers burned 300 Koryŭ boats at Kak-san. An official, Yi Tal-jung, was sent to govern the great north-eastern section of the land. He was a friend of Yi Whan-jo, the prefect of Sang-sŭng. As he approached that place his friend Yi Whan-jo came out to meet him, accompanied by his son Yi Song-gye who was to become the founder of the present dynasty, and whom we shall designate by his posthumous title T'ă-jo. When Yi Whan-jo handed his friend a cup of wine he drank it standing, but when Yi T'ă-jo handed him one, so the story runs, he drank it on his knees. When the father demanded why this greater deference was shown his son the guest replied, 'This boy is different from us,' and, turning to the young man, he continued. 'When I have passed away you must always befriend my descendants.'

The Japanese raids had now reached such alarming proportions that an extra wall was built about Song-do and all the government granaries along the coast were moved far inland to be out of the reach of piratical parties, who would naturally hesitate to go far from their boats.

The breaking up of the Mongol power was foreshadowed by the act of a certain Mongol district Hă-yang which, with its garrison of 1,800 men, now came and enrolled itself under the banner of Koryŭ. How had the mighty fallen! Less than eighty years before the world had trembled beneath the hoofbeats of the 'Golden Horde'. This was followed by the submission of a wild tribe in the north called Pang-guk-chin, and a Mongol rebel sent a messenger with gifts to the court of Koryŭ. Meanwhile the Japanese were ravaging the southern and western coasts without let or hindrance. It was a curious spectacle, a country eaten up by its own excesses receiving humble deputations from former masters and at the same time being ridden over roughshod by gangs of half-naked savages from the outlying islands of Japan.

The 'Red-Head Robbers'

There was one tribe in the north however, called the Hong-du-jŭk or 'Red-Head Robbers,' who threatened to invade the country, but forces were sent to guard against it. In the case of the Japanese marauders the difficulty was to know where they were going to strike next. There was military power enough left in Koryŭ had it been possible to so place the forces as to intercept or bring to action the robber gangs. The Japanese had really begun to threaten Song-do itself and the king wished to move the capital to Su-an in Whang-hă Province. He went so far as to send a commissioner to look over the site and report.

The king was not blessed with an heir, and in 1360 he took a second wife, which was the cause of constant quarrelling and bickering.

The 'Red-Head Robbers' were led by Kwan Sŭn-sang and P'a Tu-ban. They now took the city of Mukden and entering Liaotung, sent a letter to the king of Koryŭ saying 'We have now consolidated our power and intend to set up the Sung dynasty again.' The Mongols were thus beset on both sides and were in desperate straits. Three thousand of the 'Red-Heads' crossed the northern border and carried fire and sword into the frontier towns. A Mongol general, deserting the banners of his waning clan, took service with these people. His name was Mo Ko-gyŭng. He collected 40,000 men and crossed the Yalu. Eui-ju fell forthwith and the prefect and 1,000 men perished. Chŏng-ju soon fell and In-ju was invested, but a stubborn resistance was here encountered.

The prefect, An U, was the only prefect in the north who was not afraid of the invaders. He made light of their power and by swift countermarches and brilliant maneuvers succeeded in making them fall back to Chöng-ju. In the meantime, Gen. Yi An was sent north to P'yŏngyang to take charge of the army of defence. The tide of fortune had turned again and the invaders were in full march on P'yŏngyang.

P'yŏngyang Taken

A council of war was held at which it appeared that all the generals were about equally frightened. With a powerful force in hand and an easily defended town to hold they still considered only how best to make a retreat. Some were for burning everything behind them and retiring to some point more easy of defence; but Gen. Yi An thought they had better leave a large store of provisions in the city, for the enemy would pause and feed there until everything was gone, and this would give the Koryŭ army time to gain needed reinforcements. This course would also appear so foolish to the enemy that few preparations would be made to meet the Koryŭ troops later.

This plan was adopted and the army retired into Whang-hă Province and left the gates of P'yŏngyang open to the invaders. This caused the greatest consternation in the capital, and every citizen was under arms. The king immediately sent and deprived Gen. Yi An of the office which he had so grievously betrayed and put the command into the hands of Gen. Yi Seung-gyŭng.

The invading host was now feasting in P'yŏngyang and the king and queen in Song-do were practicing horse-back riding with the expectation that they would be obliged to leave the capital. It was the beginning of winter and the cold was intense. The Koryŭ soldiers died by hundreds and the people were being wantonly killed by foraging parties of the 'Red Heads'. The records say that they left 'heaps upon heaps' of dead in their track.

'Red Heads' Beaten

As in duty bound the Koryŭ forces went north and engaged the invaders at P'yŏngyang. At first the latter were successful and 1,000 Koryŭ troops were trampled under the hoofs of the enemy's horses; but in the end the 'Red Heads' were defeated and, retreating northwards, were hotly pursued as far as Hamjŭng. There they were reinforced and attempted to make a new stand; but the Koryŭ troops, drunk with success, attacked them with such abandon that they were obliged to build a palisade within which they intrenched themselves. The Koryŭ generals surrounded this stockade and, by a simultaneous assault of horse and foot, broke through the barrier and put the occupants, numbering 20,000, to the sword. The leader, Whang Chi-sŭn was taken alive. A remnant fled to the Yŭn-ju River where the ice broke beneath them and 2,000 perished. The few survivors made a desperate stand on a hill but were starved out and compelled to continue their flight, in which hundreds more were cut down along the road; and at last, out of 40,000 men who had come across the Yalu, just 300 recrossed it and were safe.

Hardly had this happened when seventy boatloads of these same 'Red Heads' arrived at P'yŭng-ju and soon after 100 boatloads more disembarked at An-ak and scoured the surrounding country. They were, however, soon put to flight by Gen. Yi Pang-sil whom the king rewarded richly for his services.

King Favours a Mongol Pretender

It was at this time that the king first received an envoy from Chang Sa-sŭng, a pretender to the Mongol throne. The king made the first move toward breaking away from the Mongol yoke by sending an envoy in return. The Koryŭ court evidently was in great doubt as to just how matters were going to turn out in the struggle that was under way in China. By favouring these advances on the part of a Mongol, whether of the imperial family or not, it is probable that the king lost the goodwill of the Mings who, as we shall see, looked with satisfaction upon the overthrow of Koryŭ and the founding of the present dynasty.

The alarming increase both in the frequency and the violence of the Japanese incursions gave scope for the development of the military genius of Gen. Yi Whan-jo, the father of the founder of this dynasty. He was appointed general of the west to guard against the freebooters. The people of Song-do were in dismay over the proximity of the dreaded Japanese and over the defeat of all the armies sent to put them down. Many civil officials took part in the martial preparations and even took the field in defence of their country. The Japanese were now penetrating Kyŭng-geui Province. In this year, 1360, they landed on Kang-wha, killed 300 men and stole 40,000 bags of rice. So many men were in mourning that the king was obliged to curtail the period of mourning from three years to only a few days. The palace in Han-yang had now been completed and the king removed to that place, apparently because it was further from the seashore and more difficult of access by the Japanese.

SIN-DON BECOMES THE FAVOURITE

With the opening of the year 1361 Yi Whan-jo was appointed general of all the forces in the north and north-east. This was done against the advice of one of the officials who told the king that as Gen. Yi was from the north-east it was dangerous to appoint him general over the forces there, for untoward events were likely to happen. The king turned a deaf ear to this warning, which indeed was unnecessary, for the king had no more loyal subject that Yi Whan-jo. The king, having feasted the new appointee, sent him on his mission and himself returned to Song-do.

Ere long came reports of new and terrible ravages by the Japanese along the southern coast, especially at Nam-hă, Ko-sŭng, Kö-je and Ul-ju, while at Fusan they stole a large number of Korean boats. A garrison had been stationed in the south to be used in just such emergencies, but it had been used for so many different things that it could not be concentrated upon any given point; so levies were made on the common people. These levies went under the name of Yŭn-ho-gun, or 'Smoke-house Soldiers' because from every house where smoke was seen arising a man was requisitioned. At the same time the governor of Chŭl-la Province advised the establishment of a horse relay system, but the suggestion was not acted upon.

Yi Whan-jo Dies

At this time the king lost the services of Gen. Yi Whan-jo who died at his post. His son, Yi Sŭng-gye, better known by his title Yi T'ă-jo, stepped into his father's place. At the very beginning of his martial career an opportunity presented itself for him to perform a signal service for the king. A certain Pak Eui deemed that the time was ripe for an insurrection and he began to take steps in that direction, but the king sent the young general, Yi T'ă-jo, against him and the little blaze was promptly stamped out. As a consequence the young man was confirmed in the position of military governor of the north and east, and under his command was placed a large body of troops.

New Invasion by the 'Red Heads'

And now there burst upon the country another storm of fire and blood. The 'Red Heads' had been gaining ground rapidly and were now ready to take their revenge for the terrible reverses they had suffered during the previous invasion. They crossed the Yalu 200,000 strong under the leadership of generals Pan-sŭng Sa-yu and Kwan Sŭng-săng. The king promptly sent Gen. Yi Pang-sil against them and hastened to swell the army to as high a point as possible. The officials and monks and other people of means brought horses or provisions, while the walls of Song-do were guarded with jealous care.

In the very first engagement the Koryŭ army was crumpled up like paper and one of the leading generals was killed. The 'Red Heads' sent a letter to the king saying, 'We have ten million men and there is no escape for you except in prompt surrender.' It seemed true, for the invading army swept like a cyclone though the north, and in Song-do panic reigned. Flight seemed imperative. The women and children belonging to the royal household were sent away first and the king was about to follow, when the defeated Gen. Yi Pang-sil came hurrying in and implored the king not to run away but to rally the people about him and stand the siege. The king went to the centre of the city, 'Big Bell Street,' and submitted the question to the people, asking whether they would rally round him. Just two men responded. This settled the matter and the king and queen, each on horseback, rode out the south gate, while behind them came a weeping crowd of old men, women, and children. Such was the confusion that parents lost their children and families were scattered. The king's escort consisted of only ten men. When he arrived at the Im-jin River he sent messengers in all directions summoning all loyal soldiers to rally round him.

The northern savages swept down upon the devoted city, sat down in its palaces, and gave themselves up to every form of excess. They feasted upon the cattle and horses, hanging their hides upon the city wall and pouring water over them and letting it congeal, thus preventing the citizens from making their escape from the city clandestinely.

The king in his flight carried terror with him, for the people thought the enemy would be in hot pursuit; so they scattered in every direction. This displeased the king so much that when he arrived at the capital of Ch'ung-ch'ŭng Province he imprisoned the governor. From that point he hurried southward as far as Pak-ju, now An-dong, in Kyŭng-sang Province.

Day by day the horrible orgies of the savages in Song-do increased in barbarity. It is said that they cooked and ate little children and that they cut off the breasts of women and fed on them.

Plans for Defence

In the midst of these vicissitudes the king appointed Chŏng Se-un as General-in-Chief of all the Koryŭ forces. He was a wise and loyal man and was ever thinking of ways and means of checkmating the invaders. He advised the king to send out a general letter encouraging the people and calling all the soldiers to rally to the defence of the country. The officials were also encouraged and made to feel that their utmost endeavours must be put forth in the good cause. The generals were all exhorted to do their best and were threatened with death in case they proved unfaithful. So the campaign was opened. The savages had looted all the towns about Song-do and had taken Wŭn-ju and killed its prefect. They also went north to An-byŭn in Ham-gyŭng Province where the people pretended to surrender, but, having gotten their conquerors intoxicated, they fell upon and killed them. The same tactics were tried in Kang-wha with equal success.

Gen. Chöng Se-un now appeared before Song-do with 200,000 troops. These figures must surely be an exaggeration for we can hardly suppose Koryŭ able at that time to put that number of men in the field. Snow and rain added to the difficulties of the situation. A spy returned and said that the troops of the enemy were massed inside the South Gate and that if a picked body of men could gain entrance somewhere and attack them from behind they could be easily overcome. At the dead of night a picked body of horsemen gained admittance somewhere in the rear of the city and fell with fury upon the garrison. At the same time the main body advanced to attack the South Gate. The savages, not knowing the size of the attacking force and being surprised from behind were thrown into confusion and attempted to run away. Gen. Yi T'ă-jo distinguished himself by pursuing and capturing Kwan Sŭn-săng the leader of the hostile force. In this stampede the routed savages trod on and killed each other by hundreds. In the centre of Song-do the dead were piled in heaps.

It is said, though it must be an exaggeration, that 100,000 men perished miserably on that night. As a result of this battle several Mongol seals which the savages had taken in previous fights with the imperial armies, were recovered.

Some of the generals advised that a remnant of the enemy be spared; so the Sung-in and T'an-hyŭng gates were thrown open and Pa Tu-ban and his remaining followers hastened out and made for the Yalu River.

It is related that during the fight on that eventful night a body of Koryŭ troops collided with a company of the enemy and a melée ensued near the East Gate, where the soldiers trod on each other. Gen. Yi T'ă-jo was there and was stabbed in the back with a spear. Finding himself in extremely narrow quarters he drew his sword and, hewing a path through the enemy, leaped the wall, horse and all, for he was in the saddle. The spectators thought he was a spirit. A volume might be filled with the stories of the wonderful achievements of this man, but most of them are figments of the imagination, invented at a later period to add lustre to the name of the founder of the dynasty.

The capable leader Gen. Chöng Se-un, met the fate which has been the curse of Korean history from the beginning to the present time. Kim Yong-an, a jealous official, forged a royal order for his execution and sent it to Gen. An U who promptly carried it out. When the king learned of this he thought it was an incipient revolution but soon the other generals joined in a letter to His Majesty saying that it had been done because the murdered man was a traitor. The king accepted this as true and rewarded the murderers.

The fortress of Sang-sŭng near the Tu-man River had long been under Mongol control and was governed by a Koryŭ renegade Cho Whi and afterwards by his descendants as a hereditary fief. Now when Koryŭ once more assumed control, Cho So-săng, the then chief of this anomalous settlement, fled to Mukden where he joined the banners of a wild tribe under the lead of Nap-t'ap-chul, and proposed to them to make a raid into Koryŭ. This they did, crossing the Yalu and ravaging as far as Puk-ch'ung and Hong-wŭn. This promised to become a serious matter, but the difficulty of the situation for Koryŭ was increased tenfold by a fresh invasion of the south by Japanese.

The king was on his way back to Song-do when news of these two disasters reached him. Things looked desperate, but to add to the hopelessness of the situation the same Kim Yong-an who had murdered Gen. Chöng now compelled the king to kill Gen. An U on the ground that it was he who had killed Gen Chöng. The monster then proceeded to killed his own brother, and induced the king to put to death generals Yi Pang-sil and Kim Teuk-pă, two of the best surviving generals. It is a wonder that Gen. Yi T'ă-jo was spared. Song-do had been so roughly handled that the king feared the historical records would be lost or destroyed; so he now sent men to look them up and put them in a place of safety.

Gen. Yi Brings Nap-t'ap-chul to Terms

The wild Nap-t'ap-chul having been so successful in their first venture, now once more entered Koryŭ territory and as the general sent against them was not able to check their advance Gen. Yi T'ă-jo was appointed to this place. The enemy was encamped in Hong-wŭn in Ham-gyŭng Province. Gen. Yi attacked them there and routed them with a loss of 1,000 men. Near Ham-hung they made a stand and defended themselves desperately, but he soon had them in full flight once more. Taking 600 picked cavalrymen he pursued them to Ch'a-ryăng Pass and secured another victory. Only one of the enemy fought well. This man fought aways in front of Gen. Yi. The latter feigned flight to draw him on and then suddenly turning attacked his pursuer and laid him low with an arrow from his unerring bow. The women who followed the camp of the invading army came out and taunted the men saying 'You have overcome everyone but these Koryŭ people; them you cannot conquer. You had better retreat and make for home.' The enemy called a truce and told Gen. Yi that they had come not to attack Koryŭ but the 'Red Heads'. This was a mere ruse to save time. Gen. Yi knew this and drawing an arrow to the head shot one of the leaders of the enemy through the body. At last he gave orders to his archers to shoot the horses from under the enemy. This decided the battle and the Nap-t'al-chul sued for peace. In recognition of these services the king appointed him general of all the forces in the north. The general then proceeded to annihilate all the colonies and settlements of the obnoxious Nap-t'ap-chul throughout the entire north, and having placed them where they belonged, showed them that their only hope was in making a lasting treaty with Koryŭ. This they were quite willing to do.

As the king came slowly north toward the capital the officials urged that Song-do was too small for the capital and too near the sea to be well protected from the Japanese corsairs. They therefore urged him to remain for a time at Ch'ŭng-ju, and he gave consent.

Quelpart Revolts

And now, strange to relate, Quelpart, at the instigation and under the leadership of Ho-dok-ko Pul-wha, who had been stationed there three years before to take charge of the horse breeding industry, revolted from the sway of Koryŭ and became at least nominally a part of the Yuan empire.

In order to reward the soldiers who had done such good work in the north the king levied a special tax on the people which they gave with such poor grace that they called it the 'tax without reason'.

In 1362 the emperor of China, led to it by the empress, whose seditious relatives had forfeited their lives in Koryŭ, proclaimed one Hye, called Prince Tok-heung, a relative of the king, as king in his place. But Koryŭ well knew that the old-time power of the Mongols was gone and so prepared to resist the order.

Early in 1363 the king at last re-entered his deserted capital. A strong force was sent north to guard against the pretender and an envoy was sent to Peking to ask why there were two kings for Koryŭ. The emperor replied that the newly appointed one was the right one and that he must be received in Koryŭ. To this the envoy replied, 'Though you kill me and smear my blood upon my clothes I will not accompany the pretender back to Koryŭ.' The emperor praised the envoy's bravery and did not insist upon the demand.

A Koryŭ official named Kim Yong-an, whose evil deeds we have already related, now desired to kill the king and bring in the pretender. A eunuch, An To-jok, knew of the plot and on the appointed night personated the king and was killed by the assassin's hand. The plotter was forthwith seized, drawn and quartered, and his limbs were sent throughout the land as a warning to other malcontents. The emperor was urged to send the pretender as a prisoner to Koryŭ but of course he refused. Not only so, but he also ordered the king to send the royal seals to Peking. The king refused and began preparations for defence against a possible invasion.

Mongol Invasion

He did not have to wait long, for with the opening of the year 1364 a Mongol army 10,000 strong crossed the Yalu and besieged Eui-ju. In the fight at that point the Koryŭ forces were completely routed, though not till after great valour had been shown by Gen. An U-gyŭng against overwhelming odds. The Koryŭ forces retreated in disorder to An-ju. Panic prevailed among all the people of that section for they thought the horrors of the former Mongol invasion were about to be repeated.

The king sent Gen. Ch'oé Yŭng with a considerable force to An-ju where he made all his generals swear to stand by the colours to the last. He executed a number of fugitives as an example to the rest and soon succeeded in restoring some semblance of order in the camp. Gen. Yi T'ă-jo was ordered with 1,000 soldiers from the northeast province to An-ju. Also generals Yi Sun, U Che, and Pak Ch'un were ordered to the same point, and the army thus consolidated assumed large proportions, but the men were miserably dressed and fed, and the death rate was high. Desertions were of frequent occurrence.

Gen. Yi T'ă-jo's influence in the northeast is proved by the commotion that followed when he left. The remnant of the Yŭ-jin tribe, led by Sam Seun and Sam Ka seized the whole of this northeast and the people were longing for the return of Gen. Yi. These two Sams were cousins of Gen. Yi and they had fled beyond the northern border and joined the wild Yŭ-jin folk.

Gen. Yi Drives Back the Mongols

The combination of the generals gave great confidence to the troops and when the battle was joined at Chöng-ju the Mongol forces were badly defeated. A Mongol general's body was taken and sent all about that section to encourage the people and make them believe their troubles were near an end. Gen. Yi blamed the other generals for not following up their advantage and they became angry and said, 'If you are so brave, you had better try it yourself.' So the very next day he led the army out and surrounded the Mongol forces at Su-ju near the sea, where another glorious victory was won. That night the remnant of the Mongols fled back to the Yalu. Gen. Yi gave chase and it is said that only seventeen of the Mongol army got back in safety across that Rubicon of Korea. This done, Gen. Yi returned to his northeast province and drove back to their haunts the wild tribe who had taken advantage of his absence.

Gen. Yi T'ă-jo was steadily rising in favour although like Wang Gon he wisely stayed as far as possible from his royal master. The king now conferred upon him the title of Mil-jik-sa which means 'The Messenger who Restores Confidence and Firmness'.

The Japanese had not ceased their incursions. Only a year had passed since 200 boat loads had ravaged the southern coast and now a like number swept the island of Kal-do in the south, so that from many a district no revenue rice was forthcoming. It is to be feared that this was the principal cause of uneasiness in Song-do – the loss of revenue. Troops were sent and a fleet of eighty war boats to guard the coast and to convoy the revenue junks, but these unexpectedly fell in with a Japanese fleet and were all lost. This disaster caused a panic among the people of Kang-wha and Kyo-dong Island. The governor of Chŭl-la Province came northward with troops guarding the revenue but he too met Japanese and lost all the rice and half his men.

This same year 1364 a Mongol official told the emperor that the king of Koryŭ ought to be allowed to retain his position; and the emperor listened to him. The renegade Ch'oé Yu was sent back to Koryŭ where he was imprisoned and executed. The Koryŭ envoy Yi Kong-su also returned from Peking. A very neat story is told of him. As he was pursuing his way across a wide plain which seemed to have no inhabitants he was obliged to feed his animals with the standing grain. When he was preparing to resume his way he took a bolt of linen and wrote upon it 'The price of grain', and left it among the standing barley. His attendants said, 'But the owner of the grain will never get it. Someone will steal it.' The envoy replied, 'That is not my affair. I will have done my duty.' The king wished the emperor to send the would-be king to Koryŭ but to this consent was not given.

Japanese Creep Nearer

The Japanese crept nearer and nearer to Song-do with every new expedition. They went into the temple to the dead and carried away a picture of the king. It was with great difficulty that they were dislodged and driven away.

In 1365 when the queen was confined the king ordered the monks to worship on every mountain top and at every monastery to ensure a safe delivery, but all to no avail. She died in giving birth to the child and the king was inconsolable. Treasure was poured out like water to make the funeral the most imposing that had ever been seen in Koryŭ. For three years following the king ate no meat.

The King Meets Sin-don

It was in this year that the king had that singular dream which led to such disastrous results. He dreamed that someone attempted to stab him, but a monk sprang forward and by intervening saved his life. The face of this monk remained stamped on his memory. Soon after this he met a monk, Sin-don, whose face was the same as that of the monk who had saved his life in the dream. He was the son of a slave in Ok-ch'ŭn Monastery and he was looked down upon and despised by the other monks. The king took this Sin-don to himself, raised him to high position, and lavished upon him wealth and honours. As a fact this Sin-don was a most unprincipled, licentious, and crafty man, but always when in the presence of the king he assumed the sedate demeanour of the philosopher and for many a year completely hoodwinked his royal master. The other officials expostulated in vain. In vain did they urge that this monk was a beast in human shape. The king considered him well-nigh inspired. He believed that it was jealousy that prompted their antagonism and rather enjoyed getting an outsider in and showing them that office and honours did not always go by inheritance.

This new favourite soon began to urge the banishment of this or that official and the king always complied. On this account the feeling against him rose to such a pitch that the king was obliged to send him away for a time lest he should be killed. He remained in this retreat until the king had put to death some of his worst enemies. At last the king sent and recalled him; but the crafty man answered, 'I cannot go back. It is not right that I should hold office.' When the king reiterated his pressing invitation the monk replied, 'I am afraid that you will listen to my enemies.' To this the king made answer 'I swear by the sun, the moon, the stars, heaven and earth that I will listen to no one but you.' So the wily man came back and from that day completely dominated the king. He exaggerated the faults of his enemies and so gradually supplanted them with his creatures. It is claimed of him that he built a dark vaultlike room where he indulged in almost incredible excesses. He gave out that he could cure barrenness, and by his evil practices brought down upon himself the maledictions of the whole people. The king alone would believe no ill of him. He said he was the greatest prodigy in the world.

At this time the Mongol empire was on the verge of its fall and Koryŭ envoys found it impossible to force their way through to Peking and so were compelled to desist. It is a noteworthy fact that though Koryŭ hated the Mongols she nevertheless held fast to them till the very last moment.

An Heir to the Throne

At this time it happened that the king was without an heir and both he and the court were anxious about the succession. The records say that he was so anxious to have a son that he committed an act almost if not quite unparalleled in the history of any land, civilized or savage. Having become prematurely old by his terrible excesses, he introduced a number of young men into the palace and gave them the *entré* into the queen's apartments, hoping thereby that his hopes might be realized. In this he was disappointed.

One day while passing an hour in the apartments of his favourite, Sin-don, he noticed there a newborn babe, the son of one of Sin-don's concubines. He seemed pleased with the child and Sin-don asked him to adopt it as his own. The king laughed but did not seem averse to the proposition. Returning to the palace he summoned the officials and told them that for some time he had been frequenting the apartments of Sin-don and that he had gotten a son by one of the women there. He knew well enough that if he proposed to adopt Sin-don's son the opposition would be overwhelming, so he took this means of carrying out the plan. Of course it is impossible to verify the truth of this statement. It may have been a fabrication of the historians of the following dynasty in order to justify the founder of the new dynasty in overthrowing Koryŭ. The annals of the Ming dynasty say that it was the king's son and not Sin-don's.

In 1366 the opposition to the favourite increased in intensity and the king was almost buried beneath petitions for his banishment or death. These the king answered by banishing or killing the senders and by this means the open opposition was put an end to. The wily monk knew that he needed more than the king's favour in order to maintain his position of honour, and so he began to take away the fields and other property of high officials and distribute them among the people in order to curry favour with them. This brought from the officials a new and fiercer protest and they told the king that these acts would make his reign a subject of ridicule to future generations. While this did not move the king to active steps against Sin-don it caused a coolness to spring up between them. The favourite saw that he had been going too far and he tried to smooth the matter over by returning the property that had been sequestered. At the same time he secured the liberation of many slaves. [...]

All this time the Japanese were busy at the work of pillage and destruction. They took possession of an island near Kang-wha with the intention of fortifying it and making of it a permanent rendezvous. They landed wherever they pleased and committed the most horrible excesses with impunity. The Koryŭ troops were in bad condition. They had no uniforms and their arms were of the poorest kind and mostly out of order. They dared not attack the Japanese even when there was good hope of success. The generals showed the king the ways and means of holding the freebooters in check but he would not follow their advice, probably on account of the expense. He paid dearly for his economy in the end.

Sin-don the 'Tiger'

The mother of the king could not be brought to treat Sin-don with respect. When the king expostulated with her and told her that the favourite was the pillar of the state she declared that he was a low-born adventurer and that she would not treat him as her equal. From that time she incurred the deadly enmity of the favourite who used every means in his power to influence the king against her.

He became suspicious of everyone who held any high position and caused many of the highest officials to be put to death. He was commonly called 'The Tiger'. The depth of the king's infatuation was shown when in this same year he went to a monastery to give thanks to Buddha for the cessation of famine, which he ascribed to his having taken Sin-don as counsellor. It is also shown in the impunity with which Sin-don took the king to task in public for certain things that displeased him. The favourite was playing with fire. The people sent to the king repeatedly asking if the rumours of the favourite's drunkenness and debaucheries were correct. But the king's eyes had not yet been opened to the true state of affairs and these petitioners were severely punished.

THE FALL OF SIN-DON

The year 1367 saw no diminution of the symptoms that proclaimed the deep-seated disease that was eating at the vitals of Koryŭ. Sin-don even dared to flout the emperor by scornfully casting aside an imperial missive containing a notification of his elevation to an honourary position. The king continued to abase himself by performing menial duties in Buddhistic ceremonies at his favourite monastery. Sin-don added to his other claims the power of geomancy and said the king must move the capital to P'yŏngyang. He was sent to look over the site with a view to a removal thither, but a storm of hail frightened him out of the project. Returning to Song-do he refused to see the king for four days, urging as his excuse the fatigue of the journey. His encroachments continued to such a point that at last he took no care to appear before the king in the proper court dress but came in the ordinary dress of the Koryŭ gentleman, and he ordered the historians not to mention the fact in the annals.

The Mongol horse breeders still ruffled it in high style on the island of Quelpart where they even saw fit to drive out the prefect sent by the king. For this reason an expedition was fitted out against them and they were soon brought to terms. They however appealed to the emperor. As it happened the Mongol emperor was at this time in desperate straits and foresaw the impossibility of long holding Peking against the Ming forces. He therefore formed the plan of escaping to the island of Quelpart and there finding asylum. For this purpose he sent large store of treasure and of other necessaries to this place. At the same time he sent an envoy to the court at Song-do relinquishing all claim to the island. In this way he apparently hoped to gain the goodwill of Koryŭ, of which he feared he would soon stand in need. The king, not knowing the emperor's design, feared that this was a device by which to raise trouble and he hastened to send an envoy declaring that the expeditions to Quelpart were not in reference to the Mongols there but in order to dislodge a band of Japanese freebooters. The former prefects had always treated the people of Quelpart harshly and had exacted large sums from them on any and every pretext; but the prefect now sent was determined to show the people a different kind of rule. He even carried jars of water from the mainland rather than drink the water of Quelpart. So at least the records affirm. Naturally the people idolized him.

Mongol Empire Falls

The year 1368 opened, the year which beheld the demolition of the Mongol empire. It had risen less than a century before and had increased with marvellous rapidity until it threatened the whole eastern hemisphere. Its decadence had been as rapid and as terrible as its rise. The Mongols were peculiarly unfit to resist the seductions of the more refined civilizations which they encountered. The Ming forces drove the Mongol court from Peking and the dethroned emperor betook himself northward into the desert to the town of Sa-mak.

This year also witnessed the arrival of a friendly embassy from Japan bearing gifts to the king. Here was Koryŭ's great opportunity to secure the co-operation of the Japanese government in the work of putting down the pirates who were harrying the shores of the peninsula. Proper treatment of this envoy and a little diplomacy would have saved Koryŭ untold suffering, but the low-born but all-powerful favourite, Sin-don, took advantage of the occasion to make an exhibition of his own importance and he snubbed the envoy so effectually that the latter immediately returned to Japan. The foolish favourite went so far as to withhold proper food from him and his suite, and addressed them in low forms of speech. The same year, at his instigation, the whole system of national examinations was done away with.

An Imperial Letter

Early in 1369 the first envoy, Sŭl Sa, from the Ming court arrived in Song-do. He was the bearer of an imperial letter which read as follows:

'After the Sung dynasty lost its power, a hundred years passed by without its recovering from the blow, but heaven hated the drunkenness and licentiousness of the Mongols and now after eighteen years of war the fruition of our labours has been reached. At first we entered the Mongol army and there beheld the evils of the Mongol reign. Then with heaven's help we went to the west, to Han-ju and overcame its king Chin U-ryang. Then we raised the standard of revolt against the Mongols. In the east we overcame the rebel Chang Sa-sŭng and in the south the Min-wŏl kingdom. In the north the Ho-in fell before us and now all the people of China call us emperor. The name of our dynasty is Ming and the name of this auspicious year is Hong-mu. We call upon you now as in duty bound to render allegiance to us. In times past you were very intimate with us for it was your desire to better the condition of your people thereby.'

Such was the importance of this embassy that the king went out in person to meet it. Splendid gifts were offered which, however, the envoy declined.

In accordance with the summons contained in this letter the king formally put away the Mongol calendar and assumed that of the Mings instead. An envoy was immediately sent to the Ming court to offer congratulations and perform the duties of a vassal. The emperor responded graciously by sending back to Koryŭ all citizens of that kingdom who had been held in semi-durance by the Mongols. The criminal neglect of opportunity in driving away the friendly Japanese envoy now began to bear its bitter fruit. Many Japanese had from time to time settled peacefully in southern Koryŭ and the king had given them a place to live at Nam-hă in Kyŭng-sang Province. They now broke their oath of fealty to the government, rose in open revolt and began ravaging the country right and left.

As the emperor of the Mongols had fled away north and his scheme for taking refuge in Quelpart had come to naught we would suppose the Mongol horse breeders in that island would act with considerable circumspection; but on the other hand they kept up a continual disturbance, revolting and surrendering again in quick succession much to the annoyance of the central government.

In the latter part of the year 1369 the government again took a census of the arable land of the peninsula in order to make a re-estimate of the revenue to be received. This indicates that there had been a certain degree of prosperity in spite of all untoward circumstances and that the margin of cultivation had moved at least a little way up the hillsides, and that waste land had been reclaimed. It is only by inferences from chance statements like this that we get an occasional imperfect glimpse of the condition of the common people. Oriental histories have not been written with reference to the common people.

Gen. Yi Promoted

The king had now handed over to Sin-don the whole care of public business and he was virtually the ruler of the land. Gen. Yi T'ă-jo had shown his wisdom in staying as far as possible from the capital and in not crossing the path of the dangerous favourite. He was now appointed General-in-Chief of all the north-eastern territory and at the same time Gen. Yi Im-in was appointed to a similar position in the north-west. There was some fear lest fugitive Mongols might cross the border and seek refuge in Koryŭ territory. The chief business of the army there was to guard all the approaches and see to it that such fugitives were strictly excluded. In the following year, 1370, Gen. Yi T'ă-jo even crossed the Yalu, probably in the vicinity of the present Sam-su, into what was then Yŭ-jin territory, and took 2000 bullocks and 100 horses, but gave them all to the people to be used in cultivating the fields.

Now that the Ming dynasty was firmly established the emperor turned his attention to Korea. He began by investing the king anew with the insignia of royalty and presenting him with a complete outfit of clothes of the style of the Ming dynasty. He also gave musical instruments and the Ming calendar. The important law was promulgated that after a man had passed the civil examinations in Koryŭ he should go to Nanking and there undergo further examination. The king received all the emperor's gifts and commands with complacency and soon the Ming dress was adopted throughout by the official class and more gradually by the common people. It is the style of dress in vogue in Korea today, whereas the Chinese themselves adopted later the dress of their Manchu conquerors. In this respect the Koreans today are really more Chinese than the Chinese themselves.

Gen. Yi Crosses the Yalu

With the opening of 1371 Gen. Yi led an army across the Yalu and attacked Ol-ja Fortress. The whole territory between the Yalu and the Great Wall was at this time held by the Yŭ-jin people or by offshoots of the Mongol power. The Ming emperor had as yet made no attempt to take it and therefore this expedition of Koryŭ's was not looked upon as an act of bad faith by China. Just before the attack on Ol-ja began, there came over to the Koryŭ forces a general who, formerly a Koryŭ citizen, had long been in the Mongol service. His name was Yi In-bok. Gen. Yi sent him to Song-do where the king elevated him to a high position. A bridge had been thrown across the Yalu and the army had crossed in safety, but a tremendous thunderstorm threw the army into confusion, for they feared it was a warning voice from a deity who was angered by this invasion of trans-Yalu territory. With great presence of mind one of the leaders shouted that it was a good sign for it meant that the heavenly dragon was shaking things up a bit as a presage of their victory. Their fears were thus allayed and the attack upon the fortress was successful.

Gen. Yi then led his forces toward the Liao Fortress but cautiously left all the camp baggage three days in the rear and advanced, with seven days rations in hand. The advance guard of 3,000 reached the fortress and began the assault before the main body came up. When the garrison saw the full army approach they were in despair but their commander was determined to make a fight. As he stood on the wall and in person refused Gen. Yi's terms it is said that the latter drew his bow and let fly an arrow which sped so true that it struck off the commander's helmet, whereupon Gen. Yi shouted, 'If you do not surrender I will hit your face next time.' The commander thereupon surrendered.

So Gen. Yi took the place and having dismantled it and burned all the supplies, started on the return march. Provisions ran low, and it was found necessary to kill the beasts of burden. They were in some danger from the detachments of the enemy who hung upon their rear but they were kept at a respectful distance by an ingenious strategem of Gen. Yi's, for wherever he made a camp he compelled the soldiers to make elabourate preparations even to the extent of erecting separate cattle sheds and water closets. The enemy finding these in the deserted camps deemed that the army must be in fine condition and so dared not attack them. Thus the whole army got safely back to An-ju.

As the Japanese pirates, emboldened by the impunity with which they could ravage Korea, now came even north of the capital and attacked Hă-ju the capital of Whang-hă Province, and also burned forty Koryŭ boats, Gen. Yi was detailed to go and drive them away, which he speedily did.

Sin-don Overthrown

The royal favourite was now nearing the catastrophe toward which his criminally corrupt course inevitably led. He was well known to all but the king whom he had infatuated. But now he began to see that the end was not far off. He knew that soon the king too would discover his knavery. For this cause he determined to use the little power he had left in an attempt to overthrow the government. What the plan was we are not told but it was nipped in the bud, for the king discovered it and arrested some of his accomplices and by means of torture learned the whole truth about the man whom he had before considered too good for this world. The revulsion of feeling was complete. He first banished Sin-don to Su-wŭn and then at the urgent advice of the whole court sent an executioner to make way with him. The messenger of death bore a letter with him in which the king said, 'I promised never to move against you but I never anticipated such actions as those of which you have been guilty. You have (1) rebelled, (2) you have numerous children, though a monk and unmarried, (3) you have built yourself a palace in my capital. These things I did not agree to.' So Sin-don and his two sons perished.

It is said of Sin-don that he was mortally afraid of hunting dogs and that in his feasts he insisted upon having the flesh of black fowls and white horses to eat. For these reasons the people said that he was not a man but a fox in disguise; for Korean lore affirms that if any animal drinks of water that has lain for twenty years in a human skull it will have the power to assume at will any form of man or beast. But the peculiar condition is added that if a hunting dog looks such a man in the face he will be compelled to resume his original shape.

Trouble From Three Sources

With the opening of 1372 troubles multiplied. Nap T'ap-chul, a Mongol chieftain at large, together with Ko-gan, led a mixed army of Mongol and Yŭ-jin adventurers across the Yalu and began to harry the northern border. Gen. Chi Yun was sent to put down the presumptuous robbers. At the same time the Quelpart horse breeders again revolted and when the king, at the command of the emperor, sent a man to bring horses as tribute to China the insurrectionists put him to death. But the common people of Quelpart formed a sort of militia and put down the insurrection themselves. The Japanese also made trouble, for they now began again to ravage the eastern coast, and struck as high north as An-byŭn, and Ham-ju, now Ham-heung. They also carried on operations at Nam-han near Seoul, but in both instances were driven off.

It is said that at this time the king was given over to sodomy and that he had a 'school' of boys at the palace to cater to his unnatural passions. The people were deeply indignant and talk ran very high, but the person of the king was sacred, and his acts were not to be accounted for; so he went his evil way unchecked, each step bringing him nearer the overthrow of the dynasty which was now not far away.

Late in the year the king sent a present of fifty horses to the Ming emperor.

No sooner had the spring of 1373 opened than the remnant of the Mongols in the north sent to the king and said, 'We are about to raise a mighty force to overthrow the Ming empire, and you must co-operate with us in this work.' The messenger who brought this unwelcome summons was promptly clapped into prison, but later at the advice of the courtiers he was liberated and sent back home.

It would be well-nigh impossible to describe each successive expedition of the Japanese to the shores of Koryŭ, but at this time one of unusual importance occurred. The marauders ascended the Han River in their small boats and made a swift attack on Han-yang the site of the present capital of Korea. Before leaving they burned it to the ground. The slaughter was terrific and the whole country and especially the capital was thrown into a state of unusual solicitude. The Japanese, loaded down with booty, made their way to the island of Kyo-dong just outside the island of Kang-wha, and proceeded to kill and plunder there.

A New Favourite

The boy whom the king had called his son but who was in reality an illegitimate son of Sin-don, was named Mo-ri-no, but now as he had gained his majority he was given the name of U and the rank of Kang-neung-gun, or 'Prince who is near to the king'. As Sin-don was dead the king made Kim Heung-gyŭng his favourite and pander. Gen. Kŭl Săng was put in charge of the defensive operations against the Japanese but as he failed to cashier one of his lieutenants who had suffered defeat at the hands of the Japanese the testy king took off his unoffending head. Gen. Ch'oé Yŭng was then put in charge and ordered to fit out a fleet to oppose the marauders. He was at the same time made criminal judge, but he committed so many ludicrous mistakes and made such a travesty of justice that he became a general laughingstock.

As the Ming capital was at Nanking the sending of envoys was a difficult matter, for they were obliged to go by boat, and in those days, and with the craft at their command, anything but coastwise sailing was exceedingly dangerous. So when the Koryŭ envoy Chöng Mong-ju, one of the few great men of the Koryŭ dynasty, arrived at the emperor's court, the latter ordered that thereafter envoys should come but once in three years. In reply to this the king said that if desired the envoy could be sent overland; but this the emperor forbade because of the danger from the remnants of the Mongol power.

The eventful year 1374 now came in. Gen. Yi Hyŭn told the king that without a navy Koryŭ would never be able to cope with Japanese pirates. He showed the king a plan for a navy which he had drawn up. His majesty was pleased with it and ordered it carried out, but the general affirmed that a navy never could be made out of landsmen and that a certain number of islanders should be selected and taught naval tactics for five years. In order to do this he urged that a large part of the useless army be disbanded. To all of this the royal assent was given. The quality of the army may be judged from the action of the troops sent south to Kyŭng-sang Province to oppose a band of Japanese. They ravaged and looted as badly as the Japanese themselves. And when at last the two forces did meet the Koryŭ troops were routed with a loss of 5,000 men. Meanwhile the Japanese were working their will in Whang-hă Province, north and west of the capital, and as to the details of it even the annals give up in despair and say the details were so harrowing that it was impossible to describe them.

Ming Emperor Demands Horses

The emperor of China was determined to obtain 2,000 of the celebrated horses bred on the island of Quelpart and after repeated demands the king sent to that island to procure them. The Mongol horse breeders still had the business in hand and were led by four men who said, 'We are Mongols, why should we furnish the Ming emperor with horses?' So they gave only 300 animals. The emperor insisted upon having the full 2,000 and the king reluctantly proceeded to extremities.

A fleet of 300 boats was fitted out and 25,000 men were carried across the straits. On the way a gale of wind was encountered and many of the boats were swamped, but the following morning the survivors, still a large number, arrived at Myŭng-wŭl, or 'Bright Moon,' Harbor where they found 3,000 men drawn up to oppose their landing. When the battle was joined the enemy was defeated and chased thirty *li* but they again rallied in the southern part of the island at Ho-do where they made a stand. There they were surrounded and compelled to surrender. The leader, T'ap-chi was cut in two at the waist and many others committed suicide. Several hundred others who refused to surrender were cut down. To the credit of the officers who led the expedition be it said that wherever they went the people were protected and lawless acts were strictly forbidden.

The King Assassinated

The king had now reached the moment of his fate. The blood of many innocent men was on his hands and he was destined to a violent death himself. He was stabbed by one of his most trusted eunuchs while in a drunken sleep. The king's mother was the first to discover the crime and with great presence of mind she concealed the fact and hastily summoning two of the courtiers consulted with them as to the best means of discovering the murderer. As it happened the eunuch was detected by the blood with which his clothes were stained. Put to the torture, he confessed the crime and indicated his accomplice. The cause of his act was as follows. One of the king's concubines was with child. When the eunuch informed the king the latter was very glad and asked who the father might be. The eunuch replied that one Hong Mun, one of the king's favourites, was the father. The king said that he would bring about the death of this Hong so that no one should ever know that the child was not a genuine prince. The eunuch knew that this meant his own death too, for he also was privy to the fact. So he hastened to Hung Mun and they together matured the plan for the assassination.

U, the supposed son of the king, now ascended the throne. His posthumous title is Sin-u. An envoy was sent to Nanking to announce the fact, but the emperor refused to ratify his accession to the throne. The reason may have been because he was not satisfied as to the manner of the late king's demise, or it may be that someone had intimated to him that the successor was of doubtful legitimacy; and now to add to the difficulties of the situation the Ming envoy on his way home with 200 tribute horses was waylaid by Korean renegades who stole the horses and escaped to the far north. When news of this reached Nanking the Korean envoy there hastened to make good his escape.

A conference was now held at the Koryŭ capital and as the breach with the Ming power seemed beyond remedy it was decided to make advances to the Mongols who still lingered in the north; but at the earnest desire of Chŏng Mong-ju this decision was reversed and an envoy was sent to Nanking to explain matters as best he could. The eunuch and his accomplice who had killed the king were now executed and notice of the fact was sent to the Chinese court.

There was great dissatisfaction among the Koryŭ officials for they all knew that the king was a mere usurper and it was again suggested that approaches be made to the Mongols. About this time also a Mongol envoy came demanding to know whose son the present king was. They wanted to put the king of Mukden on the throne, as he was of course favourable to the Mongols. A great and acrimonious dispute now arose between the Mongol and Ming factions in the Koryŭ court. But the Mongol sympathizers carried the day. This, however, came to nothing for when news came that the king of Mukden and many Koryŭ renegades were advancing in force on the Koryŭ frontier to take by force what the officials had decided to give unasked, there was a great revulsion of feeling and troops were sent to hold them in check. This was in 1376, and while this was in progress the Japanese were carrying fire and sword through the south without let or hindrance.

A Supernatural Proof

Pan-ya the real mother of the king came forward and claimed her position as such, but another of the former king's concubines, Han, had always passed as the boy's mother and she was now loath to give up the advantages which the position afforded. For this reason she secured the arrest and imprisonment of Pan-yu. It was decided that she must die and she was carried to the water's edge and was about to be thrown in when she exclaimed, 'When I die one of the palace gates will fall as a sign of my innocence and the truth of my claim.' The story runs that when she sank beneath the water this came true and all knew, too late, that she was indeed the mother of the king.

The Japanese now made their appearance again in Ch'ung-Ch'ŭng Province and took the town of Kong-ju. The Korean forces under Gen. Pak In-gye were there routed but not till their leader had been thrown from his horse and killed. Then an army under Gen. Ch'oé Yŭng met them at Hong-san. The general rushed forward ahead of his men to attack the marauders and was wounded by an arrow in the mouth but he did not retire from the fight. The result was a glorious victory for the Koryŭ forces. The Japanese were almost annihilated.

Some time before this the king had sent an envoy Na Heung-yu to Japan to ask the interference of the Japanese Government against the pirates, and the reply was now brought by the hand of a Japanese monk Yang Yu. It said, 'The pirates all live in western Japan in a place called Ku-ju and they are rebels against us and have been for twenty years. So we are not at fault because of the harm they have done you. We are about to send an expedition against them and if we take Ku-ju we swear that we will put an end to the piracy.' But the pirates in the meantime ravaged Kang-wha and large portions of Chŭl-la Province.

GEN. YI DEFENDS KORYŬ

Toward the close of 1377 the Mongol chieftain In-puk-wŭn sent the king a letter saying, 'Let us join forces and attack the Ming power.' At the same time he sent back all the Koryŭ people who had been taken captive at various times. The king's answer was a truly diplomatic one. He said, 'I will do so if you will first send the king of Mukden to me, bound hand and foot.' We need hardly say that this request was not granted.

The 'Revellers'

The next attack of the Japanese extended all along the southern coast. The general who had been placed in the south to guard against them spent his time feasting with courtesans and he and his officers were commonly known as 'The Revellers'. Fighting was not at all in their intentions. When the king learned of this he banished the general to a distant island. Affairs at the capital were not going well. Officials were so numerous that the people again made use of the term 'Smoke House Officials,' for there were so many that nearly every house in the capital furnished one. They tampered with the list of appointments and without the king's knowledge slipped in the names of their friends. So the people in contempt called it the 'Secret List'.

The coquetting with the Mongols brought forth fruit when early in 1378 they invested the king of Koryŭ and he adopted the Mongol name of the year. It is said that this caused great delight among the Mongols and that they now thought that with the help of Koryŭ they would be able to again establish their power in China.

Gen. Yi Takes Up Arms Against the Japanese

After the Japanese had ravaged to their hearts' content in Ch'ung-ch'ŭng Province and had killed 1,000 men on Kang-wha and had burned fifty boats, the king did what he ought to have done long before, namely, appointed Gen. Yi T'ă-jo as General-in-Chief of the Koryŭ forces. He took hold of the matter in earnest and summoned a great number of monks to aid in the making of boats for coast defence. The pirates now were ravaging the east and south and were advancing on Song-do. The king wanted to run away but was dissuaded. The Japanese were strongest in Kyŭng-sang Province. Gen Yi's first encounter with them was at Chi-ri Mountain in Chŭl-la Province and he there secured a great victory, demonstrating what has always been true, that under good leadership Koreans make excellent soldiers. When the Koryŭ troops had advanced within 200 paces of the enemy a burly Japanese was seen leaping and showing himself off before his fellows. Gen. Yi took a crossbow and at the first shot laid the fellow low. The remainder of the Japanese fled up the mountain and took their stand in a solid mass which the records say resembled a hedgehog; but Gen. Yi soon found a way to penetrate this phalanx and the pirates were slaughtered almost to a man. But Gen. Yi could not be everywhere at once and in the meantime Kang-wha again suffered. Gen. Yi was next seen fighting in Whang-hă Province at Hă-ju, where he burned the Japanese out from behind wooden defences and slaughtered them without quarter.

The Japanese government had not been able as yet to put down the pirates, but now an envoy, Sin Hong, a monk, came with gifts declaring that the government was not a party to the expeditions of the freebooters and that it was very difficult to overcome them. And so the work went on, now on one coast of the country and now on another. The king sent an envoy to the Japanese Shogun, P'ă-ga-dă, to ask his interference, but the shogun imprisoned the envoy and nearly starved him to death and then sent him back. The king wanted to send another, but the courtiers were all afraid. They all hated the wise and learned Chöng Mong-ju and told the king to send him. He was quite willing to go and, arriving at the palace of the shogun, he spoke out fearlessly and rehearsed the friendly relations that had existed between the two countries, and created a very good impression. He was very popular both with the shogun himself and with the Japanese courtiers and when he returned to Koryŭ the shogun sent a general, Chu Mang-in, as escort and also 200 Koreans who had at some previous time been taken captive. The shogun also so far complied with the king's request as to break up the piratical settlements on the Sam-do or 'Three islands'.

A man named Im Sŭn-mu had learned among the Mongols the art of making gunpowder and a bureau was now formed to attend to its manufacture but as yet there were no firearms.

Defeat Turned into Victory

With the opening of 1379 things looked blacker than ever. The Japanese were swarming in Ch'ung-ch'ŭng Province and on Kang-wha. The king was in mortal fear and had the walls of Song-do carefully guarded. Gen. Ch'oé Yŭng was sent to hold them in check. The Japanese knew that no one but he stood between them and Song-do so they attacked him fiercely and soon put him to flight; but in the very nick of time Gen. Yi T'ă-jo came up with his cavalry, turned the retreating forces about and attacked the enemy so fiercely that defeat was turned into a splendid victory. A messenger arrived breathless at the gate of Song-do saying that Gen. Ch'oé had been defeated.

All was instantly in turmoil; the king had all his valuables packed and was ready to flee at a moment's warning. But lo! another messenger followed hard upon the heels of the first announcing that Gen. Yi had turned the tide of battle and had wrested victory from the teeth of the enemy.

The goodwill of the Japanese government was shown when a prefect in western Japan sent sixty soldiers under the command of a monk, Sin Hong, to aid in the putting down of the corsairs. They made some attempts to check their lawless countrymen but soon found that they had undertaken more than they had bargained for, and so returned to Japan. As the pirates were ravaging the west coast as far north as P'yŏngyang, the king sent against them Generals Na Se and Sim Tŭk-pu who had been successful before. By the use of fire arrows they succeeded in burning several of the enemy's boats at Chin-p'o and of course had the fellows at their mercy, for they had no means of escape.

Vacillation

It is evident the king did not know his own mind in relation to Chinese suzerainty. Now he favoured the Mongols and now the Mings. A year or so before this he had adopted the Mongol name of the year but now he turns about and adopts the Ming name again. It was this vacillation, this playing fast and loose with his obligations, that alienated the goodwill of the Ming emperor and made him look with complacency upon the dissolution of the Koryŭ dynasty.

Late in the autumn of 1379 the Japanese were again in dangerous proximity to the capital and the king wanted to move to a safer place. The geomancers' book of prophecies indicated Puk-so San as 'A narrow place and good for a king to live in,' but the courtiers opposed it, saying that there was no large river flowing near by, on which the government rice could be brought by boat to the capital. So it was given up.

There was a Mongol general named Ko-ga-no who had become independent of the main body of the Mongols and had set up a separate government on his own responsibility in Liao-tung. He was wavering between natural ties on the one hand, which bound him to the Mongols, and the dictates of common sense on the other, which indicated the rising fortunes of the Ming. He chose a middle course by coming with his 40,000 men and asking the privilege of joining Koryŭ. The records do not say whether permission was given or not, but we may easily believe it was.

Japan Helps Koryŭ

In 1380 the Japanese government sent 180 soldiers under the command of Gen. Pak Kŭ-sa to aid in driving the pirates out of Koryŭ. In the midst of these dangers from freebooters, jealousy was undermining the government at Song-do. Gen. Yi T'ă-jo had a friend named Gen. Yang Păk-yŭn who now under false charges, enviously made by officials near the king, was banished and then killed. It was wonderful that the fame of Gen. Yi did not bring about his murder.

The Ming emperor thought, and rightly, that the king was a very fickle individual and sent a letter asking him why it was that he had no settled policy but did everything as the impulse of the moment led. The king's reply is not recorded but that he did not take to heart the admonitions of the emperor is quite evident, for he plunged into greater excesses than ever. His ill-timed hunting expeditions, his drunkenness and debauchery were the scandal of the country. The people thought he ought to be hunting Japanese pirates rather than wild boar and deer. Even while the Japanese were ravaging Ch'ung-ch'ŭng Province the king was trampling down the people's rice fields in the pursuit of game. He stole the people's cattle and horses whenever he needed them and if he chanced to see a good-looking girl anywhere he took means to possess himself of her person by fair means or foul. He was indeed the son of Sin-don both by blood and by disposition.

Gen. Yi's Stratagem

This year the ravages of the freebooters exceeded anything that had been known before. The southern provinces were honeycombed by them. Generals Pă Keuk-yŭm and Chöng Chi were sent against them but without result. At last the Japanese laughingly asserted that they soon would be in the city of Song-do. They might have gone there if Gen. Yi had not been sent in person to direct the campaign against them.

Hastening south he rallied around him all the available troops and came to Un-bong in Chŭl-la province. He ascended Chöng San which lay six miles from the camp of the enemy. From this point he perceived that there were two roads leading to this camp; one broad and easy and the other narrow and rough. With great sagacity he judged that the Japanese would take the narrow road, hoping to make a counter march on him. So he sent a considerable force by the broad road but selected a band of trusty men to form an ambush on the narrow one.

The Japanese acted precisely as he had foreseen. When they learned that the Koryŭ army was approaching they hastened away by the narrow road and so fell into the ambush, where they were severely handled. Fifty of their number were left dead. The remainder sought safety in the mountains but were soon brought to bay. The whole Koryŭ army was called up and the attack upon the Japanese position was begun. It was necessary to attack up a steep incline and Gen. Yi had two horses shot out from under him, and an arrow pierced his leg; but he drew it out and continued the fight.

Among the enemy was a man stronger and larger than the rest. He stood spear in hand and danced about, urging on his comrades. He was encased in armour and on his head was a copper helmet. There was no opening for an arrow to enter; so Gen. Yi said to his lieutenant, Yi Tu-ran, 'Make ready an arrow and when I strike off his helmet do you aim at his face.' Gen. Yi took careful aim and struck off the man's helmet and swift behind his arrow flew that of his lieutenant which laid the fellow low. This demoralized the enemy and they were soon hewn down. It is said that for days the stream nearby ran red with blood. As the result of this victory 1,600 horses were taken and a large amount of spoil, including implements of war.

When the victorious general returned to Song-do he was given a triumphal entry and fifty ounces of gold and other gifts were distributed among the generals who assisted him. It is said that, from that time on, whenever the news came that a Japanese band had disembarked on the southern coast the first word that was spoken was, 'Where is Gen. Yi T'ă-jo?'

The Emperor Loses Patience

The long-suffering emperor at last tired of the erratic course of the Koryŭ king and decided to bring a little pressure to bear upon him in order to bring him to his senses. He ordered the king to send him each year 1,000 horses, 100 pounds of gold, 5,000 ounces of silver and 5,000 pieces of cotton cloth. This was beyond the means of the king, but he succeeded in sending 300 ounces of gold, 1,000 ounces of silver, 450 horses, and 4,500 pieces of cotton. This large amount of tribute was delivered into the hands of the governor of Liao-tung to be sent to the imperial court, but the governor declared that as the tax was a penal one and not merely for tribute he could not accept less than the full amount required. So he drove the envoy away.

In 1382 the government adopted a new policy in the matter of coast defence. In all the larger seaport towns generals were stationed in charge of considerable bodies of troops and in the smaller towns garrisons of proportional strength. The constant coming and going of these troops was a terrible drain upon the resources of the people but there was no help for it. The piratical raids of the Japanese had now become so frequent that no attempt was made to keep a record of them. It would have been easier for the people to bear had the king showed any of the characteristics of manhood, but his feasts and revels saw no abatement. Frequently he was so intoxicated that he fell from his horse while hunting. He peopled the palace with dancing girls and it may be said of him as it was of Nero that he 'fiddled while Rome was burning'. As the king rode forth to hunt with falcon on wrist the eunuchs rode behind him singing ribald Mongol songs. When other pleasures cloyed he invented a sort of mock battle in which stones were used as missiles. It is believed by many that this was the beginning of the popular 'stone-fight,' which is such a unique custom of Korea today. Once he amused himself by pretending that he was going to bury one of his officials alive behind the palace, and he hugely enjoyed the poor fellow's shrieks and struggles. He made this same official put up his hat as a target, than which hardly anything could be a greater disgrace, for the hat in Korea is the badge of citizenship and is held in such esteem that no one will attend to the duties of nature without taking off his hat and laying it aside.

A Heavy Tribute

Being hard pressed by the emperor in the matter of tribute it is said that in 1383 he sent to the Ming court 100 pounds of gold, 10,000 ounces of silver, 10,000 pieces of linen, and 1,000 horses. The records say the emperor refused to take it, for it fell short of his demands. It is probable that this means not that it was sent back but that the emperor refused to give a receipt in full of all demands.

In this same year, 1383, the capital was again moved to Han-yang. The reasons alleged were that so many misfortunes overtook the dynasty that it seemed as if the site of the capital must be unpropitious. It was also said that wild animals entered the city, which was a bad sign. The water in the wells had boiled, fish fought with each other, and a number of other fictions were invented, all of which made it necessary to move the capital. It was affected, however, in the face of great opposition. Meanwhile the Japanese were working their will in the south, for Gen. Yi was in the north repelling an attack by the Yŭ-jin forces.

In spite of the sending of tribute to the Ming court, Koryŭ was on good terms with the Mongols. In 1384 the Mongol chief Nap-t'ap-chul came with gifts to the king and frequent envoys were exchanged. Koryŭ was neither hot nor cold but lukewarm and for this reason it was that the Mings finally spewed her out of their mouth. The capricious king now moved back to Song-do and the courtiers were put to no end of trouble and expense. When they returned to Song-do with the king they burned all their houses in Han-yang so as to make it impossible to return.

One of the most disgraceful acts of this king was his attempt to possess himself of his father's wife, or concubine. Meeting her one day he commented on her beauty and said she was more beautiful than any of his wives. He tried to force his way into her apartments at night but in some way his plan was frustrated. When one of the courtiers took him to task for his irregularities he tried to shoot him through with an arrow.

Gen. Yi Victorious in the North

Gen. Yi T'ă-jo was having a lively time in the north with the Yŭ-jin people. Their general was Ho-bal-do. His helmet was four pounds in weight. He wore a suit of red armour and he rode a black horse. Riding forth from the ranks he shouted insulting words to Gen. Yi and dared him to single combat. The latter accepted the gage and soon the two were at work striking blows that no ordinary man could withstand. Neither could gain the advantage until by a lucky chance the horse of Gen. Ho stumbled, and before the rider could recover himself Gen. Yi had an arrow in his neck. But the helmet saved him from a serious wound. Then Gen. Yi shot his horse under him.

At sight of this Gen. Ho's soldiers rushed up, as did also those of Gen. Yi, and the fight became general. The result was an overwhelming victory for Koryŭ. These flattering statements about the founder of the present dynasty are probably, in many cases, the result of hero worship but the reader has the privilege of discounting them at discretion.

The Ming court knew all about Koryŭ's coquetting with the Mongols and sent a severe letter warning her that the consequences of this would be disastrous. The king was frightened and sent an envoy in haste to the Ming court to 'make it right,' but the emperor cast him into prison and sent demanding five years' tribute at once. We may well believe that this demand was not complied with.

That there were two opinions in Japan as regards Koryŭ is shown by the fact that immediately after that government sent back 200 Koryŭ citizens, who had been carried away captive, a sanguinary expedition lauded on the coast of Kang-wŭn Province near the town of Kang-neung and ravaged right away north as far as Nang-ch'ŭn.

A Skilful Diplomat

The king, in partial compliance with the emperor's demands sent, in the spring of 1385, sent 2,000 horses to China. It was the faithful Chöng Mong-ju who accompanied this peace offering, and when he arrived in Nanking the emperor saw by the date of his commission that he had come in extreme haste. This mollified his resentment to such an extent that he gave the envoy a favourable hearing and that careful and judicious man made such good use of the opportunity that friendly intercourse was again established between China and her wayward vassal.

The state of affairs in Koryŭ was now beyond description. The *kwaga*, a literary degree of some importance, was frequently conferred upon infants still in their mothers' arms. The people, with fine sarcasm, called this the 'Pink Baby-powder Degree'. The king was struggling to pay up his arrears of tribute, but he could not secure the requisite number of horses. In lieu of these he sent large quantities of silver and cloth. The pendulum had now swung to the other extreme and a Mongol envoy was denied audience with the king.

A Grave Error

In 1386, the year following the above events, the Ming emperor formally recognized the king of Koryŭ. This event was hailed with the greatest delight by the court. But it did not have the effect of awakening the king to the dignity of his position for he gave freer rein to his passions than ever. He seized the daughter of one of his officials and made her his concubine although she was already affianced to another. This is a most grave offense in the east, for a girl affianced is considered already the same as married.

It is a relief to turn from this picture and see what Gen. Yi was doing to free his country from Japanese pirates. He was in the northeast when a band of these men landed in his vicinity, near the mouth of the Tu-man River. When they found that Gen. Yi was nearby they wanted to make their escape but he forced them into a position where they either had to fight or surrender. He informed them that immediate surrender was the only thing that could save them. They agreed to his terms but when they had thus been thrown off their guard he fell upon them and the slaughter was so great that it is said the plain was filled with the dead bodies. The records make no attempt to conceal or palliate this act of bad faith on the part of this great general. It was not an age when nice distinctions were made. The Japanese were not waging a regular warfare against the Koryŭ government but were killing helpless women and children and burning their houses. Their one aim was plunder and this put them outside the pale of whatever code of military honour prevailed.

Untold Excesses

The king's vagaries now took a new turn. Like Haroun al Raschid he went forth at night and roamed the streets in disguise accompanied by concubines and eunuchs. Crimes that cannot be described and which would have brought instant death upon a common citizen were committed with impunity. No man's honour was safe. Not only so, but other evil-minded people masquerading at night and in disguise committed like indescribable outrages under the cover of the king's name. In his hunting expeditions the king rode forth preceded by a host of harlots and concubines dressed in male attire and wherever he went the people lost their horses and cattle and whatever else the royal escort took a fancy to.

The continual trouble in Quelpart arising out of the horse breeding business grew so annoying that the king finally sent Gen. Yi Hăng with instructions to bring away every horse and to do away entirely with the business. This was done and from that day Quelpart had peace.

Kim Yu the envoy to Nanking was closely questioned by the emperor as to the cause of the late king's death and he told that potentate that it was done by Yi In-im, which indeed was true; but to the question as to whose son the king might be he returned an evasive answer. As a result of his frankness in telling who murdered the former king he was banished, for Yi In-im was all-powerful at court. The sentence of banishment meant death for he was sent to a distant place of banishment as such a breakneck pace that no man could live through it. He died of fatigue on the way as was intended. This Yi In-im and his following held the reins of power at the capital and they sold all offices and took bribes from all criminals. They thus succeeded in defeating the ends of justice and the people 'gnashed their teeth' at him. He caused the death of so many good men that he earned the popular soubriquet of 'Old Cat'.

Tribute Rejected

The year 1387 was signalized by a closer union between Koryŭ and her suzerain. The Ming emperor sent 5,000 pieces of silk to purchase horses but when the animals arrived at his capital they were such a sorry lot that he rejected them and charged the king with bad faith. The Koryŭ officials all adopted the dress and the manners of the Ming court. This they had done before but had dropped them again when they turned back to the Mongols. From that time on until the present day the clothes of the Korean have followed the fashions of the Ming dynasty.

RISE OF THE WANG DYNASTY

Koryŭ was now whirling in the outer circles of the maelstrom that was destined to engulf her. So long as the king revelled and hunted only and did not interfere with outside affairs he was endured as a necessary evil, but now in the opening of the year 1388 he determined upon an invasion of Liao-tung, a plan so utterly foolhardy as to become the laughingstock of reasonable men. It was an insane idea.

The constant inroads of the Japanese demanded the presence of all the government troops, for the sending of any of them out of the country would be the signal for the Japanese to pour in afresh and with impunity. In the second place the king could not hope to cope with the great Ming power that had just arisen and was now in the first blush of its power. The kingdom of Koryŭ was essentially bound to the Mongols and she pursued her destiny to the bitter end. In the third place the Ming power had now obtained a firm foothold in Liao-tung and an invasion there would look much like a plan to finally attack that empire itself. In the fourth place the finances of the country were utterly disorganised and the unusual taxes that would be required to carry out the plan would take away all popular enthusiasm for it and desertions would decimate the army. But in spite of all these drawbacks the stubborn king held to his point and as a preliminary measure built a wall about Han-yang where he sent all the women and children for safety. By this act he acknowledged the extreme hazard of the venture. It is not unlikely that he was so tired of all other forms of amusement that he decided to plunge into war in order to make sport for himself.

The Emperor's Letter

The emperor seems to have been aware of the plan for he now sent an envoy to announce to the Koryŭ court that 'All land north of Ch'ŭl-lyŭng belongs to the Mongols, and I am about to erect a palisade fence between you and them.' When this envoy arrived at Song-do the king feigned illness and would not see him. A letter was sent in reply saying 'We own beyond the Ch'ŭl-lyŭng as far as Sang-sŭng, so we trust it will please you not to erect a barrier there.' He then called in all the troops from the provinces in preparation for the invasion. His ostensible reason was a great hunting expedition in P'yŭng-an Province for he knew the people would rise in revolt if they knew the real purpose. The Japanese were wasting the south, the people were fainting under new exactions to cover the expense of the repairs at Han-yang and it is said the very planting of crops was dispensed with, so disheartened were the people.

Having made Ch'oé Yŭng General-in-Chief of the expedition, the king accompanied the army north to Pong-ju, now Pong-san. Gen. Ch'oé never divulged the fact that this was an army of invasion but told all the troops that they must be strong and brave and ready for any work that might be given them to do. Gen. Yi T'ă-jo was made lieutenant-general in connection with Gen. Ch'oé. He made a powerful plea against the war and the main points of his argument are preserved to us.

His objections were (1) It is bad for a small country to attack a powerful one. (2) It is bad to make a campaign in summer when the heavy rains flood the country, rendering the transporting of troops almost impossible and decimating them with disease. (3) It is bad to drain off all the soldiers from the country when the Japanese are so constant in their ravages. (4) The heat and moisture of summer will spoil the bows and make them break easily. To all these objections the king replied that having come thus far the plan must be carried out. Gen. Yi hazarded his neck by demurring; still asserting that it would mean the overthrow of the kingdom. The king in rage exclaimed 'The next man that advises against this war will lose his head.' This was an end of the debate and as the council of war dispersed the officers saw Gen. Yi weeping, and to their questions he answered, 'It means the destruction of Koryŭ'.

Gen. Yi Marches North

The Yalu was quickly bridged and Gen. Yi in company with one other generals started north from P'yŏngyang with 38,600 troops, 21,000 of whom were mounted. At the same time the king discarded the Ming calendar, dress and coiffure. The Mongol clothes were again adopted and the hair cut. The Japanese knowing that the troops had gone north, entered the open door thus invitingly left ajar and seized forty districts.

But we must follow the fortunes of the expedition that was to attack the empire of the Mings. When Gen. Yi arrived at the Yalu his plans were not laid as to what he should do. For one thing, he intended to make no invasion of China. So he crossed over to Wi-ha island, in the mouth of the Yalu, and there made his camp. Hundreds of his troops deserted and went back home. Some of these the king seized and beheaded; but it did not stop the defection. From that island a general, Hong In-ju, made a dash into Liao-tung territory and was highly complimented by the king in consequence. But Gen. Yi remained impassive. He sent a letter to the king imploring him to listen to reason and recall the army, urging history, the flooded condition of the country and the Japanese reasons for it. But the king was stubborn. Rumour said that Gen. Yi had fled but when another general was sent to ascertain whether this were true or false he was found at his post. The two generals wept together over the hopeless condition of affairs. At last they summoned the soldiers. 'If we stay here we will all be swept away by the rising flood. The king will not listen to reason. What can we do to prevent the destruction of all the people of Koryŭ? Shall we go back to P'yŏngyang, depose the General-in-Chief, Ch'oé, who urges on this unholy war against the Mings?' The soldiers shouted out acclamations of glad assent. Nothing could please them better.

The Rubicon of Korea

As Gen. Yi T'ă-jo mounted his white steed and with his red bow and white arrows stood motionless upon a mound of earth watching his soldiers recross the Yalu to the Koryŭ side against the mandate of their king and his, we see a new Caesar watching his army cross the Rubicon, an army as passionately devoted to their leader as the Roman legions ever were to Caesar. And Caesar suffers in the comparison, for he went back not to restore the integrity of the state and prevent the waste of human life, but rather to carry out to its tragic end a personal ambition. We have seen how once and again Yi T'ă-jo had plead with the king and had risked even his life to prevent this monumental folly; and we shall see how he used his power not for personal ends but with loyalty to his king, until circumstances thrust him upon the throne.

The records say that no sooner had Gen. Yi followed his army across the stream than a mighty wave, fed by mountain streams, came rolling down the valley and swept clean over the island he had just left. The people looked upon this as an omen and a sign of heaven's favour, and they made a song whose refrain runs 'The son of wood will become king.' This refers to the Chinese character for Gen. Yi's name. It is the union of the two characters 'wood' and 'son'. The whole army then took up its march toward Song-do. A magistrate in the north sent a hasty message to the king saying that the army was in full march back toward the capital. The king was at this time in Song-ch'ŭn, north of P'yŏngyang. He knew many of the generals were opposed to the war and thought that they would obey him better if he were nearby, and so had come thus far north.

Hearing this startling news he immediately dispatched Gen. Ch'oé Yu-gyŭng with whatever force he had, to oppose the march of the rebellious Gen. Yi. The associate of the latter urged him to push forward with all speed and seize the person of the king, but he was no traitor, and he replied 'If we hurry forward and encounter our countrymen many will fall. If anyone lays a finger on the king I will have no mercy on him. If a single citizen of Koryŭ is injured in any way I will never forgive the culprit.' So Gen. Yi came southward slowly, hunting along the way in order to give the king time to get back to Song-do in a leisurely manner as becomes a king. At last the king arrived at his capital and the recalcitrant army came following slowly. The people along the way hailed them as the saviours of the nation and gave them all manner of provisions and supplies, so that they lacked for nothing.

Advancing on Song-do

When Gen. Yi T'ă-jo reached the neighbourhood of Song-do he sent a letter to the king saying, 'As General-in-Chief Ch'oé-yŭng does not care for the welfare of the people he must die. Send him to me for execution.' But Gen. Ch'oé did not intend to give up without a struggle, however hopeless his case might be; so he took what troops were left and manned the walls of Song-do. It was a desperate move, for all saw what the end must be. Hundreds of soldiers who had deserted now flocked again to the standards of Gen. Yi.

When the attack came off, Gen. Yi stormed the South Gate and Gen. Yu Man-su the West Gate, and soon an entrance was affected. It is said that after entering the city the first attack upon the royal forces was made by Gen. Yu alone and that he was driven back. When this was told Gen. Yi he seemed not to care but sat on his horse and let it crop the grass along the path. After a time he partook of some food and then leisurely arose, drew up his forces and in full view of them all took a shot at a small pine that stood 100 paces away. The arrow cut it sheer off and the soldiers hailed it as a sign of victory, for was not the pine the symbol of Koryŭ? So they marched on the palace.

The Capital in Gen. Yi's Hands

The old men and boys mounted the city walls and cheered the attacking forces. Gen. Yi did not lead the attack in person and his lieutenant was beaten back by the royal forces under Gen. Ch'oé. Gen. Yi thereupon took in his hand a yellow flag, crossed the Sön-juk bridge and ascended South Mountain from which point he obtained a full view of the interior of the palace. He saw that Gen. Ch'oé and the king, with a band of soldiers, had taken refuge in the palace garden. Descending the mountain he led his troops straight through every obstacle, entered the palace and surrounded the royal party. Gen. Ch'oé was ordered to come out and surrender but as there was no response the garden gate was burst open and the king was discovered holding the hand of Gen. Ch'oé. As there was no longer hope of rescue the king, weeping, handed over the loyal general to the soldiers of Gen. Yi. He stepped forward and said 'I had no intention of proceeding to these extremes, but to fight the Ming power is out of the question. It is not only useless but suicidal to attempt such a thing. I have come back to the capital in this manner because there was no other way open to me, because it was a traitorous act to attack our suzerain, and because the people of Koryŭ were suffering in consequence of the withdrawal of protection.' Gen. Ch'oé was then banished to Ko-yang and Gen. Yi, as he sent him away, wept and said 'Go in peace.'

The records say that long before this the evil-minded Yi In-im had foretold to Gen. Ch'oé that one day Gen. Yi T'ă-jo would become king, but at the time Gen. Ch'oé laughed at it. Now he was forced to grant that the prophecy had been a true one. A popular song was composed at this time, whose refrain states that,

'Outside the wall of P'yŏngyang there is a red light,
Outside the wall of An-ju a snake.
Between them comes and goes a soldier, Yi.
May he help us.'

Gen. Yi's Demands

When Gen. Ch'oé had thus been disposed of, Gen. Yi turned to the king and said 'It was impossible to carry out the plan of conquest. The only thing left was to come back, banish the man who gave such bad advice and make a new start. We must now be firm in our allegiance to the Ming emperor, and we must change back to the Ming costume.'

The emperor, hearing of the threatened invasion, had sent a powerful army into Liao-tung, but now that the invaders had retired he recalled the troops.

We can easily imagine how the king, who had never been balked of his will, hated Gen. Yi. The moment an opportunity occurred he called about him eighty of his most trusted eunuchs, armed them with swords and sent them to kill the obnoxious dictator. But they found him so well guarded that the attempt proved abortive.

The King Banished

It will be remembered that this king was the son of Sin-don and was therefore not of the royal stock. So now the courtier Yun So-jŭng told Gen. Yi that they ought to find some blood relative of the Wang family, the genuine royal stock, and put him on the throne. To this the dictator assented. As a first move all arms were removed from the palace. The king was left helpless. He was ordered to send away one of his concubines who had formerly been a monk's slave but he replied, 'If she goes I go.' The generals went in a body to the palace and advised the king to leave the capital and retire into private life in Kang-wha. This was a polite way of saying that he was banished. He plead to be allowed to wait till the next day as it was now well along toward night. And so this evil king took his concubines, which he had always cherished more than the kingdom, and passed off the stage of history. He it was who most of all, excepting only his father, helped to bring about the fall of the dynasty.

A New King

Gen. Yi now, in 1388, was determined to put upon the throne a lineal descendant of the Wang family, but Cho Min-su with whom he had before conferred about the matter desired to put Chang, the adopted son of the banished king, on the throne. Gen. Yi demurred, but when he learned that the celebrated scholar Yi Săk had favoured this plan he acquiesced. The young king wanted to give Gen. Yi high official position but he was not anxious to receive it and it was only by strong pressure that he was induced to take it. So the records say, but we must remember in all this account that hero worship and desire to show the deeds of the founder of the new dynasty in the best light have probably coloured many of the facts which occurred at this time.

As this king was never acknowledged by the emperor nor invested with the royal insignia, his name is dropped from the list of the kings of Koryŭ. Neither he nor his foster father were given the regular posthumous title, but were known, the father as Sin-u and the son as Sin Chang.

Envoy to China

An envoy was dispatched to Nanking telling of the banishment of the king and the appointment of his successor. Cho Min-su who had been instrumental in putting this new king on the throne was not so modest as the records try to make us believe Gen. Yi was. He now held almost unlimited power. It spoiled him as it has spoiled many another good man, and he gave way to luxury and ere long had to be banished, a victim of his own excesses.

Reform now became the order of the day. First they changed the unjust and shameful manner of appointing officials that had prevailed under the banished king. The laws respecting the division of fields was changed, making the people safer in the possession of their property. The defences of the south were also looked to, for Gen. Chŏng Chi went south with a powerful force and scored a signal victory over the corsairs at Nam-wŭn. Gen. Yi T'ă-jo was now General-in-Chief of all the royal forces. His first act was to have the banished king sent further away, to the town of Yö-heung; and at the same time the banished Gen. Ch'oé Yŭng was executed. The old man died without fear, at the age of seventy. He was not a man who had given himself over to luxury and he had many good qualities, but he was unlettered and stubborn and his crime in desiring to attack China brought him to his death. The records say that when he died he said, 'If I am a true man no grass will grow on my grave,' and the Koreans say that his grave in Ko-yang is bare to this day and is called in consequence 'The Red Grave'.

The emperor's suspicions had been again roused by the new change of face on the part of Koryŭ. The celebrated scholar Yi Săk stepped forward and offered to go to the emperor's court and smooth things over. Gen. Yi praised him highly for this act of condescension and he was sent as envoy. He took with him Gen. Yi's fifth son who is known posthumously by his title T'ă-jong. He was destined to become the third king of the new dynasty. He was taken to China by Yi Săk because the latter feared that Gen. Yi might usurp the throne while he was gone and the son would then be a sort of hostage for good behaviour on the part of the father. The two great men of Koryŭ, when it fell, were Chöng Mong-ju and this Yi Săk. They were both men of education and experience and were both warm partisans of the Koryŭ dynasty. They were loyal to her even through all the disgusting scenes herein described, but their great mistake was their adherence to the Mongol power when it had plainly retired from active participation in the affairs of Asia. Yi Săk now sought the court of China not so much with a view to helping Koryŭ as to find means to get Gen. Yi into trouble. But to his chagrin the emperor never gave him an opportunity to say what he desired to say about the great dictator.

The questions the emperor asked gave no opportunity to mention the topic nearest his heart. His chagrin was so great that when he got back to Koryŭ he spoke slightingly of the emperor, to the great displeasure of the court. The king himself desired to go to Nanking and do obeisance to the emperor but was forbidden by the latter.

Offensive Against the Japanese

The year 1389 beheld some interesting and important events. In the first place Gen. Yi decided to take the offensive against the Japanese; so 100 boats were fitted out. The expedition arrived first at Tsushima where 300 of the enemy's boats were burned as well as many houses; and more than 100 prisoners were brought away. Secondly, the emperor, being asked to let the king go to Nanking and do obeisance, replied, 'This having a pretender on the throne of Koryŭ is all wrong. If you will put a real descendant of the royal family on the throne you need not send another envoy to my court for twenty years if you do not wish.' Gen Yi, to show his goodwill, sent a messenger to the banished king and gave him a feast on his birthday. The king of the Loo Choo Islands sent an envoy to Song-do with gifts, declaring his allegiance to Koryŭ. At the same time he sent back some Koryŭ captives who had fallen into his hands.

A New Wang On the Throne

Gen. Yi came to the conclusion that if the dynasty was to continue, a lineal descendant of the royal family must be put at the head of affairs. At this time Gen. Yi was of course the actuating spirit in the government and at his desire the young king, who had been on the throne but a year and who had not been formally recognized by the emperor, was sent away to Kang-wha and the seventh descendant of the seventeenth king of the line was elevated to the seat of royalty. His name was Yo and his posthumous title Kong-yang. He was forty-five years old. This move on the part of Gen. Yi was doubtless on account of the pronounced views of the emperor. A busybody named Kang Si told the newly appointed king that Gen. Yi did this not because he cared for the Wang dynasty but because he feared the Mings. When Gen. Yi learned of this the man's banishment was demanded but not insisted upon. One of the first acts of the new sovereign was to banish Yi Săk and Cho Min-su who had insisted upon putting the parvenu Chang upon the throne. An envoy was also dispatched to China announcing that at last a genuine Wang was now on the throne of Koryŭ.

The officials urged that the two banished kings be killed but when the matter was referred to Gen. Yi he advised a more lenient policy, saying, 'They have been banished and they can do no more harm. There is no sense in shedding useless blood.' But the king replied, 'They killed many good men and they deserve to die;' so executioners were sent and the two men were executed at their places of banishment. It is said that the wife of the elder of the two took the dead body of her lord in her arms and said, as she wept, 'This is all my father's fault, for it was he who advised the invasion of China.' The records say that for ten days she ate nothing and slept with the corpse in her arms. She also begged rice and with it sacrificed before the dead body of the king.

Unsuccessful Plot

In 1390 a dangerous conspiracy was gotten up with the view to assassinating Gen. Yi, but it was discovered in time and many men were killed in consequence and many more were put to the torture. Yi Săk and Cho Min-su were in some way implicated in this attempt though they were in banishment. It was advised to put them to death but after torture they were sent back to prison. The emperor in some way had the impression that Gen. Yi was persecuting these two men because they had prevented his invasion of China. Cho was executed but when the executioner approached the cell of Yi Săk, so the records say, a terrific clap of thunder was heard and a flood of water swept away part of the town in which he was imprisoned. For this reason the king dared not kill him but granted him freedom instead.

Under the supervision of Gen. Yi a war office was established and a system of conscription which secured a rotation of military duty. The king, true to the instincts of his family, was a strong adherent of Buddhism and now proceeded to take a monk as his teacher. The whole official class decided that this must not be, and the monk was forthwith expelled from the palace. In spite of the suffering it entailed upon the people the king decided to move the capital again to Han-yang and it was done, but no sooner was the court transferred to that place than the king, with characteristic Wang fickleness, went back to Song-do. The law was promulgated that women must not go to visit Buddhist monasteries. This was without doubt because the looseness of the morals of the inmates rendered it unsafe for respectable women to go to them.

The people throughout the land looked to Gen. Yi as their protector and it was the almost universal wish that he should become king. His friends tried to bring this about but they were always thwarted by the aged Chŏng Mong-ju, the only great man who now clung to the expiring dynasty. He was a man of perfect integrity and was held in much esteem by Gen. Yi himself though they differed in politics. Chong Mong-ju really believed it necessary for the preservation of the state that Gen. Yi be put out of the way and he was always seeking means for accomplishing this end.

When the crown prince came back from Nanking, whither he had gone as envoy, Gen. Yi went out to meet him. He went as far as Whang-ju where he suffered a severe fall from his horse which for a time quite disabled him. This was Chöng Mong-ju's opportunity. He hastened to have many of Gen. Yi's friends put out of the way. He had them accused to the king and six of the strongest partisans of the general were banished. Gen. Yi was at Hă-ju at the time and his son T'ă-jong hastened to him and imparted the startling news. The old man did not seem to care very much, but the son whose energy and spirit were equal to anything and who foresaw that prompt action at this juncture meant life or death to all the family, had the aged general carried on the backs of men back to Song-do. When he arrived, attempts were being made to have the six banished men put to death, but the coming of the great dictator put a stop to this. T'ă-jong urged that something must be done immediately to save the family name, but the father did not wish to proceed to extremities. The brunt of the whole business fell upon T'ă-jong and he saw that if his father was to become king someone must push him on to the throne. The first step must be the removal of Chöng Mong-ju. Nothing could be done until that was accomplished.

Chöng Mong-ju Assassinated

Gen. Yi's nephew turned traitor to him and informed Chöng Mong-ju that there was danger. About this time Gen. Yi gave a dinner to the officials and Chöng Mong-ju was invited. The latter decided to go and, by watching the face of his host, determine whether the report was true. When T'ă-jong saw Chöng Mong-ju come to the banquet he knew the time had come to make the master move. Five strong men were placed in hiding beside Sön-juk bridge which Chöng had to cross in going home. There they fell upon him and murdered him with stones, upon the bridge. Today that bridge is one of the sacred relics of the kingdom and is enclosed by a railing. On the central stone is seen a large brown blotch which turns to a dull red when it rains. This is believed to be the blood of the faithful Chöng Mong-ju which still remains a mute reproach to his murderers.

This dastardly deed having been committed, T'ă-jong conferred with his uncle, Wha, and they sent Gen. Yi's eldest living son, who is known by his posthumous title of Chöng-jong, to the king, to demand the recall of the banished friends of the general. The king was in no condition to refuse and the men came back.

Gen. Yi mourned sincerely for the death of Chöng Mong-ju for he held him to be a loyal and faithful man, but his son saw to it that the friends of the murdered man were promptly banished. Even the two sons of the king who had sided with the enemies of Gen. Yi were banished. Gen. Yi was asked to put some of the friends of Chöng Mong-ju to death but he sternly refused and would not even have them beaten. Yi Săk was again banished to a more distant point, the property of Chöng Mong-ju was confiscated and so at last all opposition was effectually silenced.

The energetic T'ă-jong next proceeded to have the king make an agreement or treaty of lasting friendship with his father. The officials opposed it on the ground that it was not in keeping with the royal office to swear an oath to a subject, but the king who had doubtless been well schooled by the young intriguer agreed to it. Gen. Yi was very loath to go and receive this honour at the king's hand and it was at last decided that the king should not attend the function in person but should do it by deputy. The oath was as follows: 'If it had not been for you I never could have become king. Your goodness and faithfulness are never to be forgotten. Heaven and earth witness to it from generation to generation. Let us abjure all harm to each other. If I ever forget this promise let this oath witness to my perfidy.'

The King Abdicates

But soon the king began to see the ludicrousness of his position. His sons had been banished, himself without a particle of power and the voice of the people clamouring to have Gen. Yi made king. The pressure was too great, and one day the unhappy king handed over the seals of office to the great dictator Gen. Yi T'ă-jo and the Wang dynasty was at an end. The king retired to private life, first to Wŭn-ju, then to Kan-Sŭng and finally to San-ch'ŭk where he died three years after abdicating. The dynasty had lasted 475 years in all.

THE JOSEON DYNASTY AND KING SE-JONG THE GREAT

Joseon [or Chosŏn], the last phase of Korean dynastic history, lasted 518 years. The Joseon dynasty has been studied far more than the early periods of the Three Kingdoms, Silla and the Koryŏ period, thanks to abundant primary sources relating to it. Since it is closer in time, scholars also feel the Joseon is more relevant to the modern period. One of the most hotly contested questions regarding Joseon is how and why Korea fell to Japanese colonization in 1910. The so-called 'sprout of capitalism' or internal development theory has been long debated. Could Korea's development include modernism and capitalism if Japan had not intervened and colonized Korea?

However, no matter how far scholars may differ on other issues, no one can deny that King Sejong's era is the peak of Joseon history and culture. He has been credited for many scientific inventions ranging from the rain gauge, sundial, water clock, celestial globes and astronomical maps to the orrery, a mechanical representation of the solar system. King Sejong's most accomplished achievement for Korean people is the creation of the Korean script *Hangul*.

With the Korean court having used Chinese writing for centuries, the king and his officials felt it necessary to create a simplified writing system using a phonetic alphabet that all Koreans could easily learn. It had been challenging for Koreans to use Chinese writing to record Korean sounds and it was almost impossible for most ordinary people to learn Chinese. The development of the 28 letters of the Korean alphabet was revolutionary for Korean culture and its people; relatively easy to learn, this simplified system enabled many more people to become literate. However, Korean literati resisted use of the Korean script; they believed that it was too simple and unsophisticated, so should be reserved for women and uneducated people. Only in the late nineteenth century did Korean script become the primary writing system for communication and publication. This final section of the book continues Hulbert's history and finishes with a deeper discussion of the Korean alphabet by James Scarth Gale.

THE FOUNDATIONS OF MODERN KOREA

It was on the sixteenth day of the seventh moon of the year 1392 that Gen. Yi ascended the throne of Koryŭ, now no longer Koryŭ. He was an old man, far past the age when he could hope to superintend in person the vigorous 'house cleaning' that the condition of things demanded. He called about him all the officials whom he knew to be personally loyal to himself and placed them in positions of trust and authority. Those who had contributed to his rise were rewarded, and a tablet was erected in the capital telling of their merits. He liberated many who had been imprisoned because of their opposition to the Wang kings and recalled many who had been banished.

Name Cho-sŭn Adopted

It was not long before a message came from the emperor saying, 'A man can become king only by the decree of Heaven. How is it then that the people of Sam-han have made Yi king?' In reply the king hastened to send an envoy to explain matters and to ask the emperor whether he would prefer to have the new kingdom called Cho-sŭn, 'Morning Freshness' or Wha-ryŭng, 'Peaceful Harmony'. The emperor probably thought there was a great deal more morning freshness than peaceful harmony in the peninsula; at any rate he ordered the former name to be adopted. It was the doubtful loyalty of the Wang kings to the Chinese throne that made it easy for king T'ă-jo to smooth over the displeasure of the emperor. The seals of the Koryŭ kings were then delivered over to China and new seals received for the new dynasty.

According to unwritten law, with the beginning of a new dynasty a new capital must be founded, and king T'ă-jo began to look about for a new site. At first he determined to build his capital at Kye-ryŭng Mountain in Ch'ung-ch'ŭng Province, and he went so far as to begin work on it; but it was found that in the days of Silla a celebrated priest, To-sŭn, had prophesied that in the days to come Yi would found a capital at Han-yang, and one of the Koryŭ kings had planted many plum trees at that place and as fast as they matured had them mutilated, hoping thus to harm the fortunes of the Yi family; for the Chinese character for Yi is the same as that for plum. Tradition also says that the king had a dream in which a spirit came and told him that Kye-ryŭng San was reserved for the capital of a future kingdom which should be founded by a member of the Chöng family. Two commissioners were thereupon sent to Han-yang to make surveys for a palace site. It is said that a monk, Mu-hak, met them at

Ha-yang and told them that the palace should face toward Pă-gak Mountain and Mong-myŭk Mountain (the present Nam-san,) but they persisted in making it face the south. 'Very well' the monk replied, 'If you do not listen to my advice you will have cause to remember it two hundred years from now.' His words were unheeded but precisely 200 years later, in the year 1592, the Japanese hordes of Hideyoshi landed on the shores of southern Korea. This is a fair sample of Korean *ex post facto* prophecy.

The courtiers urged the king to destroy the remaining relatives of the last Koryŭ kings that there might be no danger of an attempt at revolt. The royal consent was given and a considerable number of those unfortunates were put in a boat, taken out to sea and abandoned, their boat being first scuttled. The king thought better of this, however, before it had gone far and ordered this manhunt to be stopped.

As the emperor still seemed to entertain suspicions concerning the new kingdom, the king was fain to send his eldest son as envoy to the Chinese court where he carefully explained the whole situation to the satisfaction of his suzerain.

A Royal Dream

An interesting prophecy is said to have been current at the time. The king dreamed that he saw a hen swallow a silkworm. No one could explain the meaning of the dream until at last an official more imaginative than discreet averred that it meant that Kye-ryŭng would swallow Cham-du. Kye means 'hen' and Cham-du means 'silk-worm's head'. But Kye-ryong was the site of the future capital of the next kingdom according to prophecy, while 'silk-worm's head' is the name of one of the spurs of Nam-san in Seoul. So the interpretation was that the new dynasty would fall before another was founded at Kye-ryong, by Chöng. The poor fellow paid for this bright forecast with his life.

Cho Chin was charged with the work of building the wall of the new capital. To this end, in the spring of 1391, 119,000 men were brought from the provinces of P'yŭng-an and Whang-hă and they worked steadily for two months. In the autumn 89,000 men came from Kang-wŭn, Chŭl-la and Kyŭng-sang Provinces and finished it in a month more. The whole circuit of the wall was 9,975 double paces. At five feet to the double pace this would give us about nine and a half miles, its present length. It was pierced by eight gates, the South Gate, or Suk-nye-mun, the East Gate or Heung-in-mun, the West Gate, or Ton-eui-mun, the Little West Gate, or So-eui-mun, the North-east Gate, or Chang-eui-mun, the Water Mouth Gate, or Kwang-heui-mun, also called the Su-gu-mun, and finally the Suk-chang-mun, a private gate at the north by which the king may pass in time of danger to the mountain fortress of Puk-han. At the same time a law was made that dead bodies could be carried out of the city only by way of the Little West or the Water Mouth Gates. Neither of these 'dead men's gates' were roofed at first but were simply arches.

The Capital Moved

Immediately upon the completion of the wall the court was moved from Song-do to the new capital and the new palace was named the Kyŭng-bok Palace. By this time the news of the founding of a new dynasty had spread, and envoys came from Japan, the Liu-kiu Islands and from the southern kingdom of Sam-na. It will be remembered that the Mongols had absorbed a portion of the northern territory of Korea, especially in

Ham-gyŭng Province. This had never come again fully under Ko-ryŭ control, so that now the new kingdom extended only as far north as Ma-ch'ŭn Pass. Between that and the Tu-man River lived people of the Yŭ-jin tribe. The king sent Yi Tu-ran to give them a friendly introduction to the newly founded kingdom of Cho-sŭn, and he was so good a diplomat that soon he was able to form that whole region into three semi-independent districts and in course of time it naturally became incorporated into Cho-sŭn. The Koryŭ dynasty left a heavy legacy of priestcraft that was not at all to the liking of the new king. The monks had far more power with the people than seemed consistent with good government. Monasteries were constantly in process of erection and their inmates arrogated to themselves large powers that they did not by right possess. Monks were not mendicants then as they are today. Each monastery had its complement of slaves to do all menial work and the law that declared that the grandson of a slave should be free was a dead letter. The first of a long list of restrictions upon the priesthood was a restatement and an enforcement of this salutary law which made hereditary serfdom impossible.

Before his accession to the throne he had succeeded in putting down the Japanese pirates, at least for the time. He now placed high military and naval officials at all the great southern ports, who offered the people still further protection. He also set aside the three ports of Ch'e-p'o, Yŭm-p'o and Pu-san-p'o (Fusan) as places where Japanese envoys and trading parties might be entertained. At these places he built houses for the accommodation of such guests.

King T'ă-jo had a numerous family. By his first queen, Han, he had six sons, of whom the second and the fifth later became

Kings of Cho-sŭn, with the posthumous titles of Chöng-jong and T'ă-jong respectively. By his second queen, Kang, he had two sons, both of whom aspired to the crown but without hope. They were named Pang-sŭk and Pang-bon. Their ambition led them astray, for now in the sixth year of the reign they conspired to kill their two rival half-brothers and so prepare the way for their own elevation. They secured the services of two assassins who made the attempt, but being foiled they lost their heads. It was well known that the two princes were at the bottom of the plot, and the king, knowing that even he could not protect them from justice, advised them to make good their escape. They fled but were caught just outside the West Gate and put to death.

The courtiers were all homesick for Song-do and the king himself probably missed many of the comforts which he had there enjoyed. Merchants had not as yet come in large numbers to the new capital and the number of houses was comparatively small. It must be noticed that with the change of dynasty it was taken for granted that the citizens of the old capital were loyal to the fallen dynasty and so the people of Song-do were not allowed to move to Seoul in large numbers. That city was reserved as the residence of the friends of the new regime. Song-do has ever been considered less loyal than any other city in the country and the rule has been that no native of that city could hold an important office under the present government. But at first, the new capital was hardly as pleasant a place to live as the old, and so the king gave the word and the whole court moved back there for a time.

We are told that king T'ă-jo was heartily tired of the constant strife among his sons as to who should be the successor and he decided to resign the office and retire to his native Ham-heung. His choice of a successor fell upon his oldest living son, Prince

Yong-an, better known by his posthumous title Chöng-jong Kong-jŭng Tă-wang. The army and the people all desired that his fifth son, Prince Chöng-an, who is generally known as T'ă-jong, who had been so active in helping his father to the throne and who was as energetic and enterprising as his brother was slow, should become their ruler. When they heard that they could not have their will there was an angry demonstration at the palace. This led the retiring king to advise that after Chöng-jong had ruled a while he had better resign in favour of his brother, the people's choice.

King Chöng-jong's first act was a statesman-like one. He commanded the disbanding of the feudal retainers of all the officials. A few who rebelled at this as an encroachment upon their rights were promptly banished, and the rest submitted. Thus the death blow was struck at feudalism in the peninsula. It never gained the foothold here that it had in Japan, for it was thus nipped in the bud. The weakness of the fallen dynasty had been that one or more of the officials had gathered about their persons such large retinues that they succeeded in overawing the king and making him a mere puppet. But this was not to be a feature of the new regime, for King Chöng-jong by this one decree effectually stamped it out.

The retired king seemed to be determined not to be disturbed in his well-earned rest, for when his sons sent and begged him to come back to the capital and aid the government by his advice, he answered by putting the messenger to death. Later, however, he relented and returned to Seoul.

Chöng-jong Abdicates

T'ă-jo's third son, Prince Pang, was jealous because his younger brother had been selected to succeed king Chöng-jong, and so he determined to have him put out of the way. To this end he conspired with one Pak-po, but the plot was discovered, Pak Po was killed and the prince banished to T'o-san in Whang-hă Province. T'ă-jong himself, the prospective king, seems to have chafed at the delay, for we are told that King Chöng-jong's queen noticed his moody looks and advised her lord to abdicate in his favour without delay, before harm came of it. So King Chöng-jong called his brother and handed over to him the seals of office and himself retired to private life with the title Sang-wang, or 'Great king'.

It was in the centennial year 1400 that T'ă-jong, whose full posthumous title is T'ă-jong Kong-jŭng T'ă-wang, entered upon the royal office. He was a man of indomitable will, untiring energy, and ready resource. It was he who really entered upon the work of reform in earnest. T'ă-jo had been too old and Chöng-jong had lacked the energy. The year 1401 gave him an opportunity to begin these reforms.

The land was suffering from famine, and the king said, 'Why is so much grain wasted in the making of wine? Let it cease for the present.' When he found that the people would not obey he said, 'It is because I myself have not desisted from the use of wine. Let no more wine be served in the palace for the present.' It is said that this practical appeal was successful and the people also desisted. From the earliest times it had been the custom for the monks to congregate and pray for the cessation of drought, but now by one sweep of his pen the king added another limitation to the prerogatives of the monks by forbidding the observance of the custom. Large tracts of land were also taken from the monasteries and given back to the people. The king hung a great bell in the palace gate and made proclamation that anyone who failed to have a grievance righted by the proper tribunals might appeal directly to the throne, and whoever struck the drum was given instant audience. This privilege was seldom abused for it soon became known that if a man did not have right clearly on his side his rash appeal to the king brought severe punishment.

For many a decade letters had languished in the peninsula, and now with a view to their revival the king ordered the casting of copper types and provided that, as fast as new characters were found in the leading Chinese works, they should be immediately cast and added to the font. The authenticity of this statement cannot be called in question. It is attested by all the great historical works both public and private. The method of use was such that the types were practically indestructible and large numbers exist and are in active use to this day. So far as the evidence goes these were the first metal type ever made, though xylography had been known since the very earliest time.

In 1406 the emperor sent an envoy asking that a copper Buddha on the island of Quelpart be brought to Seoul for the king to do obeisance to it, and that it then be forwarded to China. The king, however, refused to bow before it. During this same year the law was promulgated forbidding the imprisonment of criminals for long periods of time. It also beheld the execution of all the brothers of the queen. We are not told the reason of this, but we may surmise that it was because they had been implicated in seditious proceedings.

In 1409 the Japanese, Wŭn-do-jin, was sent to the Korean court to present the respects of the Japanese sovereign.

The kings of Koryŭ had set aside large tracts of land in Whang-hă Province for hunting purposes. These by order of king T'ă-jong were now restored to the people and they were ordered to cultivate them. In 1413 the land suffered from a severe drought and the courtiers all advised that the monks and the female exorcists and fortune tellers be called upon to pray for rain; but the king replied, 'Buddhism is an empty religion and the exorcists and fortune tellers are a worthless lot. If I were only a better ruler Heaven would not refuse us rain.' He thereupon ordered all the sorceresses, fortune tellers, exorcists and geomancers to deliver up the books of their craft to the government and a great fire was made with them in front of the palace.

King T'ă-jong's great sorrow was his son the crown prince, Yang-yŭng. This young man was dissolute and worthless. He would not pursue the studies prescribed by his tutors but spent his time in hunting, gambling, and in less reputable pursuits. The people cried out against him and made it known that it was not their will that he should reign over them. The father saw the justice of the complaint and the young man was banished to Kwang-ju and the fourth son, Prince Ch'ung-nyŭng, was proclaimed heir to the throne.

King T'ă-jong retired in 1419 in favour of this son Ch'ung-nyŭng who is known by the posthumous title Se-jong Chang-hŭn Tă-wang.

T' ă-Jong's Claims to Greatness

T'ă-jong had been a radical reformer and worked a revolution in Korean life similar to that which Cromwell effected in England. His greatness is exhibited in three ways. (1) He was the first king who dared to break away utterly from customs whose only sanction was their antiquity. (2) He was wise enough not to force all these radical reforms at once, but spread them over a period of nearly two decades. (3) He recognized that a king is the servant of the people. It may be in place here to call attention to a peculiar custom of the east. We refer to the custom of surrendering the throne to a successor before one's death. The benefits of this custom are soon cited. The retiring sovereign becomes the tutor of the incoming one. The young ruler has the benefit of his practical suggestions and of his immense influence. He thus does away with much of the danger of revolution or rebellion which so often accompanies a change or rulers. If the new king proves inefficient or otherwise unsatisfactory it is possible, through the father's influence, to effect a change. In other words the young ruler is on trial and he undergoes a probation that is salutary for him and for the people as well. It also helps greatly in perpetuating a policy, for in such a case the father, knowing that his son is to assume the reins of government while he still lives, takes greater pains to initiate him into the secrets of government and in forming in his mind settled principles which, while they may not always perpetuate the same policy, at least ensure an easy gradation from one policy to another. This perhaps was the crowning feat of T'ă-jong's greatness. He knew enough to stop while his success was at its height and spend some years in teaching his successor how to achieve even a greater success. Let us see how these principles worked in the case of this new king.

Se-jong Reins

The young king began in a modest way by consulting with his father in regard to all matters of importance. The retired king had taken up his quarters in the 'Lotus Pond District' where he was at all times accessible to the young king and where he took cognizance of much of the public business. The new ruler was characterized by great evenness of temper, great astuteness, and untiring diligence. He is said to have risen each morning at dawn.

He ordered the making of musical instruments, including metal drums and triangles. Under his supervision a clepsydra was made and a work on astronomy was published. It is said that with his own hand he prepared works on 'The five rules of conduct,' 'The duties of King, Father, and Husband,' 'Good Government and Peace,' and a work on military tactics. The custom of collecting rare flowers and plants and growing them in the palace enclosure was done away and it was decreed that no more of the public money should be squandered in that way. He built a little straw thatched cottage beside the palace and compelled the officials to attend him there in council. He put a stop to the evil practice of letting concubines and eunuchs meddle with state affairs, for when one of his concubines asked him to give one of her relatives official position, he promptly banished her from the palace.

In the second year of his reign, 1420, the king showed his partiality for literature and literary pursuits by founding a college to which he invited thirteen of the finest scholars that the kingdom could furnish, and there they gave themselves up to the pursuit of letters.

Japanese Islands Attacked

In the early summer the dreaded Japanese again began their ravages on the coasts of Korea. Landing at Pi-in, Ch'ung-ch'ŭng Province, they easily overcame the local forces and marched northward along the coast into Whang-hă Province. They there informed the Korean generals that they did not want to ravage

Korea but that they were seeking a way into China. They lacked provisions and promised to go immediately if the Koreans would give them enough rice for their sustenance, until they should cross the border into China. Forty bags of rice were given to them, but when the king learned of it he was displeased and said, 'When they return we must destroy them.'

The southern provinces were put into a state of defence and Gen. Yi Chong-mu was put at the head of a punitive expedition. It is said that a fleet of 227 war vessels and an army of 107,285 men rendezvoused at Ma-san Harbor. They were provided with two months' rations. This powerful flotilla sailed away and soon reached the island of Tsushima. There it burned 129 Japanese boats and 1,939 houses. Over 100 Japanese were killed, twenty-one prisoners were taken, and 131 Chinese and eight Korean captives were liberated. The fleet then sailed toward Japan and arrived at Ni-ro harbor. There, the records say, they lost 120 men and so abandoned the enterprise. This is good evidence that the numbers of the army are overestimated, for a loss of 120 men from such an immense force would not have caused an abandonment of the expedition.

The emperor sent a messenger asking for the four jewels that are supposed to come from the bodies of good monks when they are incinerated.

Gradual Suppression of Buddhism

These were said to be kept at Heung-ch'ŭn monastery at Song-do. King Se-jong replied that there were no such jewels in the peninsula. He ordered the discontinuance of the custom of building monasteries at the graves of kings, and the people were commanded not to pray to Buddha in behalf of the king.

The great expense incurred in providing for the huge stone that covered the sarcophagus of a king made him change the custom and it was decreed that thereafter four smaller ones should be used instead of the one great one.

One of his most statesmanlike acts was to decree that every man charged with a capital offense should have three trials and that detailed accounts of each of these should be furnished for the royal inspection. Following out the policy of a gradual suppression of Buddhism, he interdicted the observance of the festival called the *To-ak.*

In the fourth year of his reign, his father died. It is said that at the time of his death there was a severe drought, and on his deathbed he said, 'When I die I will go and ask Heaven to send rain,' and the story goes that on the very day he died the welcome rain came. To this day it is said that it is sure to rain on the tenth day of the fifth moon, and this is called the 'T'ă-jong rain'.

Numerous Reforms

We see that under that father's tutelage he had continued the policy of reform, but what he had done was only the beginning. The law was made that if a prefect died the prefects along the road should furnish transport for his body up to the capital. The eunuchs were enjoined not to interfere in any way with the affairs of state. The term of office of the country prefects was lengthened, owing to the expense entailed upon the people by frequent changes. It was made a crime to delay the interment of a corpse simply because the geomancers could not find an auspicious spot for the burial, and all geomancers' books were ordered burned. Every adult male was required to carry on his person a wooden tag bearing his name. This was for the purpose of identification to prevent the evasion of taxes and of military service. It is but right to say that this law was never strictly carried out.

Korea has always suffered from the existence of armies on paper. The king edited a book on agriculture telling in what districts and in what kinds of soil different species of grains and vegetables would thrive best. He paid attention to penal laws as well. Beating was to be administered on the legs rather than on the back; no murderers were to be bound in prison who were under fifteen years or over seventy; no prisoner under ten or over eighty was to suffer under the rod; even the king's relatives, if guilty of crime, were not to be exempt from punishment.

These important reforms occupied the attention of the king up to the year 1432, the fourteenth of his reign, but now the border wars in the north claimed his attention. At this time the wild tribes across the Yalu were known under the collective name of Ya-in. These savages were ravaging back and forth across the border, now successful and now defeated. King Se-jong decided that the peace of the north was worth the outlay of some life and treasure; so, early in the year 1433 an expedition under Gen. Ch'oé Yun-dok crossed the Yalu in six divisions, each consisting of 1,000 men or more. These had agreed to make a common attack on Ta-ram-no, the stronghold of the robbers, on the nineteenth of the fourth moon. This was successfully done with the result that 176 of the enemy were left dead, and 236 captives and 270 head of cattle were taken. All of this was at the cost of just four men.

The Far North Colonized

The northern portion of Ham-gyŭng province was as yet but sparsely settled, and reports came in that the Ming people were coming in great numbers and settling there; so the king felt it necessary to do something to assert his rights. A great scheme for colonization was made and people from the southern part of the province were sent north to occupy the land. But there were two powerful Yŭ-jin chiefs across the Tu-man River who were constantly crossing and harrying the people along that border line. These were Ol-yang-t'ap and Hol-ja-on. It was not until the year 1436 that they were really silenced and then only after repeated and overwhelming victories on the part of the Korean forces. During these years thousands of people from the southern provinces were brought north by the government and given land in this border country.

About this time a Japanese named Chŭng Seung was Daimyo of Tsushima. He sent fifty boats across to the Korean shore and the trade relations were revived, which we may feel sure had been sadly interrupted by the long period of piratical raids. The government made these people a present of 200 bags of rice and beans. Sixty 'houses' of people also came from that island and asked to be allowed to live in the three ports, Ch'ep'o, Yŭm-p'o, and Pu-san-p'o. The king gave his assent and from that time until about the present day, with only temporary intermissions, the Japanese have resided in one or other of these three places, although Pu-san (Fusan) has always been the most important of them. In the year 1443 the custom of giving the Daimyo of Tsushima a bonus of 200 bags of grain a year was instituted. The number of trading boats that could come was strictly limited by the Korean government to fifty, but in extreme cases where sudden need arose through piratical raids or other cause the number could be increased. This custom continued without interruption until 1510.

A PHONETIC ALPHABET

The most striking feat that King Se-jong accomplished and the one that had the most far-reaching and lasting effect upon the people was the invention of a pure phonetic alphabet. This alphabet scarcely has its equal in the world for simplicity and phonetic power. He was not the first one to see the vast disadvantage under which the people laboured in being obliged to master the Chinese character before being able to read. We will remember that in the days of Silla the scholar Sŭl-chong had invented a rough way of indicating the grammatical endings in a Chinese text by inserting certain diacritical marks, but this had of course been very cumbersome and only the *ajuns* or 'clerks' were acquainted with it. Another similar attempt had been made near the end of the Koryŭ dynasty but it too had proved a failure so far as general use by the people was concerned. King Se-jong was the first man to dare to face the difficulty and overcome it by the use not of modifications of the Chinese characters but by an entirely new and different system, a phonetic alphabet[...].

The new alphabet [...] was called the *ŏn-mun* [today also spelled onmun]. [The] celebrated dictionary [derived from the alphabet] is called the *Hun-min Chŏng-eum*.

THE KOREAN ALPHABET

(Discussed by J.S. Gale)

The date of the alphabet is a matter on which all native authorities agree, namely 1446 CE, a great and expectant era in the history of the world.... The Mings were at the height of their power. It was the dawn of modern Europe. Columbus had just been born. Six years later a little child was baptized by the name of Leonardo da Vinci. Twenty-seven years later Copernicus opened his wondering eyes on this planet. Twenty-nine years later there visited the earth no less than Michaelangelo. Thirty-seven years latter came two distinguished guests, one of the Old Church, and one of the New, Raphael and Luther. About this time too, Gutenberg is reported to have issued his first book from the press of Johannes Fust. A wonderful time indeed, fruitful of great men as the megalithic age was fruitful of menhir, dolmens, and cromlechs. 1446, one of the years of the Tiger, is then the date of the alphabet....

The king was evidently solicitous for the welfare of his people. He wished that the illiterate among his subjects might have some of the joy and satisfaction that comes with literature. He himself was a great scholar and needed no simplification of the Classics, but the people, they were a distress to him, they were ignorant, and he desired that they might be enlightened. He wished also to put on record their songs and to aid and assist in music.

Opposition from the King's Ministers

His thought was not one to win him popularity with his ministers. King Se-jong completed his work three years before it was promulgated. But so great was the opposition of high officers of state and the literati against any such apparent humiliating of the noble office of the character, that they banded themselves together, in great consternation, to oppose it. Sö Kö-jöng, who wrote the *Tong-Guk T'ong-Kam*, a famous history of Korea, says,

'His Majesty the King, when he wrote the *Enmun*, found himself opposed by the great mass of the literati who determined, by all the forces at their disposal to prevent it. But the King, not granting this demand, commanded Choi Hang and his company, and they wrote the *Hun-min Cheung-Eum*, and the *Tong guk Cheung-Un* (which is simply a copy of the *Hong-Mu Cheung-Un)*. Cheung In-ji also throws light on this when he says, 'In the winter of 1443 the King wrote out the 28 letters. They were formed in this year but not promulgated till 1446. In these three years Söng Sammun and his company went thirteen times in all to Laotung to see Whang-Chan and to inquire about Rhyme. His Majesty had the persistence and patience of a Sage, and a clear decision in his own soul, and so made an independent written language. There are no words with which to praise his exalted virtue.' In the *Yel-Yö Keui-Sul* [it states] the literati wrote out a petition and begged the king not to launch this alphabet out into the world, as manifold evils would undoubtedly follow its promulgation....

'When the people cannot now master one script why attempt to make two?' was the question. 'So degraded and contemptible a substitute too!' The king was wise, however, and fixed in his purpose. He knew too, how to bide his time. 'I shall prove its capacity to be equal to that of the character itself,' said he. He then commanded Cheung In-ji to write a poem in this new script, a poem that would exalt his royal ancestors in high and noble measure, so that the *Enmun* could ride out on the wave of its popularity. It was so done and the book was called *The Flying Dragons in Heaven.* Such a book could not but be popular. At once it was placed in the national archives and the People's Alphabet went on its way rejoicing....

The Five Who Formed the Alphabet

There were five distinguished persons associated with the formation of the alphabet namely: King Se-jong, Cheung In-ji, Söng Sam-mun, Shin Sukju, and Choi Hang.

1. Se-jong was forty-seven years of age when the work was finished. He had been from his earliest school days a diligent student of the classics, had read and re-read his books 100 times, till, once, when he fell ill, his father took them all away from him except one volume. This he read through 1,000 times we are told, till he became a giant in the literary world of his day. His father before him was a great scholar, and his son after him.

He invented the water clock and sundial, and music flourished in his reign. They called him Yo-Sun of the East Peninsula, and Yo-Sun has always been a name to conjure with.

2. The second name we associate with the Alphabet is that of Cheung In-ji, who was chairman of the committee chosen to prepare it. He is said to have played as a little boy within. the precincts of the Confucian Temple located inside of the Little East-Gate of Seoul. He was born in 1396, a year before the king, and so was forty-eight years of age when the alphabet was formed. He wrote many books, one being a history of Kōryö. The king appreciated him so highly that he commanded him to marry into the royal family. This he did, becoming first Minister of State, and the strong administrator of the law.

3. Shin Suk-ju was, like Cheung, a child of ancient Silla, his family seat being Ko-Ryöng, Kyöng-sang Province. He was sent early in life to Japan as a special envoy. He went also as secretary in the train of the ambassador to the Mings. He and Söng Sam-mun met Whang Chan and consulted with him concerning Rhyme and Music. He too became Prime Minister and saw six

kings come and go. His master likened him to the greatest and most illustrious of China's sages.

4. Choi Hang was a gifted scholar and a native of Seoul. He was associated with Cheung in the History of Kōryö as well as in the creation of the Alphabet. But the state that moved on so gloriously on the high wave of scholarship fell into an awful tragedy, for the young king, like the English Princes of the Tower, was strangled by his uncle Se-jo. Choi, as did Shin and Cheung, cast in his lot with the usurper and comes down through the ages with a spot upon his fair name.

5. Söng Sam-mun. Of all the characters Söng is the most picturesque. His family name means Completeness and his given name was Sam-mun or Three Calls. It is said that when he was born some spirit voice came three times as a wireless message to him through the sky, and so he was always known as Sammun, Three Calls....

The first [records concerning the alphabet] in order of importance is the Mun-Hön Pigo the greatest of Korean literary compilations.... It was begun by King Yöngjong in 1770. Volume XXII, Section 108, is given up entirely to the People's Alphabet: 'King Se-Jong of Chosen, in the 28th year of his reign made the People's Alphabet. Said he, "Each country has its own script by which to record its speech but we have none" and so he made the twenty-eight letters calling it the Common Script.

'He opened an office in the palace and selected Cheung In-ji, Shin Suk-ju, Söng Sam-mun, and Choi Hang, to undertake the work. They used the ancient 'seal', character as a model for the forms, and divided the letters into Initials, Medials, and Finals. Though these letters are few in number and easily formed, their possible use is unlimited, so that all sounds and literary expressions can be recorded by them without exception.

'At this time a noted scholar of the Hallim, Whang Chan, a man of the Mings, was in exile in Laotung. By command of the King this Committee visited him and inquired concerning Music and Rhyme. They visited him in all thirteen times.'

Preface to the Alphabet

This is the introductory statement and we come now to the preface written by Cheung In-ji, Minister of Ceremonies.

'There are various sounds that pertain to earth and naturally there are various forms of script to indicate them. The ancients constructed their forms of writing to suit the sounds to be recorded, and made them a means of conveying all varieties of thought. It became thus the medium for recording the Doctrine of the Three Parties, Heaven, Earth, and Man, so that matters of statement might remain fixed for future generations.

'But as customs in the four quarters of the earth differ from one another, so the characteristic sounds differ likewise. Various outside nations, other than China, have sounds of speech but no letters by which to record them, and so they have made use of the character. But it has been like trying to fit a wrong wedge into a chiselled hole. How could one expect to find such an expedient satisfactory? The important matter is to find some convenience suitable to each place, and not to try to force each into the method of the other.

'Our Korean ceremonial forms, music, literature, and art are very closely allied to those of China, but our speech and dialects are altogether different. Students of the character are at a loss to get at the exact thought and oftentimes the justice of the peace is at his wits' end as to how to record definitely the judgment arrived at.

'Because of this, in ancient days Sölchong invented the Itu, which the officials use till the present day. It is a recording of sound by means of the character, a contrivance both tasteless and cumbersome, arranged in a way that is lacking in good form. As for ordinary speech, the Itu is wholly unsuitable to express one sound out of one thousand. Because of this in the winter of 1443 His Majesty began work on the 28 letters and in accordance with the use to be made of them called them the *Hun-Min Cheung-Eum*, the People's Alphabet. In their form and shape they were modelled after the ancient "seal" character of China; in sound after the Seven Primary Notes of Music. The principle of the Three Primary Forces of nature was adhered to, as well as that of the two Primary Essences and all were included in the twenty-eight letters.

'Their possibility of interchange is unlimited, simple, and yet efficient, neat of form and yet comprehensive enough for any combination. A person of intelligence can learn them in a morning, and the stupidest person in a few days. By means of these, the character can be mastered, and the thought understood in cases at law. In rhyme, too, the difference can be expressed between 'clear' and 'mixed' sounds, and songs can be written to suit the notes of music. There is no limit to their variety of use, the sound of the wind, the call of birds, cackling of fowls and barking of dogs, all can be expressed.

'His Majesty commanded us to explain it most definitely to the people, so that, even without a teacher, the reader might understand it.

'The first origin and mystery of their construction did not lie with us, but with our monarch, who, being a Sage, raised up of God, made laws and regulations that showed him superior to a hundred kings. So too, in the making of the Alphabet, he took little pattern from things seen, but rather evolved it from his own inner consciousness. It was not done by the law of men but by an infinite grasp on eternal principles.'...

This is Cheung's preface. The king then wrote 'Our speech in sound differs from that of China, and so we cannot communicate it by means of the character. Men unlearned cannot write down their thoughts. Because of this I was moved with compassion for the people, and made the 28 letters of the Alphabet so that all men could easily learn them and have something simple for everyday use.'

King Se-jong died in 1450.

ANCIENT KINGS & LEADERS

Ancient cultures often traded with and influenced each other, while others grew independently. This section provides the key leaders from a number of regions, to offer comparative insights into developments across the ancient world.

SUMERIAN KING LIST

This list is based on the *Sumerian King List* or *Chronicle of the One Monarchy*. The lists were often originally carved into clay tablets and several versions have been found, mainly in southern Mesopotamia. Some of these are incomplete and others contradict one another. Dates are based on archaeological evidence as far as possible but are thus approximate. There may also be differences in name spellings between different sources. Nevertheless, the lists remain an invaluable source of information.

As with many civilizations, lists of leaders often begin with mythological and legendary figures before they merge into the more solidly historical, hence why you will see some reigns of seemingly impossible length.

After the kingship descended from heaven, the kingship was in Eridug.

Alulim	28,800 years (8 *sars**)
Alalngar	36,000 years (10 *sars*)

Then Eridug fell and the kingship was taken to Bad-tibira.

En-men-lu-ana	43,200 years (12 *sars*)
En-mel-gal-ana	28,800 years (8 *sars*)
Dumuzid the Shepherd (or Tammuz)	36,000 years (10 *sars*)

Then Bad-tibira fell and the kingship was taken to Larag.

En-sipad-zid-ana 28,800 years (8 *sars*)

Then Larag fell and the kingship was taken to Zimbir.

En-men-dur-ana 21,000 years (5 *sars* and 5 *ners*)

Then Zimbir fell and the kingship was taken to Shuruppag.

Ubara-Tutu 18,600 years (5 *sars* and 1 *ner**)

Then the flood swept over.

*A *sar* is a numerical unit of 3,600; a *ner* is a numerical unit of 600.

FIRST DYNASTY OF KISH

After the flood had swept over, and the kingship had descended from heaven, the kingship was in Kish.

Jushur	1,200 years	Zuqaqip	900 years
Kullassina-bel	960 years	Atab (or A-ba)	600 years
Nangishlisma	1,200 years	Mashda (son of	
En-tarah-ana	420 years	Atab)	840 years
Babum	300 years	Arwium (son of	
Puannum	840 years	Mashda)	720 years
Kalibum	960 years	Etana the Shepherd	1,500 years
Kalumum	840 years	Balih (son of Etana)	400 years

En-me-nuna	660 years
Melem-Kish (son of Enme-nuna)	900 years
Barsal-nuna (son of Enme-nuna)	1,200 years
Zamug (son of Barsal-nuna)	140 years
Tizqar (son of Zamug)	305 years
Ilku	900 years
Iltasadum	1,200 years
Enmebaragesi (earliest proven ruler based on archaeological sources; Early Dynastic Period, 2900–2350 BCE)	900 years
Aga of Kish (son of Enmebaragesi) (Early Dynastic Period, 2900–2350 BCE)	625 years

Then Kish was defeated and the kingship was taken to E-anna.

FIRST RULERS OF URUK

Mesh-ki-ang-gasher (son of Utu)	324 years (Late Uruk Period, 4000–3100 BCE)
Enmerkar (son of Mesh-ki-ang-gasher)	420 years (Late Uruk Period, 4000–3100 BCE)
Lugal-banda the shepherd	1200 years (Late Uruk Period, 4000–3100 BCE)
Dumuzid the fisherman	100 years (Jemdet Nasr Period, 3100–2900 BCE)
Gilgamesh	126 years (Early Dynastic Period, 2900–2350 BCE)
Ur-Nungal (son of Gilgamesh)	30 years
Udul-kalama (son of Ur-Nungal)	15 years
La-ba'shum	9 years
En-nun-tarah-ana	8 years

Mesh-he	36 years
Melem-ana	6 years
Lugal-kitun	36 years

Then Unug was defeated and the kingship was taken to Urim (Ur).

FIRST DYNASTY OF UR

Mesh-Ane-pada	80 years
Mesh-ki-ang-Nuna (son of Mesh-Ane-pada)	36 years
Elulu	25 years
Balulu	36 years

Then Urim was defeated and the kingship was taken to Awan.

DYNASTY OF AWAN

Three kings of Awan	356 years

Then Awan was defeated and the kingship was taken to Kish.

SECOND DYNASTY OF KISH

Susuda the fuller	201 years
Dadasig	81 years
Mamagal the boatman	360 years
Kalbum (son of Mamagal)	195 years

Tuge	360 years
Men-nuna (son of Tuge)	180 years
Enbi-Ishtar	290 years
Lugalngu	360 years

Then Kish was defeated and the kingship was taken to Hamazi.

DYNASTY OF HAMAZI

Hadanish	360 years

Then Hamazi was defeated and the kingship was taken to Unug (Uruk).

SECOND DYNASTY OF URUK

En-shag-kush-ana	60 years (*c.* 25th century BCE)
Lugal-kinishe-dudu	120 years
Argandea	7 years

Then Unug was defeated and the kingship was taken to Urim (Ur).

SECOND DYNASTY OF UR

Nanni	120 years
Mesh-ki-ang-Nanna II (son of Nanni)	48 years

Then Urim was defeated and the kingship was taken to Adab.

DYNASTY OF ADAB

Lugal-Ane-mundu	90 years (*c.* 25th century BCE)

Then Adab was defeated and the kingship was taken to Mari.

DYNASTY OF MARI

Anbu	30 years	Zizi of Mari, the fuller	20 years
Anba (son of Anbu)	17 years	Limer the 'gudug' priest	30 years
Bazi the leatherworker	30 years	Sharrum-iter	9 years

Then Mari was defeated and the kingship was taken to Kish.

THIRD DYNASTY OF KISH

Kug-Bau (Kubaba)	100 years (*c.* 25th century BCE)

Then Kish was defeated and the kingship was taken to Akshak.

DYNASTY OF AKSHAK

Unzi	30 years	Ishu-Il	24 years
Undalulu	6 years	Shu-Suen (son of Ishu-Il)	7 years
Urur	6 years		
Puzur-Nirah	20 years		

Then Akshak was defeated and the kingship was taken to Kish.

FOURTH DYNASTY OF KISH

Puzur-Suen (son of Kug-bau)	25 years (*c.* 2350 BCE)
Ur-Zababa (son of Puzur-Suen)	400 years (*c.* 2300 BCE)
Zimudar	30 years
Usi-watar (son of Zimudar)	7 years
Eshtar-muti	11 years
Ishme-Shamash	11 years
Shu-ilishu	15 years
Nanniya the jeweller	7 years

Then Kish was defeated and the kingship was taken to Unug (Uruk).

THIRD DYNASTY OF URUK

Lugal-zage-si	25 years (*c.* 2296–2271 BCE)

Then Unug was defeated and the kingship was taken to Agade (Akkad).

DYNASTY OF AKKAD

Sargon of Akkad	56 years (*c.* 2270–2215 BCE)
Rimush of Akkad (son of Sargon)	9 years (*c.* 2214–2206 BCE)
Manishtushu (son of Sargon)	15 years (*c.* 2205–2191 BCE)

Naram-Sin of Akkad (son of Manishtushu)	56 years (*c*. 2190–2154 BCE)
Shar-kali-sharri (son of Naram-Sin)	24 years (*c*. 2153–2129 BCE)

Then who was king? Who was not the king?

Irgigi, Nanum, Imi and Ilulu	3 years (four rivals who fought to be king during a three-year period; *c*. 2128–2125 BCE)
Dudu of Akkad	21 years (*c*. 2125–2104 BCE)
Shu-Durul (son of Duu)	15 years (*c*. 2104–2083 BCE)

Then Agade was defeated and the kingship was taken to Unug (Uruk).

FOURTH DYNASTY OF URUK

Ur-ningin	7 years (*c*. 2091?–2061? BCE)
Ur-gigir (son of Ur-ningin)	6 years
Kuda	6 years
Puzur-ili	5 years
Ur-Utu (or Lugal-melem; son of Ur-gigir)	6 years

Unug was defeated and the kingship was taken to the army of Gutium.

GUTIAN RULE

Inkišuš	6 years (*c*. 2147–2050 BCE)
Sarlagab (or Zarlagab)	6 years

Shulme (or Yarlagash)	6 years
Elulmeš (or Silulumeš or Silulu)	6 years
Inimabakeš (or Duga)	5 years
Igešauš (or Ilu-An)	6 years
Yarlagab	3 years
Ibate of Gutium	3 years
Yarla (or Yarlangab)	3 years
Kurum	1 year
Apilkin	3 years
La-erabum	2 years
Irarum	2 years
Ibranum	1 year
Hablum	2 years
Puzur-Suen (son of Hablum)	7 years
Yarlaganda	7 years
Si'um (or Si-u)	7 years
Tirigan	40 days

Then the army of Gutium was defeated and the kingship taken to Unug (Uruk).

FIFTH DYNASTY OF URUK

Utu-hengal	427 years / 26 years / 7 years (conflicting dates; *c.* 2055–2048 BCE)

THIRD DYNASTY OF UR

Ur-Namma (or Ur-Nammu)	18 years (c. 2047–2030 BCE)
Shulgi (son of Ur-Namma)	48 years (c. 2029–1982 BCE)
Amar-Suena (son of Shulgi)	9 years (c. 1981–1973 BCE)
Shu-Suen (son of Amar-Suena)	9 years (c. 1972–1964 BCE)
Ibbi-Suen (son of Shu-Suen)	24 years (c. 1963–1940 BCE)

Then Urim was defeated. The very foundation of Sumer was torn out. The kingship was taken to Isin.

DYNASTY OF ISIN

Ishbi-Erra	33 years (c. 1953–1920 BCE)
Shu-Ilishu (son of Ishbi-Erra)	20 years
Iddin-Dagan (son of Shu-Ilishu)	20 years
Ishme-Dagan (son of Iddin-Dagan)	20 years
Lipit-Eshtar (son of Ishme-Dagan or Iddin Dagan)	11 years
Ur-Ninurta (son of Ishkur)	28 years
Bur-Suen (son of Ur-Ninurta)	21 years
Lipit-Enlil (son of Bur-Suen)	5 years
Erra-imitti	8 years
Enlil-bani	24 years
Zambiya	3 years
Iter-pisha	4 years
Ur-du-kuga	4 years
Suen-magir	11 years
Damiq-ilishu (son of Suen-magir)	23 years

ANCIENT EGYPTIAN PHARAOHS

There is dispute about the dates and position of pharaohs within dynasties due to several historical sources being incomplete or inconsistent. This list aims to provide an overview of the ancient Egyptian dynasties, but is not exhaustive and dates are approximate. There may also be differences in name spellings between different sources. Also please note that the throne name is given first, followed by the personal name – more commonly they are known by the latter.

ANCIENT EGYPTIAN DEITIES

Ancient Egyptian gods and goddesses were worshipped as deities. They were responsible for maat (divine order or stability), and different deities represented different natural forces, such as Ra the Sun God. After the Egyptian state was first founded in around 3100 BCE, pharaohs claimed to be divine representatives of these gods and were thought to be successors of the gods.

While there are many conflicting Egyptian myths, some of the significant gods and goddesses and their significant responsibilities are listed here.

Amun/Amen/Amen-Ra	Creation
Atem/Tem	Creation, the sun

Ra	The sun
Isis	The afterlife, fertility, magic
Osiris	Death and resurrection, agriculture
Hathor	The sky, the sun, motherhood
Horus	Kingship, the sky
Set	Storms, violence, deserts
Maat	Truth and justice, she personifies *maat*
Anubis	The dead, the underworld

PREDYNASTIC AND EARLY DYNASTIC PERIODS (*c.* 3000–2686 BCE)

First Dynasty (*c.* 3150–2890 BCE)

The first dynasty begins at the unification of Upper and Lower Egypt.

Narmer (Menes/M'na?)	*c.* 3150 BCE
Aha (Teti)	*c.* 3125 BCE
Djer (Itej)	54 years
Djet (Ita)	10 years
Merneith (possibly the first female Egyptian pharaoh)	*c.* 2950 BCE
Khasti (Den)	42 years
Merybiap (Adjib)	10 years
Semerkhet (Iry)	8.5 years
Qa'a (Qebeh)	34 years
Sneferka	*c.* 2900 BCE
Horus-Ba (Horus Bird)	*c.* 2900 BCE

Second Dynasty (*c.* 2890–2686 BCE)

Little is known about the second dynasty of Egypt.

Hetepsekhemwy (Nebtyhotep)	15 years
Nebra	14 years
Nynetjer (Banetjer)	43–45 years
Ba	unknown
Weneg-Nebty	*c*. 2740 BCE
Wadjenes (Wadj-sen)	*c*. 2740 BCE
Nubnefer	unknown
Senedj	*c*. 47 years
Peribsen (Seth-Peribsen)	unknown
Sekhemib (Sekhemib-Perenmaat)	*c*. 2720 BCE
Neferkara I	25 years
Neferkasokkar	8 years
Horus Sa	unknown
Hudejefa (real name missing)	11 years
Khasekhemwy (Bebty)	18 years

OLD KINGDOM (*c*. 2686–2181 BCE)

Third Dynasty (*c*. 2686–2613 BCE)

The third dynasty was the first dynasty of the Old Kingdom. Its capital was at Memphis.

Djoser (Netjerikhet)	*c*. 2650 BCE
Sekhemkhet (Djoser-Teti)	2649–2643 BCE
Nebka? (Sanakht)	*c*. 2650 BCE
Qahedjet (Huni?)	unknown
Khaba (Huni?)	2643–2637 BCE
Huni	2637–2613 BCE

Fourth Dynasty (*c.* 2613–2498 BCE)

The fourth dynasty is sometimes known as the 'golden age' of Egypt's Old Kingdom.

Snefru (Nebmaat)	2613–2589 BCE
Khufu, or Cheops (Medjedu)	2589–2566 BCE
Djedefre (Kheper)	2566–2558 BCE
Khafre (Userib)	2558–2532 BCE
Menkaure (Kakhet)	2532–2503 BCE
Shepseskaf (Shepeskhet)	2503–2498 BCE

Fifth Dynasty (*c.* 2498–2345 BCE)

There is some doubt over the succession of pharaohs in the fifth dynasty, especially Shepseskare.

Userkaf	2496/8–2491 BCE
Sahure	2490–2477 BCE
Neferirkare-Kakai	2477–2467 BCE
Neferefre (Izi)	2460–2458 BCE
Shepseskare (Netjeruser)	few months between 2458 and 2445 BCE
Niuserre (Ini)	2445–2422 BCE
Menkauhor (Kaiu)	2422–2414 BCE
Djedkare (Isesi)	2414–2375 BCE
Unis (Wenis)	2375–2345 BCE

Sixth Dynasty (*c.* 2345–2181 BCE)

Teti	2345–2333 BCE
Userkare	2333–2332 BCE
Meryre (Pepi I)	2332–2283 BCE

Merenre I (Nemtyemsaf I)	2283–2278 BCE
Neferkare (Pepi II)	2278–2183 BCE
Merenre II (Nemtyemsaf II)	2183 or 2184 BCE
Netjerkare (Siptah I) or Nitocris	2182–2179 BCE

FIRST INTERMEDIATE PERIOD (*c.* 2181–2040 BCE)

Seventh and Eighth Dynasties (*c.* 2181–2160 BCE)

There is little evidence on this period in ancient Egyptian history, which is why many of the periods of rule are unknown.

Menkare	*c.* 2181 BCE
Neferkare II	unknown
Neferkare III (Neby)	unknown
Djedkare (Shemai)	unknown
Neferkare IV (Khendu)	unknown
Merenhor	unknown
Sneferka (Neferkamin I)	unknown
Nikare	unknown
Neferkare V (Tereru)	unknown
Neferkahor	unknown
Neferkare VI (Peiseneb)	unknown to 2171 BCE
Neferkamin (Anu)	*c.* 2170 BCE
Qakare (Ibi)	2175–2171 BCE
Neferkaure	2167–2163 BCE
Neferkauhor (Khuwihapi)	2163–2161 BCE
Neferiirkkare (Pepi)	2161–2160 BCE

Ninth Dynasty (*c.* 2160–2130 BCE)

There is little evidence on this period in ancient Egyptian history which is why many of the periods of rule are unknown.

Maryibre (Khety I)	2160 BCE to unknown
Name unknown	unknown
Naferkare VII	unknown
Seneh (Setut)	unknown

The following pharaohs and their dates of rule are unknown or widely unconfirmed.

Tenth Dynasty (*c.* 2130–2040 BCE)

Rulers in the Tenth dynasty were based in Lower Egypt.

Meryhathor	2130 BCE to unknown
Neferkare VIII	2130–2040 BCE
Wahkare (Khety III)	unknown
Merykare	unknown to 2040 BCE
Name unknown	unknown

Eleventh Dynasty (*c.* 2134–1991 BCE)

Rulers in the eleventh dynasty were based in Upper Egypt.

Intef the Elder	unknown
Tepia (Mentuhotep I)	unknown to 2133 BCE
Sehertawy (Intef I)	2133–2117 BCE
Wahankh (Intef II)	2117–2068 BCE
Nakhtnebtepefer (Intef III)	2068–2060/40 BCE

MIDDLE KINGDOM (*c.* 2040–1802 BCE)

Eleventh Dynasty Continued (*c.* 2134–1991 BCE)

This period is usually known as the beginning of the Middle Kingdom.

Nebhepetre (Mentuhotep II) 2060–2040 BCE as king of Upper Egypt, 2040–2009 BCE as King of Upper and Lower Egypt

Sankhkare (Mentuhotep III)	2009–1997 BCE
Nebtawyre (Mentuhotep IV)	1997–1991 BCE

Twelfth Dynasty (*c.* 1991–1802 BCE)

The twelfth dynasty was one of the most stable prior to the New Kingdom, and is often thought to be the peak of the Middle Kingdom.

Sehetepibre (Amenemhat I)	1991–1962 BCE
Kheperkare (Senusret I / Sesostris I)	1971–1926 BCE
Nubkaure (Amenemhat II)	1929–1895 BCE
Khakheperre (Senusret II / Sesostris II)	1898–1878 BCE
Khakaure (Senusret III / Sesostris III)	1878–1839 BCE
Nimaatre (Amenemhat III)	1860–1815 BCE
Maakherure (Amenemhat IV)	1815–1807 BCE
Sobekkare (Sobekneferu/Nefrusobek)	1807–1802 BCE

SECOND INTERMEDIATE PERIOD (*c.* 1802–1550 BCE)

Thirteenth Dynasty (*c.* 1802–*c.* 1649 BCE)

There is some ambiguity on the periods of rule of the thirteenth dynasty, but it is marked by a period of several short rules. This dynasty is often combined with the eleventh, twelfth and fourteenth dynasties under the Middle Kingdom.

Sekhemre Khutawy (Sobekhotep I)	1802–1800 BCE
Mehibtawy Sekhemkare (Amenemhat Sonbef)	1800–1796 BCE
Nerikare (Sobek)	1796 BCE
Sekhemkare (Amenemhat V)	1796–1793 BCE
Ameny Qemau	1795–1792 BCE
Hotepibre (Qemau Siharnedjheritef)	1792–1790 BCE
Lufni	1790–1788 BCE
Seankhibre (Amenemhat VI)	1788–1785 BCE
Semenkare (Nebnuni)	1785–1783 BCE
Sehetepibre (Sewesekhtawy)	1783–1781 BCE
Sewadijkare I	1781 BCE
Nedjemibre (Amenemhat V)	1780 BCE
Khaankhre (Sobekhotep)	1780–1777 BCE
Renseneb	1777 BCE
Awybre (Hor)	1777–1775 BCE
Sekhemrekhutawy Khabaw	1775–1772 BCE
Djedkheperew	1772–1770 BCE
Sebkay	unknown
Sedjefakare (Kay Amenemhat)	1769–1766 BCE
Khutawyre (Wegaf)	*c.* 1767 BCE
Userkare (Khendjer)	*c.* 1765 BCE
Smenkhkare (Imyremeshaw)	started in 1759 BCE
Sehetepkare (Intef IV)	*c.* 10 years
Meribre (Seth)	ended in 1749 BCE
Sekhemresewadjtawy (Sobekhotep III)	1755–1751 BCE
Khasekhemre (Neferhotep I)	1751–1740 BCE

Menwadjre (Sihathor)	1739 BCE
Khaneferre (Sobekhotep IV)	1740–1730 BCE
Merhotepre (Sobekhotep V)	1730 BCE
Knahotepre (Sobekhotep VI)	c. 1725 BCE
Wahibre (Ibiau)	1725–1714 BCE
Merneferre (Ay I)	1714–1691 BCE
Merhotepre (Ini)	1691–1689 BCE
Sankhenre (Sewadjtu)	1675–1672 BCE
Mersekhemre (Ined)	1672–1669 BCE
Sewadjkare II (Hori)	c. 5 years
Merkawre (Sobekhotep VII)	1664–1663 BCE
Seven kings (names unknown)	1663–? BCE

Note: the remaining pharaohs of the thirteenth dynasty are not listed here as they are either unknown or there is a lot of ambiguity about when they ruled.

Fourteenth Dynasty (*c.* 1805/1710–1650 BCE)

Rulers in the fourteenth dynasty were based at Avaris, the capital of this dynasty.

Sekhaenre (Yakbim)	1805–1780 BCE
Nubwoserre (Ya'ammu)	1780–1770 BCE
Khawoserre (Qareh)	1770–1745 BCE
Aahotepre ('Ammu)	1760–1745 BCE
Maaibre (Sheshi)	1745–1705 BCE
Aasehre (Nehesy)	c. 1705 BCE
Khakherewre	unknown
Nebefawre	c. 1704 BCE
Sehebre	1704–1699 BCE

Merdjefare	c. 1699 BCE

Note: the remaining pharaohs of the fourteenth dynasty are not listed here as they are either unknown or there is a lot of ambiguity about when they ruled.

Fifteenth Dynasty (*c.* 1650–1544 BCE)

The fifteenth dynasty was founded by Salitas and covered a large part of the Nile region.

Salitas	c. 1650 BCE
Semqen	1649 BCE to unknown
'Aper-'Anat	unknown
Sakir-Har	unknown
Seuserenre (Khyan)	c. 30 to 35 years
Nebkhepeshre (Apepi)	1590 BCE?
Nakhtyre (Khamudi)	1555–1544 BCE

Sixteenth Dynasty (*c.* 1650–1580 BCE)

Rulers in the sixteenth dynasty were based at Thebes, the capital of this dynasty. The name and date of rule of the first pharaoh is unknown.

Sekhemresementawy (Djehuti)	3 years
Sekhemresemeusertawy (Sobekhotep VIII)	16 years
Sekhemresankhtawy (Neferhotep III)	1 year
Seankhenre (Mentuhotepi)	less than a year
Sewadjenre (Nebiryraw)	26 years
Neferkare (?) (Nebiryraw II)	c. 1600 BCE
Semenre	c. 1600 BCE

Seuserenre (Bebiankh)	12 years
Djedhotepre (Dedumose I)	*c*. 1588–1582 BCE
Djedneferre (Dedumose II)	*c*. 1588–1582 BCE
Djedankhre (Montensaf)	*c*. 1590 BCE
Merankhre (Mentuhotep VI)	*c*. 1585 BCE
Seneferibre (Senusret IV)	unknown
Sekhemre (Shedwast)	unknown

Seventeenth Dynasty (*c.* 1650–1550 BCE)

Rulers in the seventeenth dynasty ruled Upper Egypt.

Sekhemrewahkhaw (Rahotep)	*c*. 1620 BCE
Sekhemre Wadjkhaw (Sobekemsaf I)	*c*. 7 years
Sekhemre Shedtawy (Sobekemsaf II)	unknown to *c*. 1573 BCE
Sekhemre-Wepmaat (Intef V)	*c*. 1573–1571 BCE
Nubkheperre (Intef VI)	*c*. 1571–1565 BCE
Sekhemre-Heruhirmaat (Intef VII)	late 1560s BCE
Senakhtenre (Ahmose)	*c*. 1558 BCE
Seqenenre (Tao I)	1558–1554 BCE
Wadkheperre (Kamose)	1554–1549 BCE

NEW KINGDOM (*c.* 1550–1077 BCE)

Eighteenth Dynasty (*c.* 1550–1292 BCE)

The first dynasty of Egypt's New Kingdom marked the beginning of ancient Egypt's highest power and expansion.

Nebpehtire (Ahmose I)	*c*. 1550–1525 BCE
Djeserkare (Amenhotep I)	1541–1520 BCE

Aakheperkare (Thutmose I)	1520–1492 BCE
Aakheperenre (Thutmose II)	1492–1479 BCE
Maatkare (Hatshepsut)	1479–1458 BCE
Menkheperre (Thutmose III)	1458–1425 BCE
Aakheperrure (Amenhotep II)	1425–1400 BCE
Menkheperure (Thutmose IV)	1400–1390 BCE
Nebmaatre 'the Magnificent' (Amehotep III)	1390–1352 BCE
Neferkheperure Waenre (Amenhotep IV)	1352–1336 BCE
Ankhkheperure (Smenkhkare)	1335–1334 BCE
Ankhkheperure mery Neferkheperure (Neferneferuaten III)	1334–1332 BCE
Nebkheperure (Tutankhamun)	1332–1324 BCE
Kheperkheperure (Aya II)	1324–1320 BCE
Djeserkheperure Setpenre (Haremheb)	1320–1292 BCE

Nineteenth Dynasty (*c.* 1550–1292 BCE)

The nineteenth dynasty is also known as the Ramessid dynasty as it includes Ramesses II, one of the most famous and influential Egyptian pharaohs.

Menpehtire (Ramesses I)	1292–1290 BCE
Menmaatre (Seti I)	1290–1279 BCE
Usermaatre Setpenre 'the Great', 'Ozymandias' (Ramesses II)	1279–1213 BCE
Banenre (Merneptah)	1213–1203 BCE
Menmire Setpenre (Amenmesse)	1203–1200 BCE
Userkheperure (Seti II)	1203–1197 BCE
Sekhaenre (Merenptah Siptah)	1197–1191 BCE
Satre Merenamun (Tawosret)	1191–1190 BCE

Twentieth Dynasty (*c.* 1190–1077 BCE)

This, the third dynasty of the New Kingdom, is generally thought to mark the start of the decline of ancient Egypt.

Userkhaure (Setnakht)	1190–1186 BCE
Usermaatre Meryamun (Ramesses III)	1186–1155 BCE
Heqamaatre Setpenamun (Ramesses IV)	1155–1149 BCE
Heqamaatre Setpenamun (Ramesses IV)	1155–1149 BCE
Usermaatre Sekheperenre (Ramesses V)	1149–1145 BCE
Nebmaatre Meryamun (Ramesses VI)	1145–1137 BCE
Usermaatre Setpenre Meryamun (Ramesses VII)	1137–1130 BCE
Usermaatre Akhenamun (Ramesses VIII)	1130–1129 BCE
Neferkare Setpenre (Ramesses IX)	1128–1111 BCE
Khepermaatre Setpenptah (Ramesses X)	1111–1107 BCE
Menmaatre Setpenptah (Ramesses XI)	1107–1077 BCE

Twenty-first Dynasty (*c.* 1077–943 BCE)

Rulers in the twenty-first dynasty were based at Tanis and mainly governed Lower Egypt.

Hedjkheperre-Setpenre (Nesbanadjed I)	1077–1051 BCE
Neferkare (Amenemnisu)	1051–1047 BCE
Aakkheperre (Pasebakhenniut I)	1047–1001 BCE
Usermaatre (Amenemope)	1001–992 BCE
Aakheperre Setepenre (Osorkon the Elder)	992–986 BCE
Netjerikheperre-Setpenamun (Siamun)	986–967 BCE
Titkheperure (Pasebakhenniut II)	967–943 BCE

Twenty-second Dynasty (*c.* 943–728 BCE)

Sometimes called the Bubastite dynasty. Its pharaohs came from Libya.

Hedjkheneperre Setpenre (Sheshonq I)	943–922 BCE
Sekhemkheperre Setepenre (Osorkon I)	922–887 BCE
Heqakheperre Setepenre (Sheshonq II)	887–885 BCE
Tutkheperre (Sheshonq Llb)	c. the 880s BCE
Hedjkheperre Setepenre (Takelot I Meriamun)	885–872 BCE
Usermaatre Setpenre (Sheshonq III)	837–798 BCE
Hedjkheperre Setepenre (Sheshonq IV)	798–785 BCE
Usermaatre Setpenre (Pami Meriamun)	785–778 BCE
Aakheperre (Sheshonq V)	778–740 BCE
Usermaatre (Osorkon IV)	740–720 BCE

Twenty-third and Twenty-fourth Dynasties (*c.* 837–720 BCE)

These dynasties were led mainly by Libyans and mainly ruled Upper Egypt.

Hedjkheperre Setpenre (Takelot II)	837–813 BCE
Usermaatre Setpenamun (Meriamun Pedubaste I)	826–801 BCE
Usermaatre Meryamun (Sheshonq VI)	801–795 BCE
Usermaatre Setpenamun (Osorkon III)	795–767 BCE
Usermaatre-Setpenamun (Takelot III)	773–765 BCE
Usermaatre-Setpenamun (Meriamun Rudamun)	765–762 BCE
Shepsesre (Tefnakhte)	732–725 BCE
Wahkare (Bakenrenef)	725–720 BCE

Twenty-fifth Dynasty (*c.* 744–656 BCE)

Also known as the Kushite period, the twenty-fifth dynasty follows the Nubian invasions.

Piankhy (Piye)	744–714 BCE
Djedkaure (Shebitkku)	714–705 BCE
Neferkare (Shabaka)	705–690 BCE
Khuinefertemre (Taharqa)	690–664 BCE

LATE PERIOD (c. 664–332 BCE)

Twenty-sixth Dynasty (c. 664 – 525 BCE)

Also known as the Saite period, the twenty-sixth dynasty was the last native period before the Persian invasion in 525 BCE.

Wahibre (Psamtik I)	664–610 BCE
Wehemibre (Necho II)	610–595 BCE
Neferibre (Psamtik II)	595–589 BCE
Haaibre (Apreis)	589–570 BCE
Khemibre (Amasis II)	570–526 BCE
Ankhkaenre (Psamtik III)	526–525 BCE

Twenty-seventh Dynasty (c. 525–404 BCE)

The twenty-seventh dynasty is also known as the First Egyptian Satrapy and was ruled by the Persian Achaemenids.

Mesutre (Cambyses II)	525–1 July 522 BCE
Seteture (Darius I)	522–November 486 BCE
Kheshayarusha (Xerxes I)	November 486–December 465 BCE
Artabanus of Persia	465–464 BCE
Arutakhshashas (Artaxerxes I)	464–424 BCE
Ochus (Darius II)	July 423–March 404 BCE

Twenty-eighth Dynasty (*c.* 404–398 BCE)

The twenty-eighth dynasty consisted of a single pharaoh.

Amunirdisu (Amyrtaeus)	404–398 BCE

Twenty-ninth Dynasty (*c.* 398–380 BCE)

The twenty-ninth dynasty was founded following the overthrow of Amyrtaeus.

Baenre Merynatjeru (Nepherites I)	398–393 BCE
Khnemmaatre Setepenkhnemu (Hakor)	c. 392–391 BCE
Userre Setepenptah (Psammuthis)	c. 391 BCE
Khnemmaatre Setepenkhnemu (Hakor)	c. 390–379 BCE
Nepherites II	c. 379 BCE

Thirtieth Dynasty (*c.*379–340 BCE)

The thirtieth dynasty is thought to be the final native dynasty of ancient Egypt.

Kheperkare (Nectanebo I)	c. 379–361 BCE
Irimaatenre (Teos)	c. 361–359 BCE
Snedjemibre Setepenanhur (Nectanebo II)	c. 359–340 BCE

Thirty-first Dynasty (*c.* 340–332 BCE)

The thirty-first dynasty is also known as the Second Egyptian Satrapy and was ruled by the Persian Achaemenids.

Ochus (Artaxerxes III)	c. 340–338 BCE
Arses (Artaxerxes IV)	338–336 BCE
Darius III	336–332 BCE

MACEDONIAN/ARGEAD DYNASTY (*c.* 332–309 BCE)

Alexander the Great conquered Persia and Egypt in 332 BCE.

Setpenre Meryamun (Alexander III of Macedon 'the Great')	332–323 BCE
Setpenre Meryamun (Philip Arrhidaeus)	323–317 BCE
Khaibre Setepenamun (Alexander IV)	317–309 BCE

PTOLEMAIC DYNASTY (*c.* 305–30 BCE)

The Ptolemaic dynasty in Egypt was the last dynasty of ancient Egypt before it became a province of Rome.

Ptolemy I Soter	305–282 BCE
Ptolemy II Philadelphos	284–246 BCE
Arsinoe II	*c.* 277–270 BCE
Ptolemy III Euergetes	246–222 BCE
Berenice II	244/243–222 BCE
Ptolemy IV Philopater	222–204 BCE
Arsinoe III	220–204 BCE
Ptolemy V Epiphanes	204–180 BCE
Cleopatra I	193–176 BCE
Ptolemy VI Philometor	180–164, 163–145 BCE
Cleopatra II	175–164 BCE, 163–127 BCE and 124–116 BCE
Ptolemy VIII Physcon	171–163 BCE, 144–131 BCE and 127–116 BCE
Ptolemy VII Neos Philopator	145–144 BCE

Cleopatra III	142–131 BCE, 127–107 BCE
Ptolemy Memphites	113 BCE
Ptolemy IX Soter	116–110 BCE
Cleopatra IV	116–115 BCE
Ptolemy X Alexander	110–109 BCE
Berenice III	81–80 BCE
Ptolemy XI Alexander	80 BCE
Ptolemy XII Auletes	80–58 BCE, 55–51 BCE
Cleopatra V Tryphaena	79–68 BCE
Cleopatra VI	58–57 BCE
Berenice IV	58–55 BCE
Cleopatra VII	52–30 BCE
Ptolemy XIII Theos Philopator	51–47 BCE
Arsinoe IV	48–47 BCE
Ptolemy XIV Philopator	47–44 BCE
Ptolemy XV Caesar	44–30 BCE

In 30 BCE, Egypt became a province of the Roman Empire.

ANCIENT GREEK MONARCHS

This list is not exhaustive and dates are approximate. Where dates of rule overlap, emperors either ruled jointly or ruled in opposition to one another. There may also be differences in name spellings between different sources.

Because of the fragmented nature of Greece prior to its unification by Philip II of Macedon, this list includes mythological and existing rulers of Thebes, Athens and Sparta as some of the leading ancient Greek city-states. These different city-states had some common belief in the mythological gods and goddesses of ancient Greece, although their accounts may differ.

KINGS OF THEBES (*c.* 753–509 BCE)

These rulers are mythological. There is much diversity over who the kings actually were, and the dates they ruled.

Calydnus (son of Uranus)
Ogyges (son of Poseidon, thought to be king of Boeotia or Attica)
Cadmus (Greek mythological hero known as the founder of Thebes, known as Cadmeia until the reign of Amphion and Zethus)
Pentheus (son of Echion, one of the mythological Spartoi, and Agave, daughter of Cadmus)

Polydorus (son of Cadmus and Harmonia, goddess of harmony)
Nycteus (like his brother Lycus, thought to be the son of a Spartoi and a nymph, or a son of Poseidon)
Lycus (brother of Nyceteus)
Labdacus (grandson of Cadmus)
Lycus (second reign as regent for Laius)
Amphion and Zethus (joint rulers and twin sons of Zeus, constructed the city walls of Thebes)
Laius (son of Labdacus, married to Jocasta)
Oedipus (son of Laius, killed his father and married his mother, Jocasta)
Creon (regent after the death of Laius)
Eteocles and Polynices (brothers/sons of Oedipus; killed each other in battle)
Creon (regent for Laodamas)
Laodamas (son of Eteocles)
Thersander (son of Polynices)
Peneleos (regent for Tisamenus)
Tisamenus (son of Thersander)
Autesion (son of Tisamenes)
Damasichthon (son of Peneleos)
Ptolemy (son of Damasichton, 12 century BCE)
Xanthos (son of Ptolemy)

KINGS OF ATHENS

Early legendary kings who ruled before the mythological flood caused by Zeus, which only Deucalion (son of Prometheus) and a few others survived (date unknown).

Periphas (king of Attica, turned into an eagle by Zeus)
Ogyges (son of Poseidon, thought to be king of either Boeotia or Attica)
Actaeus (king of Attica, father-in-law to Cecrops I)

Erechtheid Dynasty (1556–1127 BCE)

Cecrops I (founder and first king of Athens; half-man, half-serpent who married Actaeus' daughter)	1556–1506 BCE
Cranaus	1506–1497 BCE
Amphictyon (son of Deucalion)	1497–1487 BCE
Erichthonius (adopted by Athena)	1487–1437 BCE
Pandion I (son of Erichthonius)	1437–1397 BCE
Erechtheus (son of Pandion I)	1397–1347 BCE
Cecrops II (son of Erechtheus)	1347–1307 BCE
Pandion II (son of Cecrops II)	1307–1282 BCE
Aegeus (adopted by Pandion II, gave his name to the Aegean Sea)	1282–1234 BCE
Theseus (son of Aegeus, killed the minotaur)	1234–1205 BCE
Menestheus (made king by Castor and Pollux when Theseus was in the underworld)	1205–1183 BCE
Demophon (son of Theseus)	1183–1150 BCE
Oxyntes (son of Demophon)	1150–1136 BCE
Apheidas (son of Oxyntes)	1136–1135 BCE
Thymoetes (son of Oxyntes)	1135–1127 BCE

Melanthid Dynasty (1126–1068 BCE)

Melanthus (king of Messenia, fled to Athens when expelled)	1126–1089 BCE
Codrus (last of the semi-mythological Athenian kings)	1089–1068 BCE

LIFE ARCHONS OF ATHENS (1068–753 BCE)

These rulers held public office up until their deaths.

Medon	1068–1048 BCE	Pherecles	864–845 BCE
Acastus	1048–1012 BCE	Ariphon	845–825 BCE
Archippus	1012–993 BCE	Thespieus	824–797 BCE
Thersippus	993–952 BCE	Agamestor	796–778 BCE
Phorbas	952–922 BCE	Aeschylus	778–755 BCE
Megacles	922–892 BCE	Alcmaeon	755–753 BCE
Diognetus	892–864 BCE		

From this point, archons led for a period of 10 years up to 683 BCE, then a period of one year up to 485 CE. Selected important leaders – including archons and tyrants – in this later period are as follows:

SELECTED LATER LEADERS OF ATHENS

Peisistratos 'the Tyrant of Athens'	561, 559–556, 546–527 BCE
Cleisthenes (archon)	525–524 BCE
Themistocles (archon)	493–492 BCE
Pericles	*c.* 461–429 BCE

KINGS OF SPARTA

These rulers are mythological and are thought to be descendants of the ancient tribe of Leleges. There is much diversity over who the kings actually were, and the dates they ruled.

Lelex (son of Poseidon or Helios, ruled Laconia)	c. 1600 BCE
Myles (son of Lelex, ruled Laconia)	c. 1575 BCE
Eurotas (son of Myles, father of Sparta)	c. 1550 BCE

From the Lelegids, rule passed to the Lacedaemonids when Lacedaemon married Sparta.

Lacedaemon (son of Zeus, husband of Sparta)
Amyklas (son of Lacedaemon)
Argalus (son of Amyklas)
Kynortas (son of Amyklas)
Perieres (son of Kynortas)
Oibalos (son of Kynortas)
Tyndareos (first reign; son of Oibalos, father of Helen of Troy)
Hippocoon (son of Oibalos)
Tyndareos (second reign; son of Oibaos, father of Helen of Troy)

From the Lacedaemons, rule passed to the Atreids when Menelaus married Helen of Troy.

Menelaus (son of Atreus, king of Mycenae, and husband of Helen)	c. 1250 BCE
Orestes (son of Agamemnon, Menelaus' brother)	c. 1150 BCE
Tisamenos (son of Orestes)	
Dion	c. 1100 BCE

From the Atreids, rule passed to the Heraclids following war.

Aristodemos (son of Aristomachus, great-great-grandson of Heracles)

Theras (served as regent for Aristodemes' sons, Eurysthenes and Procles)
Eurysthenes *c.* 930 BCE

From the Heraclids, rule passed to the Agiads, founded by Agis I. Only major kings during this period are listed here.

Agis I (conceivably the first historical Spartan king) *c.* 930–900 BCE
Alcamenes *c.* 740–700 BCE, during First Messenian War
Cleomenes I (important leader in the Greek resistance against the Persians) 524 – 490 BCE
Leonidas I (died while leading the Greeks – the 300 Spartans – against the Persians in the Battle of Thermopylae, 480 BCE) 490–480 BCE
Cleomenes III (exiled following the Battle of Sellasia) *c.* 235–222 BCE

KINGS OF MACEDON

Argead Dynasty (808–309 BCE)

Karanos	*c.* 808–778 BCE	Alcetas I	*c.* 576–547 BCE
Koinos	*c.* 778–750 BCE	Amyntas I	*c.* 547–498 BCE
Tyrimmas	*c.* 750–700 BCE	Alexander I	*c.* 498–454 BCE
Perdiccas I	*c.* 700–678 BCE	Alcetas II	*c.* 454–448 BCE
Argaeus I	*c.* 678–640 BCE	Perdiccas II	*c.* 448–413 BCE
Philip I	*c.* 640–602 BCE	Archelaus I	*c.* 413–339 BCE
Aeropus I	*c.* 602–576 BCE	Craterus	*c.* 399 BCE

Orestes	*c.* 399–396 BCE
Aeropus II	*c.* 399–394/93 BCE
Archelaus II	*c.* 394–393 BCE
Amyntas II	*c.* 393 BCE
Pausanias	*c.* 393 BCE
Amyntas III	*c.* 393 BCE; first reign
Argeus II	*c.* 393–392 BCE
Amyntas III	*c.* 392–370 BCE
Alexander II	*c.* 370–368 BCE
Perdiccas III	*c.* 368–359 BCE
Amyntas IV	*c.* 359 BCE
Philip II	*c.* 359–336 BCE
Alexander III 'the Great' (also King of Persia and Pharaoh of Egypt by end of reign)	*c.* 336–323 BCE
Philip III	*c.* 323–317 BCE
Alexander IV	*c.* 323/317–309 BCE

Note: the Corinthian League or Hellenic League was created by Philip II and was the first time that the divided Greek city-states were unified under a single government.

Post-Argead Dynasty (309–168 BCE, 149–148 BCE)

Cassander	*c.* 305–297 BCE
Philip IV	*c.* 297 BCE
Antipater II	*c.* 297–294 BCE
Alexpander V	*c.* 297–294 BCE

Antigonid, Alkimachid and Aeacid Dynasties (294–281 BCE)

Demetrius	*c.* 294–288 BCE
Lysimachus	*c.* 288–281 BCE
Pyrrhus	*c.* 288–285 BCE; first reign

Ptolemaic Dynasty (281–279 BCE)

Ptolemy Ceraunus (son of Ptolemy I of Egypt)	*c.* 281–279 BCE
Meleager	279 BCE

Antipatrid, Antigonid, Aeacid Dynasties, Restored (279–167 BCE)

Antipater	*c.* 279 BCE
Sosthenes	*c.* 279–277 BCE
Antigonus II	*c.* 277–274 BCE; first reign
Pyrrhus	*c.* 274–272 BCE; second reign
Antigonus II	*c.* 272–239 BCE; second reign
Demetrius II	*c.* 239–229 BCE
Antigonus III	*c.* 229–221 BCE
Philip V	*c.* 221–179 BCE
Perseus (deposed by Romans)	*c.* 179–168 BCE
Revolt by Philip VI (Andriskos)	*c.* 149–148 BCE

SELEUCID DYNASTY (*c.* 320 BCE–63 CE)

Seleucus I Nicator	*c.* 320–315, 312–305, 305–281 BCE
Antiochus I Soter	*c.* 291, 281–261 BCE
Antiochus II Theos	*c.* 261–246 BCE
Seleucus II Callinicus	*c.* 246–225 BCE
Seleucus III Ceraunus	*c.* 225–223 BCE
Antiochus III 'the Great'	*c.* 223–187 BCE
Seleucus IV Philopator	*c.* 187–175 BCE
Antiochus (son of Seleucus IV)	*c.* 175–170 BCE
Antiochus IV Epiphanes	*c.* 175–163 BCE
Antiochus V Eupater	*c.* 163–161 BCE
Demetrius I Soter	*c.* 161–150 BCE
Alexander I Balas	*c.* 150–145 BCE
Demetrius II Nicator	*c.* 145–138 BCE; first reign
Antiochus VI Dionysus	*c.* 145–140 BCE

Diodotus Tryphon	*c*. 140–138 BCE
Antiochus VII Sidetes	*c*. 138–129 BCE
Demetrius II Nicator	*c*. 129–126 BCE; second reign
Alexander II Zabinas	*c*. 129–123 BCE
Cleopatra Thea	*c*. 126–121 BCE
Seleucus V Philometor	*c*. 126/125 BCE
Antiochus VIII Grypus	*c*. 125–96 BCE
Antiochus IX Cyzicenus	*c*. 114–96 BCE
Seleucus VI Epiphanes	*c*. 96–95 BCE
Antiochus X Eusebes	*c*. 95–92/83 BCE
Demetrius III Eucaerus	*c*. 95–87 BCE
Antiochus XI Epiphanes	*c*. 95–92 BCE
Philip I Philadelphus	*c*. 95–84/83 BCE
Antiochus XII Dionysus	*c*. 87–84 BCE
Seleucus VII	*c*. 83–69 BCE
Antiochus XIII Asiaticus	*c*. 69–64 BCE
Philip II Philoromaeus	*c*. 65–63 BCE

Ptolemaic Dynasty (305–30 BCE)

The Ptolemaic dynasty in Greece was the last dynasty of ancient Egypt before it became a province of Rome.

Ptolemy I Soter	305–282 BCE
Ptolemy II Philadelphos	284–246 BCE
Arsinoe II	*c*. 277–270 BCE
Ptolemy III Euergetes	246–222 BCE
Berenice II	244/243–222 BCE
Ptolemy IV Philopater	222–204 BCE
Arsinoe III	220–204 BCE
Ptolemy V Epiphanes	204–180 BCE

Cleopatra I	193–176 BCE
Ptolemy VI Philometor	180–164, 163–145 BCE
Cleopatra II	175–164 BCE, 163–127 BCE and 124–116 BCE
Ptolemy VIII Physcon	171–163 BCE, 144–131 BCE and 127–116 BCE
Ptolemy VII Neos Philopator	145–144 BCE
Cleopatra III	142–131 BCE, 127–107 BCE
Ptolemy Memphites	113 BCE
Ptolemy IX Soter	116–110 BCE
Cleopatra IV	116–115 BCE
Ptolemy X Alexander	110–109 BCE
Berenice III	81–80 BCE
Ptolemy XI Alexander	80 BCE
Ptolemy XII Auletes	80–58 BCE, 55–51 BCE
Cleopatra V Tryphaena	79–68 BCE
Cleopatra VI	58–57 BCE
Berenice IV	58–55 BCE

In 27 BCE, Caesar Augustus annexed Greece and it became integrated into the Roman Empire.

ANCIENT ROMAN LEADERS

This list is not exhaustive and some dates are approximate. The legitimacy of some rulers is also open to interpretation. Where dates of rule overlap, emperors either ruled jointly or ruled in opposition to one another. There may also be differences in name spellings between different sources.

KINGS OF ROME (753–509 BCE)

Romulus (mythological founder and first ruler of Rome)	753–716 BCE
Numa Pompilius (mythological)	715–672 BCE
Tullus Hostilius (mythological)	672–640 BCE
Ancus Marcius (mythological)	640–616 BCE
Lucius Tarquinius Priscus (mythological)	616–578 BCE
Servius Tullius (mythological)	578–534 BCE
Lucius Tarquinius Superbus (Tarquin the Proud; mythological)	534–509 BCE

ROMAN REPUBLIC (509–27 BCE)

During this period, two consuls were elected to serve a joint one-year term. Therefore, only a selection of significant consuls are included here.

Lucius Junius Brutus (semi-mythological)	509 BCE
Marcus Porcius Cato (Cato the Elder)	195 BCE
Scipio Africanus	194 BCE
Cnaeus Pompeius Magnus (Pompey the Great)	70, 55 and 52 BCE
Marcus Linius Crassus	70 and 55 BCE
Marcus Tullius Cicero	63 BCE
Caius Julius Caesar	59 BCE
Marcus Aemilius Lepidus	46 and 42 BCE
Marcus Antonius (Mark Anthony)	44 and 34 BCE
Marcus Agrippa	37 and 28 BCE

PRINCIPATE (27 BCE–284 CE)

Julio-Claudian Dynasty (27 BCE–68 CE)

Augustus (Caius Octavius Thurinus, Caius Julius Caesar, Imperator Caesar Divi filius)	27 BCE–14 CE
Tiberius (Tiberius Julius Caesar Augustus)	14–37 CE
Caligula (Caius Caesar Augustus Germanicus)	37–41 CE
Claudius (Tiberius Claudius Caesar Augustus Germanicus)	41–54 CE
Nero (Nero Claudius Caesar Augustus Germanicus)	54–68 CE

Year of the Four Emperors (68–69 CE)

Galba (Servius Sulpicius Galba Caesar Augustus)	68–69 CE
Otho (Marcus Salvio Otho Caesar Augustus)	Jan–Apr 69 CE
Vitellius (Aulus Vitellius Germanicus Augustus)	Apr–Dec 69 CE

Note: the fourth emperor, Vespasian, is listed below.

Flavian Dynasty (66–96 CE)

Vespasian (Caesar Vespasianus Augustus)	69–79 CE
Titus (Titus Caesar Vespasianus Augustus)	79–81 CE
Domitian (Caesar Domitianus Augustus)	81–96 CE

Nerva-Antonine Dynasty (69–192 CE)

Nerva (Nerva Caesar Augustus)	96–98 CE
Trajan (Caesar Nerva Traianus Augustus)	98–117 CE
Hadrian (Caesar Traianus Hadrianus Augustus)	138–161 CE
Antonius Pius (Caesar Titus Aelius Hadrianus Antoninus Augustus Pius)	138–161 CE
Marcus Aurelius (Caesar Marcus Aurelius Antoninus Augustus)	161–180 CE
Lucius Verus (Lucius Aurelius Verus Augustus)	161–169 CE
Commodus (Caesar Marcus Aurelius Commodus Antoninus Augustus)	180–192 CE

Year of the Five Emperors (193 CE)

Pertinax (Publius Helvius Pertinax)	Jan–Mar 193 CE
Didius Julianus (Marcus Didius Severus Julianus)	Mar–Jun 193 CE

Note: Pescennius Niger and Clodius Albinus are generally regarded as usurpers, while the fifth, Septimius Severus, is listed below

Severan Dynasty (193–235 CE)

Septimius Severus (Lucius Septimus Severus Pertinax)	193–211 CE
Caracalla (Marcus Aurelius Antonius)	211–217 CE
Geta (Publius Septimius Geta)	Feb–Dec 211 CE
Macrinus (Caesar Marcus Opellius Severus Macrinus Augustus)	217–218 CE
Diadumenian (Marcus Opellius Antonius Diadumenianus)	May–Jun 218 CE
Elagabalus (Caesar Marcus Aurelius Antoninus Augustus)	218–222 CE
Severus Alexander (Marcus Aurelius Severus Alexander)	222–235 CE

Crisis of the Third Century (235–285 CE)

Maximinus 'Thrax' (Caius Julius Verus Maximus)	235–238 CE
Gordian I (Marcus Antonius Gordianus Sempronianus Romanus)	Apr–May 238 CE
Gordian II (Marcus Antonius Gordianus Sempronianus Romanus)	Apr–May 238 CE
Pupienus Maximus (Marcus Clodius Pupienus Maximus)	May–Aug 238 CE
Balbinus (Decimus Caelius Calvinus Balbinus)	May–Aug 238 CE
Gordian III (Marcus Antonius Gordianus)	Aug 238–Feb 244 CE
Philip I 'the Arab' (Marcus Julius Philippus)	244–249 CE
Philip II 'the Younger' (Marcus Julius Severus Philippus)	247–249 CE
Decius (Caius Messius Quintus Traianus Decius)	249–251 CE
Herennius Etruscus (Quintus Herennius Etruscus Messius Decius)	May/Jun 251 CE

Trebonianus Gallus (Caius Vibius Trebonianus Gallus) 251–253 CE
Hostilian (Caius Valens Hostilianus Messius Quintus) Jun–Jul 251 CE
Volusianus (Caius Vibius Afinius Gallus Veldumnianus Volusianus) 251–253 CE
Aemilian (Marcus Aemilius Aemilianus) Jul–Sep 253 CE
Silbannacus (Marcus Silbannacus) Sep/Oct 253 CE
Valerian (Publius Licinius Valerianus) 253–260 CE
Gallienus (Publius Licinius Egnatius Gallienus) 253–268 CE
Saloninus (Publius Licinius Cornelius Saloninus Valerianus) Autumn 260 CE
Claudius II Gothicus (Marcus Aurelius Claudius) 268–270 CE
Quintilus (Marcus Aurelius Claudias Quintillus) Apr–May/Jun 270 CE
Aurelian (Luciua Domitius Aurelianus) 270–275 CE
Tacitus (Marcus Claudius Tacitus) 275–276 CE
Florianus (Marcus Annius Florianus) 276–282 CE
Probus (Marcus Aurelius Probus Romanus; in opposition to Florianus) 276–282 CE
Carus (Marcus Aurelias Carus) 282–283 CE
Carinus (Marcus Aurelius Carinus) 283–285 CE
Numerian (Marcus Aurelius Numerianus) 283–284 CE

DOMINATE (284–610)

Tetrarchy (284–324)

Diocletian 'Lovius' (Caius Aurelius Valerius Diocletianus) 284–305
Maximian 'Herculius' (Marcus Aurelius Valerius Maximianus; ruled the western provinces) 286–305/late 306–308

Galerius (Caius Galerius Valerius Maximianus; ruled the eastern provinces)	305–311
Constantius I 'Chlorus' (Marcus Flavius Valerius Constantius; ruled the western provinces)	305–306
Severus II (Flavius Valerius Severus; ruled the western provinces)	306–307
Maxentius (Marcus Aurelius Valerius Maxentius)	306–312
Licinius (Valerius Licinanus Licinius; ruled the western, then the eastern provinces)	308–324
Maximinus II 'Daza' (Aurelius Valerius Valens; ruled the western provinces)	316–317
Martinian (Marcus Martinianus; ruled the western provinces)	Jul–Sep 324

Constantinian Dynasty (306–363)

Constantine I 'the Great' (Flavius Valerius Constantinus; ruled the western provinces then whole)	306–337
Constantine II (Flavius Claudius Constantinus)	337–340
Constans I (Flavius Julius Constans)	337–350
Constantius II (Flavius Julius Constantius)	337–361
Magnentius (Magnus Magnentius)	360–353
Nepotianus (Julius Nepotianus)	Jun 350
Vetranio	Mar–Dec 350
Julian 'the Apostate' (Flavius Claudius Julianus)	361–363
Jovian (Jovianus)	363–364

Valentinianic Dynasty (364–392)

Valentinian I 'the Great' (Valentinianus)	364–375
Valens (ruled the eastern provinces)	364–378

Procopius (revolted against Valens)	365–366
Gratian (Flavius Gratianus Augustus; ruled the western provinces then whole)	375–383
Magnus Maximus	383–388
Valentinian II (Flavius Valentinianus)	388–392
Eugenius	392–394

Theodosian Dynasty (379–457)

Theodosius I 'the Great' (Flavius Theodosius)	Jan 395
Arcadius	383–408
Honorius (Flavius Honorius)	395–432
Constantine III	407–411
Theodosius II	408–450
Priscus Attalus; usurper	409–410
Constantius III	Feb–Sep 421
Johannes	423–425
Valentinian III	425–455
Marcian	450–457

Last Emperors in the West (455–476)

Petronius Maximus	Mar–May 455
Avitus	455–456
Majorian	457–461
Libius Severus (Severus III)	461–465
Anthemius	467–472
Olybrius	Apr–Nov 472
Glycerius	473–474
Julius Nepos	474–475
Romulus Augustulus (Flavius Momyllus Romulus Augustulus)	475–476

Leonid Dynasty (East, 457–518)

Leo I (Leo Thrax Magnus)	457–474
Leo II	Jan–Nov 474
Zeno	474–475
Basiliscus	475–476
Zeno (second reign)	476–491
Anastasius I 'Dicorus'	491–518

Justinian Dynasty (East, 518–602)

Justin I	518–527
Justinian I 'the Great' (Flavius Justinianus, Petrus Sabbatius)	527–565
Justin II	565–578
Tiberius II Constantine	578–582
Maurice (Mauricius Flavius Tiberius)	582–602
Phocas	602–610

LATER EASTERN EMPERORS (610–1059)

Heraclian Dynasty (610–695)

Heraclius	610–641
Heraclius Constantine (Constantine III)	Feb–May 641
Heraclonas	Feb–Nov 641
Constans II Pogonatus ('the Bearded')	641–668
Constantine IV	668–685
Justinian II	685–695

Twenty Years' Anarchy (695–717)

Leontius	695–698
Tiberius III	698–705

Justinian II 'Rhinometus' (second reign)	705–711
Philippicus	711–713
Anastasius II	713–715
Theodosius III	715–717

Isaurian Dynasty (717–803)

Leo III 'the Isaurian'	717–741
Constantine V	741–775
Artabasdos	741/2–743
Leo V 'the Khazar'	775–780
Constantine VI	780–797
Irene	797–802

Nikephorian Dynasty (802–813)

Nikephoros I 'the Logothete'	802–811
Staurakios	July–Oct 811
Michael I Rangabé	813–820

Amorian Dynasty (820–867)

Michael II 'the Amorian'	820–829
Theophilos	829–842
Theodora	842–856
Michael III 'the Drunkard'	842–867

Macedonian Dynasty (867–1056)

Basil I 'the Macedonian'	867–886
Leo VI 'the Wise'	886–912
Alexander	912–913
Constantine VII Porphyrogenitus	913–959
Romanos I Lecapenus	920–944

Romanos II	959–963
Nikephoros II Phocas	963–969
John I Tzimiskes	969–976
Basil II 'the Bulgar-Slayer'	976–1025
Constantine VIII	1025–1028
Romanus III Argyros	1028–1034
Michael IV 'the Paphlagonian'	1034–1041
Michael V Kalaphates	1041–1042
Zoë Porphyrogenita	Apr–Jun 1042
Theodora Porphyrogenita	Apr–Jun 1042
Constantine IX Monomachos	1042–1055
Theodora Porphyrogenita (second reign)	1055–1056
Michael VI Bringas 'Stratioticus'	1056–1057
Isaab I Komnenos	1057–1059

ANCIENT KOREAN LEADERS

This list is not exhaustive and dates are approximate. Where dates of rule overlap, rulers either ruled jointly or ruled in opposition to one another. There may also be differences in name spellings between different sources.

ANCIENT KOREAN MONARCHS

The first rulers of Korea were mythological and descended from Hwanin (Lord of Heaven), and his son Hwanung, who was permitted to descend to Earth to found the Sinsi (City of God).

GOJOSEON (2333–108 BCE)

The first Korean kingdom was founded by a legendary ruler in 2333 BCE:

Dangun (mythological son of Ungnyeo, the bear-woman)	2333–? BCE
Gija (semi-mythological, thought to be descended from the Chinese Shang dynasty)	1122? –? BCE

(The first historical ruler of Gojoseon is unknown.)

King Bu	(232–220 BCE)
King Jun	(220–195 BCE)

Wiman Joseon (194–108 BCE)

Wiman Jodeon was a dynasty of Gojoseon.

Wi Man	(194–? BCE)
? (son of Wi Man)	(?–?)
King Ugeo	(?–108 BCE)

THREE KINGDOMS PERIOD (57 BCE–668 CE)

During this period there were three kingdoms existing on the Korean peninsula.

Goguryeo (37 BCE–668 CE)

Note: the rules of Goguryeo may have used the title 'Greatest King'.

Chumoseong (Chumo the Holy)	37–19 BCE	Sansang	197–227 CE
Yuri	19 BCE–18 CE	Dongcheon	227–248 CE
Daemusin	18–44 CE	Jungcheon	248–270 CE
Minjung	44–48 CE	Seocheon	270–292 CE
Mobon	48–53 CE	Bongsang	292–300 CE
Taejo (the Great) (disputed)	53–146 CE	Micheon	300–331 CE
		Gogugwon	331–371 CE
		Sosurim	371–384 CE
Chadae	146–165 CE	Gogugyang	384–391 CE
Sindae	165–179 CE	Gwanggaeto	391–413 CE
Gogukcheon	179–197 CE	Jangsu	413–491 CE

Munjamyeong	491–519 CE	Pyeongwon	559–590 CE
Anjang	519–531 CE	Yeongyang	590–618 CE
Anwon	531–545 CE	Yeongnyu	618–642 CE
Yangwon	545–559 CE	Bojang	642–668 CE

Baekje (18 BCE–660 CE)

Onjo	18 BCE–28 CE	Asin	392–405 CE
Daru	28–77 CE	Jeonji	405–420 CE
Giru	77–128 CE	Guisin	420–427 CE
Gaeru	128–166 CE	Biyu	427–455 CE
Chogo	166–214 CE	Gaero	455–475 CE
Gusu	214–234 CE	Munju	475–477 CE
Saban	234 CE	Samgeun	477–479 CE
Goi	234–286 CE	Dongseong	479–501 CE
Chaekkye	286–298 CE	Munyeong	501–523 CE
Bunseo	298–304 CE	Seong	523–554 CE
Biryu	304–344 CE	Wideok	554–598 CE
Gye	344–346 CE	Hye	598–599 CE
Geun Chogo	346–375 CE	Beob	599–600 CE
Geun Gusu	375–384 CE	Mu	600–641 CE
Chimnyu	384–385 CE	Uija	641–660 CE
Jinsa	385–392 CE		

Silla (57 BCE–935 CE)

Hyeokkeose Geoseogan	57 BCE–4 CE	Pasa Isageum	80–112 CE
		Jima Isageum	112–134 CE
Namhae Chachaung	4 BCE–24 CE	Ilseong Isageum	134–154 CE
		Adalla Isageum	154–184 CE
Yuri Isageum	24–57 CE	Beorhyu Isageum	184–196 CE
Tarhae Isageum	57–80 CE	Naehae Isageum	196–230 CE

Jobun Isageum	230–247 CE
Cheomhae Isageum	247–261 CE
Michu Isageum	261–284 CE
Yurye Isageum	284–298 CE
Girim Isageum	298–310 CE
Heurhae Isageum	310–356 CE
Naemul Maripgan	356–402 CE
Silseong Maripgan	402–417 CE
Nulji Maripgan	417–458 CE
Jabi Maripgan	458–479 CE
Soji Maripgan	479–500 CE
Jijeung	500–514 CE
Beopheung	514–540 CE
Jinheung	540–576 CE
Jinji	576–579 CE
Jinpyeong	579–632 CE
Queen Seondeok (first reigning queen)	632–647 CE
Queen Jindeok	647–654 CE
Taejong Muyeol	654–661 CE

The period which follows is known as the United Silla Dynasty.

Mumnu	661–681 CE
Sinmun	681–692 CE
Hyoso	692–702 CE
Seongdeok	661–681 CE
Hyoseong	737–742 CE
Gyeongdeok	742–765 CE
Hyegong	765–780 CE
Seondeok	780–785 CE
Weonseong	785–798 CE
Soseong	798–800 CE
Aejang	800–809 CE
Heondeok	809–826 CE
Heungdeok	826–836 CE
Huigang	836–838 CE
Minae	838–839 CE
Sinmu	839 CE
Munseong	839–857 CE
Heonan	857–861 CE
Gyeongmun	861–875 CE
Heongang	875–886 CE
Jeonggang	886–887 CE
Queen Jinseong	887–897 CE
Hyogong	897–912 CE
Sindeok	912–917 CE
Gyeongmyeong	917–924 CE
Gyeongae	924–927 CE
Gyeongsun	927–935 CE

BARHAE (698/9–926)

The Barhae state was established after Goguryeo fell, and coexisted with the Unified Silla Dynasty.

Go	699–719	Seon	818–830
Mu	719–737	Dae/Wang Ijin	830–858
Mun	737–793	Dae/Wang Geonhwang	858–870/1
Dae/Wang Won-ui	793–794	Dae/Wang Hyeonseok	870/1–892
Seong	794–795	Dae/Wang Wihae	892–906
Gang	795–809	Dae/Wang Inseon	906–926
Jeong	809–813		
Hui	813–817		
Gan	817–818		

GORYEO DYNASTY (918–1392)

Goryeo was ruled by the Wang Dynasty.

Taejo	918–943	Seonjong	1084–1094
Hyejong	943–945	Heonjong	1094–1095
Jeongjong	945–949	Sukjong	1095–1105
Gwangjong	949–975	Yejong	1105–1122
Gyeongjong	975–981	Injong	1122–1146
Seongjong	981–997	Uijong	1146–1170
Mokjong	997–1009	Myeongjong	1170–1197
Hyeonjong	1009–1031	Sinjong	1197–1204
Deokjong	1031–1034	Huijong	1204–1211
Jeongjong	1034–1046	Gangjong	1211–1213
Munjong	1046–1083	Gojong	1213–1259
Sunjong	1083	Wonjong	1259–1274

Chungnyeol wang	1274–1298, 1298–1308	Chungmok wang	1344–1348
Chungseon wang	1308–1313	Chungjeong wang	1348–1351
Chungsuk wang	1313–1330, 1332–1339	Gongmin wang	1351–1374
Chunghye wang	1330–1332, 1339–1344	U wang	1374–1388
		Chang wang	1388–1389
		Gongyang wang	1389–1392

JOSEON DYNASTY (1392–1910)

Also known as the Yi Dynasty.

Taejo	1392–1398	Kwanghae-gun	1608–1623
Jeongjong	1398–1400	Injo	1623–1649
Taejong	1400–1418	Hyojong	1649–1659
Sejong	1418–1450	Hyeonjong	1659–1674
Munjong	1450–1452	Sukjong	1674–1720
Danjong	1452–1455	Gyeongjong	1720–1724
Sejo	1455–1468	Yeongjo	1724–1776
Yejong	1468–1469	Jeongjo	1776–1800
Seongjong	1469–1494	Sunjo	1800–1834
Yeonsan-gun	1494–1506	Heonjong	1834–1849
Chungjong	1506–1544	Cheoljong	1849–1863
Injong	1544–1545	Gojong	1863–1907
Myeongjong	1545–1567	Sunjong	1907–1910
Seonjo	1567–1608		

Joseon become known as the Korean Empire in 1897. The dynasty ended with the Japanese annexation of Korea in August 1910.

ANCIENT CHINESE MONARCHS

This list focuses on emperors with at least some proven legitimate claim and dates are approximate. Where dates of rule overlap, rulers either ruled jointly or ruled in opposition to one another. There may also be differences in name spellings between different sources.

THREE SOVEREIGNS OR PRIMEVAL EMPERORS, AND FIVE PREMIER EMPERORS (*c.* 2852–2070 BCE)

These are generally thought to be mythological figures. The history of China's rulers begins with a group of three *huáng* ('sovereigns') and a group of five *di* (emperors). There is much diversity over who the three sovereigns and five emperors actually were, and the dates they ruled.

Fuxi (Heavenly Sovereign)	18,000 years
NuWa (Earthly Sovereign)	11,000 years
Shennong (Human Sovereign)	45,600 years

Yellow Emperor (Xuanyuan)	100 years
Zhuanxu (Gaoyang)	78 years
Emperor Ku (Gaoxin)	70 years
Emperor Yao of Tang (Yiqi, Taotang or Fangxun)	100 years
Emperor Shun of Yu (Yao, Youyu or Chonghua)	42 years

XIA DYNASTY (*c.* 2070–1600 BCE)

This dynasty was thought to be established after the legendary Shun handed his throne to Yu the Great, also a legendary leader, whose historicity is debated.

Yu the Great	2150–2106 BCE	Bu Jiang	1851–1792 BCE
Qi of Xia	2106–2077 BCE	Jiong of Xia	1792–1771 BCE
Tai Kang	2077–2048 BCE	Jin of Xia (Yin Jia)	1771–1750 BCE
Zhong Kang	2048–2036 BCE	Kong Jia	1750–1719 BCE
Xiang of Xia	2036–2008 BCE	Gao of Xia	1719–1708 BCE
Shao Kang	1968–1946 BCE	Fa of Xia (Hou Jin)	1708–1689 BCE
Zhu of Xia	1946–1929 BCE	Jie of Xia (Lu Gui)	1689–1658 BCE
Huai of Xia	1929–1885 BCE		
Mang of Xia	1885–1867 BCE		
Xie of Xia	1867–1851 BCE		

SHANG DYNASTY (*c.* 1600–1046 BCE)

Tang of Shang	1658–1629 BCE	Wai Ren	1452–1437 BCE
Wai Bing	1629–1627 BCE	He Dan Jia	1437–1428 BCE
Zhong Ren	1627–1623 BCE	Zu Ji	1428–1409 BCE
Tai Jia	1623–1611 BCE	Zu Xin	1409–1393 BCE
Wo Ding	1611–1592 BCE	Wo Jia	1393–1368 BCE
Tai Geng	1592–1567 BCE	Zu Ding	1368–1336 BCE
Xiao Jia	1567–1550 BCE	Nan Geng	1336–1307 BCE
Yong Ji	1550–1538 BCE	Yang Jia	1307–1290 BCE
Tai Wu	1538–1463 BCE	Pan Geng	1290–1262 BCE
Zhong Ding	1463–1452 BCE	Xiao Xin	1262–1259 BCE

Xiao Yi	1259–1250 BCE	Wu Yi	1147–1112 BCE
Wu Ding	1250–1192 BCE	Wen Wu Ding	1112–1102 BCE
Zu Geng	1192–1185 BCE	Di Yi	1101–1076 BCE
Zu Jia	1185–1158 BCE	King Zhou of Shang	1075–1046 BCE
Lin Xin	1158–1152 BCE		
Geng Ding	1152–1147 BCE		

ZHOU DYNASTY (*c.* 1046–256 BCE)

Western Zhou (1046–771 BCE)

King Wu of Zhou	1046–1043 BCE
King Cheng of Zhou	1042–1021 BCE
King Kang of Zhou	1020–996 BCE
King Zhao of Zhou	995–977 BCE
King Mu of Zhou	976–922 BCE
King Gong of Zhou	922–900 BCE
King Yi of Zhou (Jian)	899–892 BCE
King Xiao of Zhou	891–886 BCE
King Yi of Zhou (Xie)	885–878 BCE
King Li of Zhou	877–841 BCE

Gonghe Regency (827–827 BCE)

King Xuan of Zhou	827–782 BCE
King You of Zhou	781–771 BCE

Eastern Zhou (770–256 BCE)

Spring and Autumn Period (770–476 BCE)

King Ping of Zhou	770–720 BCE

King Huan of Zhou	719–697 BCE
King Zhuang of Zhou	696–682 BCE
King Xi of Zhou	681–677 BCE
King Hui of Zhou	676–652 BCE
King Xiang of Zhou	651–619 BCE
King Qing of Zhou	618–613 BCE
King Kuang of Zhou	612–607 BCE
King Ding of Zhou	606–586 BCE
King Jian of Zhou	585–572 BCE
King Ling of Zhou	571–545 BCE
King Jing of Zhou (Gui)	544–521 BCE
King Dao of Zhou	520 BCE
King Jing of Zhou (Gai)	519–476 BCE

Warring States Period (475–221 BCE)

King Yuan of Zhou	475–469 BCE
King Zhending of Zhou	468–442 BCE
King Ai of Zhou	441 BCE
King Si of Zhou	441 BCE
King Kao of Zhou	440–426 BCE
King Weilie of Zhou	425–402 BCE
King An of Zhou	401–376 BCE
King Lie of Zhou	375–369 BCE
King Xian of Zhou	368–321 BCE
King Shenjing of Zhou	320–315 BCE
King Nan of Zhou	314–256 BCE

QIN DYNASTY (*c.* 221–207 BCE)

Qin Shi Huang declared himself emperor rather than king, and this period is often thought to mark the beginning of Imperial China.

Qin Shi Huang	221–210 BCE
Qin Er Shi	209–207 BCE
Ziying	207 BCE

HAN DYNASTY (*c.* 202 BCE–9 CE, 25–220 CE)

Western Han (202 BCE–9 CE)

Emperor Gaozu of Han	202–195 BCE
Emperor Hui of Han	195–188 BCE
Emperor Qianshao of Han	188–184 BCE
Emperor Houshao of Han	184–180 BCE
Emperor Wen of Han	179–157 BCE
Emperor Jing of Han	156–141 BCE
Emperor Wu of Han	140–87 BCE
Emperor Zhao of Han	86–74 BCE
Marquis of Haihun	74 BCE
Emperor Xuan of Han	73–49 BCE
Emperor Yuan of Han	48–33 BCE
Emperor Cheng of Han	32–7 BCE
Emperor Ai of Han	6–1 BCE
Emperor Ping of Han	1 BCE–5 CE
Ruzi Ying	6–8 CE
Interregnum (9 CE–23 CE; see Xin dynasty below)	
Gengshi Emperor	23–25 CE

XIN DYNASTY (*c.* 9–23 CE)

Wang Mang; possible usurper	9–23CE

Eastern Han (25–220 CE)

Emperor Guangwu of Han	25–57 CE
Emperor Ming of Han	58–75 CE
Emperor Zhang of Han	76–88 CE
Emperor He of Han	89–105 CE
Emperor Shang of Han	106 CE
Emperor An of Han	106–125 CE
Emperor Shun of Han	125–144 CE
Emperor Chong of Han	144–145 CE
Emperor Zhi of Han	145–146 CE
Emperor Huan of Han	146–168 CE
Emperor Ling of Han	168–189 CE
Prince of Hongnong	189 CE
Emperor Xian of Han	189–220 CE

THREE KINGDOMS (*c.* 220–280 CE)

Cao Wei (220–266 CE)

Cao Pi	220–226 CE	Cao Mao	254–260 CE
Cao Rui	226–239 CE	Cao Huan	260–266 CE
Cao Fang	239–254 CE		

Shu Han (221–263 CE)

Liu Bei	221–223 CE
Liu Shan	223–263 CE

Eastern Wu (222–280 CE)

Sun Quan	222–252 CE	Sun Xiu	258–264 CE
Sun Liang	252–258 CE	Sun Hao	264–280 CE

JIN DYNASTY (c. 266–420 CE)

Western Jin (266–316 CE)

Emperor Wu of Jin	266–290 CE	Emperor Huai of Jin	307–313 CE
Emperor Hui of Jin	290–306 CE	Emperor Min of Jin	313–317 CE

Eastern Jin (317–420 CE)

Emperor Yuan of Jin	317–322 CE	Emperor Fei of Jin	365–371 CE
Emperor Ming of Jin	322–325 CE	Emperor Jianwen of Jin	371–372 CE
Emperor Cheng of Jin	325–342 CE	Emperor Xiaowu of Jin	372–396 CE
Emperor Kang of Jin	342–344 CE	Emperor An of Jin	396–418 CE
Emperor Mu of Jin	345–361 CE	Emperor Gong of Jin	419–420 CE
Emperor Ai of Jin	361–365 CE		

SIXTEEN KINGDOMS (c. 304–439 CE)

Han Zhao (304–329 CE)

Northern Han (304–318 CE)

Liu Yuan	304–310 CE
Liu He	7 days in 310 CE
Liu Cong	310–318 CE
Liu Can	a month+ in 318 CE

Former Zhao (318–329 CE)

Liu Yao 318–329 CE

Cheng Han (304–347 CE)

Cheng (304–338 CE)

Li Te	303 CE
Li Lui	several months in 303 CE
Li Xiong	303–334 CE
Li Ban	7 months in 334 CE
Li Qi	334–338 CE

Han (338–347 CE)

Li Shou	338–343 CE
Li Shi	343–347 CE

Later Zhao (319–351 CE)

Shi Le	319–333 CE
Shi Hong	333–334 CE
Shi Hu	334–349 CE
Shi Shi	73 days in 349 CE
Shi Zun	183 days in 349 CE
Shi Jian	73 days in 349–350 CE
Shi Zhi	350–351 CE

Former Liang (320–376 CE)

Zhang Mao	320–324 CE
Zhang Jun	324–346 CE
Zhang Chonghua	346–353 CE
Zhang Yaoling	3 months in 353 CE
Zhang Zuo	353–355 CE
Zhang Xuanjing	355–363 CE
Zhang Tianxi	364–376 CE

Former Yan (337–370 CE)

Murong Huang	337–348 CE
Murong Jun	348–360 CE
Murong Wei	360–370 CE

Former Qin (351–394 BCE)

Fu Jian	351–355 CE	Fu Pi	385–386 CE
Fu Sheng	355–357 CE	Fu Deng	386–394 CE
Fu Jian	357–385 CE	Fu Chong	394 CE

Later Yan (384–409 CE)

Murong Chui	384–396 CE	Murong Sheng	398–301 CE
Murong Bao	396–398 CE	Murong Xi	401–407 CE

Later Qin (384–417 CE)

Yao Chang	384–393 CE	Yao Hong	416–417 CE
Yao Xing	394–416 CE		

Western Qin (385–400 CE, 409–431 CE)

Qifu Guoren	385–388 CE	Qifu Chipan	412–428 CE
Qifu Qiangui	388–400 CE, 409–412 CE	Qifu Mumo	428–431 CE

Later Liang (386–403 CE)

Lü Guang	386–399 CE	Lü Zuan	399–401 CE
Lü Shao	399 CE	Lü Long	401–403 CE

Southern Liang (397–414 CE)

Tufa Wugu	397–399 CE	Tufa Rutan	402–414 CE
Tufa Lilugu	399–402 CE		

Northern Liang (397–439 CE)

Duan Ye	397–401 CE	Juqu Wuhui	442–444 CE
Juqu Mengxun	401–433 CE	Juqu Anzhou	444–460 CE
Juqu Mujian	433–439 CE		

Southern Yan (398–410 CE)

Murong De	398–405 CE	Murong Chao	405–410 CE

Western Liang (400–421 CE)

Li Gao	400–417 CE	Li Xun	420–421 CE
Li Xin	417–420 CE		

Hu Xia (407–431 CE)

Helian Bobo	407–425 CE	Helian Ding	428–431 CE
Helian Chang	425–428 CE		

Northern Yan (407–436 CE)

Gao Yun	407–409 CE	Feng Hong	430–436 CE
Feng Ba	409–430 CE		

NORTHERN AND SOUTHERN DYNASTIES (*c.* 386–589 CE)

Northern Dynasties (386–581 CE)

Northern Wei (386–535 CE)

Emperor Daowu of Northern Wei	386–409 CE
Emperor Mingyuan of Northern Wei	409–423 CE
Emperor Taiwu of Northern Wei	424–452 CE
Tuoba Yu	452 CE
Emperor Wencheng of Northern Wei	452–465 CE
Emperor Xianwen of Northern Wei	466–471 CE
Emperor Xiaowen of Northern Wei	471–499 CE
Emperor Xuanwu of Northern Wei	499–515 CE
Emperor Xiaoming of Northern Wei	516–528 CE

Yuan Zhao	528 CE
Emperor Xiaozhuang of Northern Wei	528–530 CE
Yuan Ye	530–531 CE
Emperor Jiemin of Northern Wei	531–532 CE
Yuan Lang	531–532 CE
Emperor Xiaowu of Northern Wei	532–535 CE

Eastern Wei (534–550 CE)

Emperor Xiaojing of Eastern Wei	534–550 CE

Western Wei (535–557 CE)

Emperor Wen of Western Wei	535–551 CE
Emperor Fei of Western Wei	552–554 CE
Emperor Gong of Western Wei	554–557 CE

Northern Qi (550–577 CE)

Emperor Wenxuan of Northern Qi	550–559 CE
Emperor Fei of Northern Qi	559–560 CE
Emperor Xiaozhao of Northern Qi	560–561 CE
Emperor Wucheng of Northern Qi	561–565 CE
Gao Wei	565–577 CE
Gao Heng	577 CE
Gao Shaoyi	577–579? CE

Northern Zhou (557–581 CE)

Emperor Xiaomin of Northern Zhou	557 CE
Emperor Ming of Northern Zhou	557–560 CE
Emperor Wu of Northern Zhou	561–578 CE
Emperor Xuan of Northern Zhou	578–579 CE
Emperor Jing of Northern Zhou	579–581 CE

Southern dynasties (420–589 CE)

Liu Song (420–497 CE)

Emperor Wu of Liu Song	420–422 CE
Emperor Shao of Liu Song	423–424 CE
Emperor Wen of Liu Song	424–453 CE
Emperor Xiaowu of Liu Song	454–464 CE
Emperor Ming of Liu Song	465–472 CE
Emperor Houfei of Liu Song	473–477 CE
Emperor Shun of Liu Song	477–479 CE

Southern Qi (479–502 CE)

Emperor Gao of Southern Qi	479–482 CE
Emperor Wu of Southern Qi	482–493 CE
Xiao Zhaoye	493–494 CE
Xiao Zhaowen	494 CE
Emperor Ming of Southern Qi	494–498 CE
Xiao Baojuan	499–501 CE
Emperor He of Southern Qi	501–502 CE

Liang Dynasty (502–557 CE)

Emperor Wu of Liang	502–549 CE
Emperor Jianwen of Liang	549–551 CE
Xiao Dong	551–552 CE
Emperor Yuan of Liang	552–555 CE
Xiao Yuanming	555 CE
Emperor Jing of Liang	555–557 CE

Western Liang (555–587 CE)

Emperor Xuan of Western Liang	555–562 CE

Emperor Ming of Western Liang	562–585 CE
Emperor Jing of Western Liang	585–587 CE

Chen Dynasty (557–589 CE)

Emperor Wu of Chen	557–559 CE
Emperor Wen of Chen	559–566 CE
Emperor Fei of Chen	566–568 CE
Emperor Xuan of Chen	569–582 CE
Chen Shubao	583–589 CE

SUI DYNASTY (*c.* 581–610 CE)

Emperor Wen of Sui	581–604 CE
Emperor Yang of Sui	605–617 CE
Yang You	617–618 CE
Yang Hao	618 CE
Yang Tong	618–619 CE

TANG DYNASTY (*c.* 618–690 CE, 705–907 CE)

Emperor Gaozu of Tang	618–626 CE
Emperor Taizong of Tang	627–649 CE
Emperor Gaozong of Tang	650–683 CE
Emperor Zhongzong of Tang	684 and 705–710 CE
Emperor Ruizong of Tang	684–690 and 710–712 CE
Emperor Shang of Tang	710 CE
Emperor Xuanzong of Tang	712–756 CE
Emperor Suzong of Tang	756–762 CE

Emperor Daizong of Tang	762–779 CE
Emperor Dezong of Tang	780–805 CE
Emperor Shunzong of Tang	805 CE
Emperor Xianzong of Tang	806–820 CE
Emperor Muzong of Tang	821–824 CE
Emperor Jingzong of Tang	824–826 CE
Emperor Wenzong of Tang	826–840 CE
Emperor Wuzong of Tang	840–846 CE
Emperor Xuanzong of Tang	846–859 CE
Emperor Yizong of Tang	859–873 CE
Emperor Xizong of Tang	873–888 CE
Emperor Zhaozong of Tang	888–904 CE
Emperor Ai of Tang	904–907 CE

Wu Zhou (690 – 705 CE)

Wu Zetian (only female considered legitimate)	690–705 CE

Huang Qi (881–884 CE)

Huang Chao	881–884 CE

FIVE DYNASTIES AND TEN KINGDOMS (c. 907–979 CE)

Five Dynasties (907–960 CE)

Later Liang (907–923 CE)

Zhu Wen	907–912 CE
Zhu Yougui	912–913 CE
Zhu Zhen	913–923 CE

Later Tang (923–937 CE)

Li Cunxu	923–926 CE
Li Siyuan (Li Dan)	923–926 CE
Li Conghou	933–934 CE
Li Congke	934–937 CE

Later Jin (936–947 CE)

Shi Jingtang	936–942 CE
Shi Chonggui	942–947 CE

Later Han (947–951 CE)

Liu Zhiyuan	947–948 CE
Liu Chengyou	948–951 CE

Later Zhou (951–960 CE)

Guo Wei	951–954 CE
Chai Rong	954–959 CE
Chai Zongxun	959–960 CE

Ten Kingdoms (907–979 CE)

Former Shu (907–925 CE)

Wang Jian	907–918 CE
Wang Zongyan	918–925 CE

Yang Wu (907–937 CE)

Yang Xingmi	904–905 CE
Yang Wo	905–908 CE
Yang Longyan	908–921 CE
Yang Pu	921–937 CE

Ma Chu (907–951 CE)

Ma Yin	897–930 CE
Ma Xisheng	930–932 CE
Ma Xifan	932–947 CE
Ma Xiguang	947–950 CE
Ma Xi'e	950 CE
Ma Xichong	950–951 CE

Wuyue (907–978 CE)

Qian Liu	904–932 CE
Qian Yuanguan	932–941 CE
Qian Hongzuo	941–947 CE
Qian Hongzong	947 CE
Qian Chu (Qian Hongchu)	947–978 CE

Min (909–945 CE) and Yin (943–945 CE)

Wang Shenzhi	909–925 CE
Wang Yanhan	925–926 CE
Wang Yanjun	926–935 CE
Wang Jipeng	935–939 CE
Wang Yanxi	939–944 CE
Wang Yanzheng	943–945 CE

Southern Han (917–971 CE)

Liu Yan	917–925 CE
Liu Bin	941–943 CE
Liu Sheng	943–958 CE
Liu Chang	958–971 CE

Jingnan (924–963 CE)

Gao Jixing	909–928 CE
Gao Conghui	928–948 CE
Gao Baorong	948–960 CE
Gao Baoxu	960–962 CE
Gao Jichong	962–963 CE

Later Shu (934–965 CE)

Meng Zhixiang	934 CE
Meng Chang	938–965 CE

Southern Tang (937–96 CE)

Li Bian	937–943 CE
Li Jing	943–961 CE
Li Yu	961–976 CE

Northern Han (951–979 CE)

Liu Min	951–954 CE
Liu Chengjun	954–968 CE
Liu Ji'en	970 CE
Liu Jiyuan	970–982 CE

ANCIENT JAPANESE EMPERORS

This list is not exhaustive and dates are approximate. Where dates of rule overlap, emperors either ruled jointly or ruled in opposition to one another. There may also be differences in name spellings between different sources.

MYTHOLOGICAL FIGURES AND THE AGE OF THE GODS

The first descendants of Japan are the mythological deities or *kami*. There were seven generations of *kami*, including Izanagi (Izanagi-no-Mikoto) and Izanami (Izanami-no-Mikoto), who are generally thought of as the creator deities of Japan. Among their many offspring are the Three Precious Children: Amaterasu (sun goddess), Susanoo (storm god) and Tsukuyomi (moon god). Ninigi, a grandson of Amaterasu, was sent to earth to rule. His great-grandson was the first Emperor, Jimmu.

IMPERIAL HOUSE OF JAPAN

Early History

Emperor Jimmu (Hikohohodemi; presumed mythological and thought descended from

Amaterasu, the sun goddess)	660–585 BCE
Emperor Suizei (Kamununakawamimi; presumed mythological)	581–549 BCE
Emperor Annei (Shikitsuhikotamatemi; presumed mythological)	549–511 BCE
Emperor Itoku (Ōyamatohikosukitomo; presumed mythological)	510–477 BCE
Emperor Kōshō (Mimatsuhikokaeshine; presumed mythological)	475–393 BCE
Emperor Kōan (Yamatotarshihiko*kuni*oshihito; presumed mythological)	392–291 BCE
Emperor Kōrei (Ōyamatonekohikofutoni; presumed mythological)	290–215 BCE
Emperor Kōgen (Ōyamatonekohiko*kuni*kuru; presumed mythological)	214–158 BCE
Emperor Kaika (Wakayamato Nekohiko Ōbibi; presumed mythological)	157–98 BCE
Emperor S*uji*n (Mimaki; presumed mythological but possibly existed)	97–30 BCE
Emperor Suinin (Ikume; presumed mythological)	29 BCE–70 CE
Emperor Keikō (Ōtarashihiko; presumed mythological)	71–130 CE
Emperor Seimu (Wakatarashihiko; presumed mythological)	131–190 CE
Emperor Chūai (Tarashinakatsuhiko; presumed mythological)	192–200 CE
Empress Jingū (Okinagatarashi; presumed mythological, not officially counted as Emperor)	201–269 CE

Kofun Period (*c.* 300–538 CE)

Emperor Ōjin (Homutawake; deified)	270–310 CE
Emperor Nintoku (Ohosazaki)	313–399 CE
Emperor Richū (Ōenoizahowake)	400–405 CE
Emperor Hanzei (Mizuhawake)	406–410 CE
Emperor Ingyō (Oasatsuma Wakugo no Sukune)	411–453 CE
Emperor Ankō (Anaho)	453–456 CE
Emperor Yūrayaku (Ōhatuse no Wakatakeru)	456–479 CE
Emperor Seinei (Shiraka)	480–484 CE
Emperor Kenzō (Woke)	485–487 CE
Emperor Ninken (Oke)	488–498 CE
Emperor Buretsu (Ohatsuse no Wakasazaki)	499–506 CE
Emperor Keitai (Ohodo)	507–531 CE
Emperor Ankan (Magari)	534–535 CE
Emperor Senka (Hinokuma-no-takata)	536–539 CE

Asuka Period (*c.* 538–710 CE)

Emperor Kinmei is the first emperor for which historical evidence exists.

Emperor Kinmei (Ame*kuni*oshiharakihironiwa)	540–571 CE
Emperor Bidatsu (Nunakura no Futotamashiki)	572–585 CE
Emperor Yōmei (Tachibana no Toyohi)	586–587 CE
Emperor Sushun (Hatsusebe)	588–592 CE
Emperor Suiko (Nukatabe)	593–628 CE
Emperor Jomei (Tamura)	629–641 CE
Empress Kōgyoku (Takara; first reign)	642–645 CE
Emperor Kōtoku (Karu)	645–654 CE
Empress Saimei (Takara; second reign)	655–661 CE

Emperor Tenchi (Kazuraki)	662–672 CE
Emperor Kōbun (Ōtomo)	672 CE
Emperor Temnu (Ōama)	673–686 CE
Empress Jitō (Unonosarara)	687–697 CE
Emperor Monmu (Karu)	697–707 CE
Empress Genmei (Ahe)	707–715 CE

Nara Period (*c.* 710–794 CE)

Empress Genshō (Hidaka)	715–724 CE
Emperor Shōmu (Obito)	724–749 CE
Empress Kōken (Abe; first reign)	749–758 CE
Emperor Junnin (Ōi)	758–764 CE
Empress Shōtoku (Abe; second reign)	764–770 CE
Emperor Kōnin (Shirakabe)	770–781 CE
Emperor Kanmu (Yamabe)	781–806 CE

Heian Period (*c.* 794–1185 CE)

Emperor Heizei (Ate)	806–809 CE
Emperor Saga (*Kam*ino)	809–823 CE
Emperor Junna (Ōtomo)	823–833 CE
Emperor Ninmyō (Masara)	833–850 CE
Emperor Montoku (Michiyasu)	850–858 CE
Emperor Seiwa (Korehito)	858–876 CE
Emperor Yōzei (Sadaakira)	876–884 CE
Emperor Kōkō (Tokiyasu)	884–887 CE
Emperor Uda (Sadami)	887–897 CE
Emperor Daigo (Atsuhito)	897–930 CE
Emperor Suzaku (Yutaakira)	930–946 CE
Emperor Murakami (Nariakira)	946–967 CE
Emperor Reizei (Norihara)	967–969 CE

Emperor En'yū (Morihira)	969–984 CE
Emperor Kazan (Morosada)	984–986 CE
Emperor Ichijō (Kanehito)	986–1011 CE
Emperor Sanjō (Okisada)	1011–1016 CE
Emperor Go-Ichijō (Atsuhira)	1016–1036 CE
Emperor Go-Suzaku (Atsunaga)	1036–1045 CE
Emperor Go-Reizei (Chikahito)	1045–1068 CE
Emperor Go-Sanjō (Takahito)	1068–1073 CE
Emperor Shirakawa (Sadahito)	1073–1087 CE
Emperor Horikawa (Taruhito)	1087–1107 CE
Emperor Toba (Muhehito)	1107–1123 CE
Emperor Sutoku (Akihito)	1123–1142 CE
Emperor Konoe (Narihito)	1142–1155 CE
Emperor Go-Shirakawa (Masahito)	1155–1158 CE
Emperor Nijō (Morihito)	1158–1165 CE
Emperor Rokujō (Nobuhito)	1165–1168 CE
Emperor Takakura (Norihito)	1168–1180 CE
Emperor Antoku (Tokohito)	1180–1185 CE

Kamakura Period (*c.* 1185–1333 CE)

Emperor Go-Toba (Takahira)	1183–1198 CE
Emperor Tsuchi*mikado* (Tamehito)	1198–1210 CE
Emperor Juntoku (Morinari)	1210–1221 CE
Emperor Chūkyō (Kanenari)	1221 CE
Emperor Go-Horikawa (Yuahito)	1221–1232 CE
Emperor Shijō (Mitsuhito)	1232–1242 CE
Emperor Go-Saga (Kuninito)	1242–1246 CE
Emperor Go-Fukakusa (Hisahito)	1246–1260 CE
Emperor Kameyama (Tsunehito)	1260–1274 CE
Emperor Go-Uda (Yohito)	1274–1287 CE

Emperor Fushimi (Hirohito)	1287–1298 CE
Emperor Go-Fushimi (Tanehito)	1298–1301 CE
Emperor Go-Nijō (Kuniharu)	1301–1308 CE
Emperor Hanazono (Tomihito)	1308–1318 CE

Nanbokucho Period (*c.* 1336–1392 CE)

Emperor Go-Daijo (Takaharu; first emperor of the Southern Court)	1318–1339 CE
Emperor Kōgen (Kazuhito; first emperor of the Northern Court	1331–1333 CE
Emperor Kōmyō (Yutahito; second emperor of the Northern Court)	1336–1348 CE
Emperor Go-Murakami (Noriyoshi; second emperor of the Southern Court)	1339–1368 CE
Emperor Sukō (Okihito; third emperor of the Northern Court)	1348–1351 CE
Emperor Go-Kōgon (Iyahito; fourth emperor of the Northern Court)	1352–1371 CE
Emperor Chōkei (Yutanari; third emperor of the Southern Court)	1368–1383 CE
Emperor Go-En'yu (Ohito; fifth emperor of the Northern Court)	1371–1382 CE
Emperor Go-Komatsu (Motohito; sixth and final emperor of the Northern Court)	1382–1392 CE
Emperor Go-Kameyama (Hironari; fourth and final emperor of the Southern Court)	1383–1392 CE

Muromachi Period (*c.* 1392–1573 CE)

Emperor Go-Komatsu (Motohito)	1392–1412 CE
Emperor Shōkō (Mihito)	1412–1428 CE

Emperor Go-Hanazono (Hikohito)	1428–1464 CE
Emperor Go-Tsuchi*mikado* (Fusahito)	1464–1500 CE
Emperor Go-Kashiwabara (Katsuhito)	1500–1526 CE
Emperor Go-Nara (Tomohito)	1526–1557 CE
Emperor Ōgimachi (Michihito)	1557–1586 CE